DATE DUE

DIAHANN

AN AUTOBIOGRAPHY

by *Diahann Carroll*
with *Ross Firestone*

LITTLE, BROWN AND COMPANY · BOSTON · TORONTO

FIRST EDITION

Library of Congress Catalog Card No 85-82452

HAL

Designed by Jeanne F. Abboud

Published simultaneously in Canada
by Little, Brown & Company (Canada) Limited

PRINTED IN THE UNITED STATES OF AMERICA

DEDICATION

To my mother, Mabel, and my daughter, Suzanne
From where it came, to where it is going.

Preface

I'm standing in a strange room. There is death in the air. My father is lying in the bed before me, and he is dying. Since my father has never acknowledged that I am his daughter, he and I have not been face to face since I was an infant. He looks old, and sick, and I realize that he is a complete stranger.

I feel sadness and anger, because I did not know him, and because he is now dying. As if he knows that, he begins to speak.

"You are as lovely as your mother," he says quietly, knowing that this phrase means everything in the world to me. It means that my father, a wealthy white man, has acknowledged that I, a black woman, am his daughter.

"Cut," says Nancy Malone, the director. "It's a take."

"The Will," Script Number 100, *Dynasty,* Air date — January 9, 1985; Supervising Producer, Elaine Rich; a Richard and Esther Shapiro Production in association with Aaron Spelling Productions.

And I, Diahann Carroll, am one of the stars. I have just completed one of my favorite scenes — when John Forsythe and I, Blake Carrington and Dominique Deveraux, brother and sister, confront our dying father to make him declare publicly, before he dies, that I am indeed his daughter. It means a great deal, socially and financially, for Dominique. It means at least as much, if not more, to Diahann Carroll.

I am forty-nine years old. I have been a singer, an actress, a daughter, a mother, a wife, a lover, a friend. I have had my ups, a lot of downs, and now I am at the highest point of my career, at the top of my life. I am in a hit television series, I sing all over the world, and my life is in order.

All I ever wanted to do was sing.

What happened was more.

Chapter One

It was about 1:30 in the afternoon and I was rushing back to home room when the boy stopped me in the hall.

"They want you at The House," he said. The hint of a smile flickered across his face. "You know what that is, don'tcha?"

I knew, all right. All the kids knew. The House was a broken-down old wooden building a block and a half away from our junior high school. It had been vacant for years until the Imperial Lords took it over for their clubhouse. One never, ever, went anywhere near there — the Lords were one of the most ferocious teenage gangs in Washington Heights, so full of hatred and rage that the whole neighborhood was terrified of them. There was good reason to be terrified — they carried knives, they used zip guns, and they killed people.

Having delivered his message, he continued on his way. I stood on the steps, paralyzed. My heart was pounding so hard and loud that I started to shake. Go to The House? Alone? Me? Why? But, of course, the messenger hadn't spelled out why they wanted me at The House. He didn't have to. I had heard the stories at school. And when they ordered you to go there, you went. If you hid from them today, they would look for you tomorrow.

I cut my last class, slipped out of the building, and walked — very, very slowly — down 164th Street. It was a bright, crisp autumn afternoon. It was very quiet, which surprised me. Here I was, caught in a nightmare, trembling with fear, and everything around me seemed so normal. I wanted to scream for help or run home and hide. But I had to keep putting one foot in front of the other. I had to face it. And the worst was — I wasn't quite sure what "it" was. I was only thirteen years old.

I made it to The House. The boy guarding the front door barely looked at me — just motioned me toward the room in the back. I tiptoed, afraid that any sound I might make would set something off. When I got there I stopped short and stared. There, in the middle of the room, was a girl standing in her underwear, ironing her dress on an old table as if it were the most ordinary of circumstances. When she raised her head, I recognized her as one of my classmates.

The sight of a familiar face helped quell the terror — maybe things weren't so bad, maybe it was all a mistake — but that lasted only for a moment. It pounced back with a vengeance as soon as she began to speak.

"Don't fight them," she said. "And don't argue. Whatever they tell you to do, you just do it. And then get the hell out of here."

I looked over at her defeated face and half-naked body and I knew that I couldn't. Not me. Not Carol Diann Johnson. But what would I do? I had to think. I had to have some time. But before I even had a chance to think of my next move, the guard summoned me to the front room. The window shades were drawn, but through the darkness I could see half-a-dozen boys sitting around on chairs or sprawled on the floor. Some of them had their hats on, and I remember having this ridiculous thought that their mothers would be very angry to see their sons sitting inside the house wearing hats. When I looked around, I couldn't help noticing the bare mattress over in the corner. My heart started to pound even louder, and I felt faint.

The boys were talking but I couldn't hold on to the words long enough to make sense of them. Instinctively, without even realizing what I was doing, I blanked out, removing myself completely from the reality of the moment, becoming so cold and distant they might as well have been talking to a wall.

It seemed to take an eternity before the boy named George, who seemed to be their leader, finally grumbled, "Aw, get the hell out of here," and motioned me to leave. I looked around to see who he was talking to. Me? Could he mean me? Did he mean I could go? That's it? I couldn't believe it! I just couldn't believe that I was getting off so easily. Before he had a chance to change his mind, I muttered a quick "Thank you" and ran. I ran for my life.

A week or so later I had a second run-in with the gang. Just as I was passing the candy store on my way home from school, they spilled out on the sidewalk and swarmed around me. I started to tremble, remembering that familiar fear, when George smiled at me and said in a surprisingly gentle voice, "Come on, I'll walk you to 155th Street." His henchmen walked with us, teasing him and punching him on the arm for flirting with this square little schoolgirl. He tried staying cocky and tough — "Go 'way, man. Can't you see I'm busy?" — and I began to relax, thinking maybe things would be all right after all.

But when school ended the next afternoon, one of the tough girls in the eighth grade was waiting for me on the street with a bunch of her pals and there was murder in her eyes.

"You! Yeah, you with the curls!" she yelled, stomping over and planting herself in front of my face. "You stay the hell away from George, you hear! He's my man! That's right, I'm gonna have his baby. I catch you messin' with him again, I'll knock your fuckin' teeth down your throat."

I turned on my heels and ran as fast as I could, hoping against hope that a bus would be waiting at the bus stop by the time I reached it. The girls followed close behind me, cursing and taunting and pulling at my hair to goad me into fighting. Through the grace of God one of my schoolmates — a large, strong girl named Evelyn — materialized from somewhere and told them to leave me alone. That made them back off a little. When the bus finally lumbered up to the stop, Evelyn got on with me, but I wasn't safe yet. Half the kids started yelling and screaming to distract the driver, and the other half sneaked in the back door. A police car rounding the corner pulled over to see what was going on. The policemen seemed to think Evelyn was the one causing all the trouble, so they yanked her off the bus and I was left alone.

My whole body was shaking as I counted off the streets to my stop. "Just ten more blocks and home! . . . Only eight more blocks to go. . . . Another two blocks, and I'll be safe." When we finally arrived at my stop, I ran out the door and kept on running. They were right behind me.

I made it to my front stoop. My mother couldn't imagine why

I was so disheveled and out of breath. There wasn't time to explain. The girls were outside in the front yard yelling and cursing and banging on the windows. When Mom opened the window to shoo them away, they reached in through the bars and tried to grab her. She went out to the yard to confront them, but they still held their ground, spitting at her and calling her names. They didn't leave until she telephoned the police.

By now I was calmer, but my mom was furious. Until that moment I don't think she realized just how ugly and vicious it could be in our neighborhood. It had never occurred to her that a bunch of thirteen-year-old girls would threaten us on our own property.

"We have to get out of here," she pleaded with my father when he came home from work that night. I rarely saw my mom cry, but that night, she burst into tears. "We have to move. I don't want her in this environment. I'm afraid for her." Dad listened silently, as was his way, and nodded his head in agreement.

Eventually, we did get out, leaving Harlem for the middle-class safety of Yonkers. But that was a few years off. Right now I still had to face whatever was waiting for me in school the next day. And there was nothing I could do.

It started as we were filing back up the stairs after lunch period. "There she is with her curls," someone behind me muttered, and then the pushing and shoving began. I made it up to the landing before the wave of bodies knocked me down. As my head hit the slate floor, I felt the hands grabbing and pulling at my hair. This time there was no place to run and no Evelyn to scare them off. I could either just lie there and take it or try to fight back. To me, there wasn't much of a choice. I had to show them that I would not let people push me around.

I fought back as hard and violently as I could, punching and kicking and scratching with every ounce of strength I had in me. Finally they stopped. To this day, I'm not sure if I won or lost. I was covered with bruises. My pretty, freshly ironed blouse was torn to shreds. Large clumps of hair had been ripped out of my head. But I seemed to have proved something to them, to have passed some kind of test.

I saw the change a few days later when three of the girls followed me into the bathroom between classes.

"Listen, we just want to talk to you," the first one said. "Look, you're not really all that square, but you can't dress this way. As long as you look like Miss Goody Two-Shoes, you're looking to get your ass kicked every day."

"That's right," her friend chimed in. "It's stupid to be walking around with your socks turned down like that. You gotta pull them up and put some rubber bands around the top. And you gotta get rid of those dumb shoes."

"Yeah, and you gotta show more leg," the third one added. "Your skirt's way too long. Fold the waistband to make it shorter. And comb those damn curls out of your hair. You know, mess it up a little. If you don't, you're gonna always be . . . uh — well, different."

They were right. I *was* different.

❧

Many things set me apart from the world around me. The most important difference — and the one that would have the greatest impact on my character and personality — was the relationship I had with my parents. My parents' lives revolved around me. In the world we lived in — surrounded mostly by black families headed by working parents, by people struggling every day to survive — my childhood seemed like a perfect fairy tale.

To the have-nots on the street, we were the haves. I cringed whenever my folks picked me up from school in our shiny new Chrysler, but they were so proud of their accomplishments they couldn't really understand my embarrassment. My parents owned a brownstone. My dad worked at the Department of Transportation of the City of New York (he was a subway conductor), and my mother stayed home to take care of me.

And take care of me she did! From the minute we got up in the morning, until she tucked me into bed, her day was spent caring for my needs, my wants, and sometimes my demands.

Unlike many mothers in my neighborhood, every morning my mother made breakfast for me — a hot cereal to "give me energy and keep me healthy." I hated it, but she insisted. And every morning I threw it up. Every morning my mother waited, thinking, "Maybe tomorrow morning . . ." But the next morning I'd throw up again. Finally, we went to the doctor, because she was convinced that I was ill, and the doctor said, "Don't make her eat it. She'll be fine."

Respectability, achievement, hard work — those were the values my parents lived by, and my mother worked hard to instill them in me. She inherited that determination from her mother, Grandma Faulk, who, after my grandfather died, brought up nine children on her own while running a cotton and tobacco farm. This was unusual in those days — a black woman running a business was unheard of! I remember walking around the farm with her while she gave the orders and checked up on the workers. "Good morning, Miz Rebecca," they would say with much respect in their voices as she checked how much tobacco they had hung up to dry that day. Grandma Faulk persevered against huge odds, and that kind of stubborn dedication to working hard and doing the best you could possibly do was a gift she gave directly to my mother.

I always understood that my parents' expectations were very high. There were rules in our house. School ended at three, and I was expected home at 3:45, not a second later. After having a piece of fruit, it was time to do my homework, which I had to do at my desk because the lighting was correct. Homework was followed by piano practice. (Once a week I went to Mrs. Shepherd's brownstone on Convent Avenue for my piano lessons.) Mom would place the clock on top of the piano, and I sat there running scales until the alarm went off exactly sixty minutes later. Thursday afternoon was set aside for religious instruction, Sunday mornings for Sunday school and church.

One of my mother's favorite mottoes was "Idleness is the devil's workshop." I was to stay busy, to be productive — to do, to learn, to go and be a part of something. "What have you done today to earn the salt in your daily bread?" Mom was forever asking. "Idle people don't sleep well at night. They can't get up in the morning and take advantage of the day and produce something worthwhile."

"Where have you *been?*" Mom would demand the second I walked through the door if I were five minutes late returning from school or running an errand to the grocery store. "Oh, I was just standing on the corner talking to my friend." That's all she had to hear. "No, no. You don't stand on the corner. We don't do that. Loose children, children who don't know where their parents are, stand on the corner."

The way my mother sent me to school set me completely apart from the other girls, which is why they picked on me so often. Every night before I went to bed she neatly laid out my clothes for the next day — the freshly ironed white middy blouse, the navy blue skirt, the polished oxford shoes and little white socks folded down at the ankles. And every night she set aside time to dress my hair — applying the Vaseline, then wrapping each curl in pieces of brown grocery bag paper so that I would have curls just as nice as Shirley Temple's.

It was my mother's way to prepare me for life and, for better or worse, she made me different. She made me feel better and stronger; she made me feel I could do anything. She had her dreams for her little girl, and she was determined to make them come true. For herself. And for me. Mabel, who grew up on Grandma Faulk's farm in Bladenboro, North Carolina, had had to struggle all her young life just to survive; she wanted, like all mothers, the best for her little girl.

Thus I knew that I was loved. And I knew that none of the luxuries I had came easy — I had roller skates and a new bike and lots of wonderful children's books my father brought home. My hair was always washed and curled. I had a closet full of beautiful dresses, which I adored. I loved the attention because — as my mother constantly reminded me — I looked so pretty and stood out in a special, nice way.

But at the same time I felt so different at school — so unlike the girls around me. And that's why after the attack at school, when the girls let me know that different was not better, I did my best to try in little ways to fit in with the other kids. I saved my lunch money and, for $4.99, went to Miles Shoe Store and bought a pair of high-heeled black shoes, which I hid in my book bag so I could change into them before classes began. I left the house with my socks folded neatly at my ankles, but before school began I unrolled them and fastened them with rubber bands. And one day I finally convinced my mother that it was okay to let me carry my books loose in my arms rather than haul that neat little book bag. I even messed my hair after I left the house, and tried to recurl it around my fingers before I returned home. These were small things, but they made me feel less alone among the other kids. If my mom noticed what I had done to her handiwork — and I'm sure she must have — she never said one word.

The protective camouflage helped some. I wasn't picked on as often. But the girls never really accepted me. And I wasn't supposed to be accepted, not according to my parents' plans. My father and mother made that abundantly clear from the time I was old enough to set foot outside alone. Through years of unrelenting hard work they had struggled to improve the condition of their lives, and now that they had managed to pull themselves a rung or two up the ladder, they weren't about to lose their daughter to the disreputable ways of the street.

I still remember how upset my father became when I was taken into the bar down the block for a ginger ale when I was six or seven years old. Fat Man's was the local hangout for the sporting crowd in the neighborhood. Snappily dressed men and women could be seen sauntering in and out of the place at all hours of the day when everyone else was at work. The bar was a source of great mystery to me, especially since I had been ordered to give it a wide berth. "Don't you dillydally when you pass there," my mother warned me time and time again. "You keep your eyes right in front of you and walk by as fast as your legs can move."

Then one afternoon on my way home from school I caught the attention of Eddie Mallory (gossip said that he was Ethel Waters's man), who was lounging outside by his Cadillac, talking to Fat Man.

"Who is that child?" he asked. "My goodness, she's dressed just like a little princess."

"That's Mr. Johnson's daughter, Carol Diann," Fat Man told him. (My father supplemented his salary by renting out rooms in two or three apartments in the area, and he was somewhat known. Black men who found other ways to make money and achieved a certain standard of living all recognized one another.)

"Well, isn't she cute," Mr. Mallory answered, then picked me up, carried me up the stairs, and placed me on top of the bar. He didn't think he was doing anything wrong. Who could possibly object to a celebrity like Ethel Waters's man buying this little girl a ginger ale? When I mentioned that maybe my dad might not be too pleased, he dismissed my concern with a wave of his hand. "No, no, it'll be all right," he assured me, flashing a big, beautiful smile. "It's okay. You're with *me*."

That wasn't quite how my father saw it. He must have come home early and heard what was going on from one of the neighborhood gossips, because the next thing I knew, he burst through the door and scooped me up in his arms.

"Don't you ever bring my child here again," he seethed, trying hard to hold on to his composure. "She doesn't belong here."

"All right, Mr. Johnson," Eddie Mallory answered, still smiling as he threw up his hands in surrender. "Sorry if I was out of line."

As young as I was, I didn't fail to notice the respect he accorded my father. He seemed to understand immediately that this gentleman was bringing up his daughter a certain way and that's how it was going to be. And though it didn't relate to his own way of life, he liked my father for it.

∝℘

Despite the meticulous planning and strong hold my parents had over my life, there was plenty of time for fun. Saturdays, Mom would take me to the local movie theater if there was a film that met with her approval, or we would take the subway and ride downtown to watch Uncle Don on his radio program or see a puppet show or go to the circus. Somehow, she managed to find things for me to do all over the city, not just in Harlem. Every now and then she would even buy balcony seats to a Broadway play, where live actors performed on stage, making a movie right before your eyes. Sundays, after church, there were all sorts of marvelous family excursions. We would go to Radio City Music Hall and eat at the Automat, drive out to Long Island to visit relatives and have a huge family dinner, stroll down the hill to the park on Edgecombe Avenue for a picnic. There I'd help my folks spread the blanket, then Mom would unpack the picnic basket and lay out the napkins and a full array of plates and silverware. And I remember it so clearly — we didn't just eat; we dined.

Afterward, the three of us would play ball together, then, while Mom sat down to rest with her book, Dad would rent a bicycle and take me off for a ride. He was so big and strong and smelled so deliciously clean when I snuggled up next to him that I couldn't have felt more safe and protected and happy. When the sun began to set, we would walk back up the hill, nodding hello to our neighbors. I could almost hear them whisper, "There are Mr. and Mrs. Johnson and their daughter." We were the living image of a perfect storybook family. My parents were pursuing a fairy tale. I didn't know it then, and it didn't matter then — for their reality was mine.

But like every fairy tale, there's a little more than meets the eye. Things were not always as lovely as they seemed.

Let me back up a little. Mom met my father when she traveled to Long Island to find work during her summer vacation. A girl friend invited her to a local carnival, and as they strolled down the midway, the friend stopped to say hello to this tall, handsome man in a white suit. My mother fell in love with him on the spot. "That's the man I'm going to marry," she announced, and a few months later she did. She was twenty. He was twenty-one.

Like so many black men of his generation, my father had come North to make a better life for himself. He was bright and hard-working and fiercely ambitious, but with only a grammar school education, it was difficult to find a job that paid a decent salary. After the wedding, my parents lived in a tiny apartment on West 151st Street. To help pay the rent, Mom went to work as a domestic. Dad hated her doing that — he just hated it — especially after I came along thirteen months later. Sending your wife to work as someone's maid or cleaning woman meant you couldn't support your family and weren't a real man. I knew he felt a sense of shame.

Because they both had to work, they were forced to leave me with one of my mother's sisters in North Carolina when I was one and a half. My mother took me there, ostensibly for a visit. But Mom put me to bed, kissed me goodnight, and when I woke up the next morning, she was gone.

They tell me I never screamed or cried when I realized she had left me. Even at that age, I adjusted. I repressed my feelings of abandonment and immediately adopted my aunt and uncle as my new parents. The determination and adjustment of that two-year-old amazes me today. A personality, a habit was being formed — let's make the best of it; let's deal with it the best way we can.

My parents intended to leave me there only a short while, just until they managed to get on their feet. But that took much longer than they expected. I didn't see or hear from either of them for over a year.

When Mother finally came to get me, I barely remembered her face. I know today that my parents had to leave me. But the fact that they did leave me changed my life. The experience was so devastating to me that I was too terrified to sit on the toilet once they brought me home — I was afraid of being lost, flushed away, gotten rid of again. For months I behaved like an animal — whenever I went to the bathroom, my mother had to cover the tile floor with newspapers.

My parents felt so guilty about having sent me away that they never acknowledged it; we never talked about it all through the years I was growing up. As was their way, disturbing incidents were not discussed. Believe it or not, I didn't discover what had happened until my late twenties when I had gone into LSD therapy to try to find out why I was plagued by such terrible feelings of insecurity and rejection in relationships. (When a man would tell me he loved me, I didn't believe it and always insisted he keep proving it over and over again.)

Finally, one day when I was twenty-eight, during one of my therapy sessions, my mind traveled back to my childhood, and there I was, in my aunt's home again, without my parents. I suddenly remembered being left — the experience was so overwhelming and overpowering I knew it had to be real.

I was somehow relieved — I felt as though I had changed my life in a moment. I'm sure you know how it feels when the truth is uncovered. I was frightened because it was so painfully clear, and it hurt so much. But it explained so many things in my personality — the need to be good so that no one would leave me; the need to make those who loved me prove it; the need to be led by those who took care of me.

I knew then that I had to call my mother. I also knew that she was not going to be able to understand that I had to talk to her about what had happened. After all, she had refused to acknowledge the existence of this trauma. I hated to make that phone call (I couldn't face seeing her in person!). But I knew that I had to have all the information — even if it meant that she never spoke to me again.

"I think I've found it, Mom," I announced as soon as she answered the phone. "I think I've found out what is wrong with me."

"What are you talking about? There's nothing wrong with you," she answered. I could hear the nervousness in her voice.

"Mom, you've got to help me. I have to know — did you leave me when I was a baby?"

My mother hung up. I called again, and my father answered. "Don't call this house again!" he screamed.

But I did. This time my mother answered. "What are you asking me? What are you doing to me? What kind of question is that?" she asked, her voice breaking more with each question. "I wish you'd stop seeing that awful psychiatrist."

By this time my stomach was in knots. I was clutching the telephone for dear life. But I had to know that there was a reason for my pain.

"Please, Mom," I begged. "Please, Mom. Please tell me what happened."

Finally, resigned, defeated, and frightened, she gave in. "Yes, my child, I did leave you," she sobbed. "I left you. I left you. I had to. There was no other choice."

❧

And so I was different.

At twenty-eight I could deal with this knowledge. It helped me understand what made me me. But at eight, ten, thirteen, I didn't know anything except that I needed to be with my parents — I needed their love, their support, their constant guidance. And I had it.

Even when times were rough — particularly whenever racial prejudice threatened to disrupt our rather idyllic existence — my parents tried to shield me from the pain while at the same time insisting on teaching me about prejudice. They taught me to believe that I could do whatever I wanted in life, I could be whatever I wanted to be, despite the color of my skin.

Sometimes, surprisingly, the prejudice came from other blacks. When I was very young I overheard one of my aunts insinuate that because my skin was so dark perhaps Dad wasn't my real father. It was said as a joke, but I could tell she really meant it. To her peculiar way of thinking, a brown-skinned man and a light tan woman should have produced a lighter-skinned child. Mom threw her a wicked look, then grabbed me in her arms to comfort me and keep the hurt from sinking in. "If your father and I had lots of children," she said, "they'd probably be every color of the rainbow. So what? None of that means anything." And I believed her.

She responded the same way when I returned from my friend Sylvia's home one afternoon, crushed by her mother's insensitivity. "Where's Sylvia?" I had asked, and Mrs. O'Gilvie answered, "Oh, she went out to play with one of her real friends. You know, she has to play with her *real friends* sometime." "Real friends" meant girls whose mothers and fathers came from the West Indies, who preferably had lighter skin and straighter hair. Mrs. O'Gilvie felt that her children's skin color conferred on her family a kind of natural superiority. Thus, sometimes when the two families visited together, a little of that snobbery leaked through, but Mom always made me feel it had nothing to do with us. She would stand behind Mrs. O'Gilvie and motion with a wave of her hand that this was just empty rhetoric that didn't merit a response. The fact that Mom was secure enough to have a sense of humor about that pathetic kind of prejudice impressed me greatly. If anything, it strengthened my confidence and sense of self-worth.

Obviously, my parents tried to protect me from the more serious kinds of prejudice, the cruelties of white racism. I remember, when I was about six, how tactfully Mom handled the situation when we took the train south. During the northern portion of the trip the train was totally integrated and we laughed and joked easily with the white soldiers and sailors sitting across the aisle. But then, around Baltimore, the conductor came through and asked if we would move to another car. I remember wondering why he asked us to move. Then I heard my mother answer, in her most offhand, ladylike manner, "Why certainly. Of course we'll move." Gathering the suitcases and parcels, she told the soldiers, "Well, goodbye. Awfully nice to have met you," as if we were tearing ourselves away from some pleasant little tea party. I was confused, to say the least, and I didn't understand any of this. Later, when Mom tried to explain, she emphasized that we had run up against someone else's ignorance and stupidity. It wasn't my fault nor my problem. It wasn't me — it was their problem, their ignorance, and I wasn't ever to take it personally.

It was a lesson — a gift — I would always remember. Throughout my life, whenever I was in a situation where someone was rude to me because I was black, I always knew that I was dealing with a person who had a problem and it was *his* problem.

There were other instances when my mother tried to rise above those situations by remaining dignified and composed, but dignity and composure didn't always work. Sometimes I would be thrown head-on into the reality from which my parents wanted to shield me.

That's what happened the day after Christmas in 1941. Dad

took me along to visit his boss (at that time he worked for a printing company). Mr. Miller was fond of my father with that "you're-a-nice-boy-and-a-good-worker" kind of fondness white bosses could feel for their black help as long as they stayed in their place. Every Christmas he and Dad exchanged presents. When we entered his house that morning, I was immediately confronted by a large, growling dog that scared the hell out of me. I grabbed hold of my father's leg, and with tears in my eyes I begged him to pick me up. As he started to bend down, Mr. Miller told him not to bother. "Don't worry about Old Redd," he smiled. "He's perfectly harmless."

Well, that was the white man Dad worked for and he had to do what he said. But I was too young and too confused to understand my father's dilemma. My father always responded when I was threatened or frightened. If anything, he overresponded. So why was he just standing there while I whimpered and tugged away at his leg? Why did he keep whispering under his breath, "It's all right, it's all right," when he could see that it wasn't? Why did he wait until the dog snapped at me before changing back to the father I knew and finally scooping me up in his arms? Years later I would know why he acted the way he did, and still feel his pain at that moment.

There were other incidents when my dad found himself in situations that made him feel powerless and impotent. When I was about eight years old, we took a trip to North Carolina. My father was always a little apprehensive about driving that big, shiny Chrysler through the South — imagine, a black man driving a beautiful new shiny Chrysler through poor white neighborhoods in the South. But his pride made him defy the risk. He was very, very careful about observing speed limits and traffic signals, but one night we were stopped.

Suddenly, the flashing red lights of a police car came up behind us, and we were ordered to pull over. Again I was terrified. A large white man in a ten-gallon hat stuck his head through the window.

"Where you goin', boy?" he demanded. "Whose car are you drivin'?"

Dad answered his questions politely and directly, but that didn't seem to satisfy the policeman.

"Well, you just follow us," he ordered.

We did what he said, following him down the main highway,

then off onto a dirt road that took us deeper and deeper into the woods. No one spoke in our car, and the silence was frightening. It was the blackest night I had ever seen. There were no streetlights, there was no moon, not even a single star — only the beams from our headlights to cut through the dark.

We drove on for what seemed like miles without saying one word. Eventually we saw the lights of a house. It didn't look like a police station to me, and it wasn't. We were in the middle of nowhere. Even at that young age, I remember thinking that this was the end. We would die. And no one would be able to help us.

The police approached the car and then told Mom and me to wait. They took my father inside. I could see white men interrogating him through the basement window. Once again, I witnessed his terrible helplessness. The fear was so thick I could barely breathe. I thought I would choke, and held on to my mother for dear life.

It seemed to take forever, but they finally did let my father go — why, we'll never know. When he climbed back into the car and stepped on the gas, I could sense both his anger and his relief. And, even then, I knew that with their power, these men had stripped him of his manhood, of his humanity.

My dad drove through the night without speaking, and although this was not unusual, since my parents never discussed anything that bothered them, I remember thinking that this deadly silence made me right to have felt afraid. I can still feel how awful it was to see my parents, who had always taken care of me and protected me, become totally helpless. I can still feel the pain and hurt I felt then for my father's shame and humiliation.

And that was yet another lesson learned in my young life — I had seen my father powerless, and I understood why he was so determined that I should never feel this way. I vowed that I would someday gain enough power to insure that I would never be made to feel that helpless. (It worked well for me in my professional life, that kind of determination, but it was a harder lesson for me to learn in my personal life.)

Other stories are burned in my memory. One day when my dad was about ten years old, three or four white men burst into his classroom. "We're here to fetch John," they announced. "Where is he?"

Two boys stood up from their desks. One of them was my father.

"All right," they asked, "which is the John who walked home with that little white girl yesterday?"

Fortunately for my father, the other boy was courageous enough to answer, "I am." Otherwise they probably would have killed them both. There was pain in my father's eyes as he described how the men took the child out to the woods behind the schoolhouse and tied him to a tree. Then they built two circles of firewood around him, doused them with kerosene, and set a match to the outer pile. The idea was to keep the child screaming as long as possible so the entire neighborhood would hear him and understand that acts like walking a white girl home were punishable by the most horrible kind of death.

I never forgot that story. Never. It is as fresh in my mind as the incident that was always to remind me how dangerous it is to feel powerless, helpless, alone.

When I entered the High School of Music and Art, the school sent me to a doctor on Park Avenue for my physical examination. When I showed up for my appointment, the doctor was too rushed to see me, and for the next few hours I busied myself with homework while a steady stream of patients came and went. I couldn't understand why I was still sitting there, but wait I did. Remember, I was the good girl who was brought up to listen to authority.

At six o'clock the receptionist put on her coat and said goodnight, and I was left alone in the empty waiting room. Finally, the doctor's assistant stuck his head through the doorway and motioned me inside. Handing me a robe, he told me to undress so he could take my X rays. When the doctor, an elderly white man, entered the room, the assistant disappeared. The doctor started off quite matter-of-factly, examining my body and questioning me about my medical history. But then, slowly, almost imperceptibly, he began to change.

"Open your robe," he told me. "I want to have another look at your chest."

Something funny was beginning to happen. He was examining my breasts, but his touch felt a little too familiar.

"Do you have a boy friend?" he asked.

"Yes, I do, but I don't understand what that has to do with —"

"Just answer the questions. Have you ever had sexual intercourse?"

His hands were still on my breasts.

"I don't think that's any of —"

"Do you enjoy having sex?"

"Wait a minute! I —"

"Oh, your nipples are getting hard. What does that mean? Does it mean you're getting excited?"

A gray veil dropped before my eyes, cutting me off from his presence. I don't know how I stopped him. I don't know what I said or how I managed to get my clothes back on. I only know I did what I had done before in difficult situations — I blanked out the problem and forged ahead. The next thing I remember, I was riding uptown on the subway, counting off the minutes until I arrived home.

Mom was resting in bed when I burst into her room. I threw myself on top of her and began sobbing like a baby. When I finished telling her the story, I waited for her reaction. She was strangely quiet.

"So what are we going to do, Mom? Do we call the police? Are we going back down there to get him?"

There was a long pause before she answered, "No."

"Well, what *are* we going to do? We can't just let him get away with this!"

"I don't know," she told me. "I just don't know."

I couldn't understand why she was so hesitant. Where was the anger? Where was the need for revenge for what someone had done to *her* little girl?

"Are you sure that's what happened?" I couldn't believe what I was hearing. "Are you certain?" she asked, quietly. "It would be your word against his."

My word against his? What was she talking about? Why would I lie? She knew I never lied. Besides, why would I say this old man did what he did unless it were true?

I stormed into my room, confused by my mother's response and consumed by my own anger. But then I began to understand why she reacted as she had. Yes, he had done it, and she knew it. But she was powerless, and so was I. Because he was white and rich and more powerful than we were, there wasn't a thing we could do.

I was devastated. I cried for hours. But I knew one thing for certain. I vowed I would never, ever, if I could ever help it, allow myself to be trapped in this sort of helplessness again.

⁓❧⁓

My childhood was complicated. The feelings surrounding me were so often contradictory. I was adored, catered to, given as many advantages as my parents could have possibly given any child, yet I often felt estranged. I remember wondering about the meaning of being different. Different meant behaving "properly," the way my parents taught me, which was not the way most of the girls around me behaved. Different was feeling my father's and mother's pain at being treated unfairly because they were black. Different was never seeing any black faces in the magazines I bought, never seeing any black models in those beautiful evening gowns, or selling toothpaste or cereal in the bus and subway ads.

Different was going to the movies and watching black maids and shiftless handymen who rolled their eyes like idiots and were afraid of ghosts. (I was embarrassed whenever I saw Willie Best on the screen, because he was always the handyman who was lazy and dumb. Years later I realized that he was a brilliant talent who understood timing and how best to use the camera. The same was true of the television show *Amos and Andy* — I didn't discover the brilliance of those shows then because my parents refused to let me watch them; they portrayed the wrong image of blacks, the stereotypes my parents wanted no part of.)

The messages were indeed confusing, and, even then, I was doing what I would be accused of doing all my life — crossing between the white and black worlds. I was proud to be black — the black my parents allowed me to see. But the culture I saw in magazines and movies, the one my parents held up as successful and profitable, was white — and that was my model. Magazines convinced me that Rita Hayworth was beautiful — the epitome of perfect beauty. I never saw a picture of Dorothy Dandridge or Lena Horne until years later, and by then I knew that they, too, were beautiful.

And so the conflicts. Even though my parents tried hard to give me a sense of self, to make me feel special, to shield me from the pain of the outside world, I still knew, deep inside, that I was somehow different. And so I did what I would do for the rest of my life. I took the fact that I was loved, that I was sheltered, that

I was secure (at least on the surface) and ran with it. I was stubborn in my conviction that, no matter the circumstances, I would hold my head up. I became relentless in my ambition to stand out in the crowd, to be somebody that people would notice, that people would respect.

And, I was determined to sing.

Chapter Two

I began singing in public when I was six years old as part of the Tiny Tots choir in Adam Clayton Powell's Abyssinian Baptist Church. From the very beginning I loved everything about it. I loved the rehearsing. I loved getting my hair done and dressing up in my beautiful white and black choir robe that was floor length, almost like a gown. I loved the high of the actual performance. Most of all, I loved standing in front of the other Tiny Tots as I belted out my solo in "No Hiding Place Down There" or "There Is a Balm in Gilead." Even then I knew I wanted to be where everyone could see me. I wasn't shy or apprehensive about singing a solo or being out in front — I loved every minute of it. Hearing that little voice come out of my mouth as the rest of the choir harmonized behind me gave me a feeling of exultation that kept me on top of the world for days! I was a natural singer and a born ham. Even at that young age, it felt familiar. It felt right.

A few years later I started taking singing lessons in downtown Manhattan. An organization affiliated with the Metropolitan Opera came to my school, offering scholarships to children with talent. I auditioned and won myself a scholarship. I loved everything about taking the lessons. I enjoyed visiting the voice teachers' homes and seeing how their lives revolved around their music. I even enjoyed struggling with the German lieder and Italian art songs they assigned me. I felt the same about my piano lessons. I never minded the lessons — I loved to hear the music. I loved being able to execute what they wanted. I didn't really love all the time that practicing entailed, but I quickly caught on to the fact that the more I practiced, the better I became, and I loved sounding good. I practiced my scales and exercises over and over again every day, doggedly pursuing the ideal of excellence the teacher had set as my goal. I began to feel a sense of identity, a place where I might belong.

Mom couldn't have been more supportive. She encouraged me to practice. She shepherded me back and forth for my lessons. When it was time for the yearly piano recital, she made sure I had a pretty new silk organza gown (which was no small feat!). We always went to the stalls under the Third Avenue Bridge to buy the fabric. When she spotted some fabric she liked, she would bunch it up in her hand to see if it wrinkled, and if it didn't spring back to life the second she opened her fist, we would continue the search until she found something of better quality. Then she'd take me to one of the seamstresses in the Father Divine compound, who, for a dollar or two, would make it into a gown. She was always very finicky about detail. "I want pleats in the back," she would tell the lady. "And pearl buttons." The following week we'd return for a fitting to make sure the finished garment came up to her standards. That was my first lesson on dressing right. And soon I was giving the orders. I would say to my mother, often in one big breath: "I have the solo and I want a satin robe and I don't want the waistline at the waistline, I'd like it here, under the bosom, and I'd like a yoke and a Peter Pan collar and long sleeves with a cuff and I want a bow in the back but I don't want to see it from the front." My mom would very often look at me and think, "This child has been here before" or "She's really forty-five years old."

Often on weekends when there was no schoolwork, Mom would take me downtown to the Broadway theater. I loved it! The instant the curtain went up and the actors came to life I was swept away by the magic, and the rest of the world disappeared. The first play I saw off-Broadway was *The Voice of the Turtle,* because my mother saw an ad in the paper and assumed that it was about animals, and that it would be youthful, funny, and light, the perfect children's play. When we got there, my mother learned that we were in the midst of an adult comedy-drama and was a bit concerned, particularly when we heard one of the actors curse. That's when she leaned forward and said, "Diann, you must remember: you did not hear this."

I also saw every production of *Cinderella, Snow White, Pinocchio* — whatever my mother would find. It was important to her that I be exposed to everything cultural, and it became important to me, too. The biggest thrill of all was experiencing Ethel Merman in *Annie Get Your Gun*. I thought she was the most beautiful, the most talented human being I had ever seen. I sat there on the edge of my seat, watching her sing "Anything You Can Do I Can Do Better," then throw a chicken in the air and shoot it with her rifle, and I knew without question that to be able to stand on the stage and give that kind of powerful performance had to be just about the best thing anybody could hope to accomplish in life. And I wanted to do it, too.

❦

All this time I was attending Stitt Junior High School, which was not a happy experience for me — not because I couldn't handle the work, but because, as I've said, it was a rough school and I was different. Mrs. Humphries, the guidance counselor at Stitt, is a woman I will never forget. She called my mother and explained to her that my life wouldn't be easier when I moved on to George Washington High the following year. She suggested I think about a place called the High School of Music and Art. I doubt if my mother had heard of the school before, but she asked a lot of questions and came to the conclusion that this was where I belonged.

At first I was a little uncertain. I liked the idea of studying music and art but didn't want to be separated from the few friends that I had. I didn't want to start all over again in a strange school. But Mom was insistent. "I want you to go to this school," she kept saying. "I promise you, you'll never regret it." I still wasn't convinced, so to swing the vote in her favor she offered a bribe. "All right," she said, "I'll tell you what. Just take the entrance exam and your father and I will give you a hundred dollars and we'll go shopping." My mother knew that was a proposition I would never refuse. I said yes on the spot.

I filled out the application and went to look the place over on visiting day. It was an extraordinary school, a whole new world, unlike anything I had ever seen or even imagined possible. (This was one of two schools that were the inspiration for the movie *Fame*.) As I walked from classroom to classroom, I was staggered by the obvious rapport between the students and teachers, by the enthusiasm and involvement everyone seemed to share. The students weren't angry or sullen or defeated, as most of us were at Stitt. They were happy to be there. And so were the teachers. It seemed that everyone liked each other and everyone wanted to learn. The more I listened and watched and absorbed everything around me, the more certain I became that this was where I belonged. That day changed my life.

I took the test — I played the piano and I sang "Why Was I Born?" and "More Than You Know." And, wonder of wonders, I was accepted. And that was a new beginning. But I had a lot of catching up to do. My new classmates talked constantly about studying and achieving, the colleges they planned to attend, what they wanted to do with their lives. I had never heard this sort of talk from children my own age. I didn't know anything at all about studying so hard — school started at eight, let out at four, and in between we handled a difficult academic curriculum plus music, voice, art, and theory of music. That's some load for a girl who didn't even know she could go to the library and ask the librarian to help her find the information she needed for her assignments.

"You're about the most uninformed young lady I've ever met," my history teacher told me. "We have to do something about that. I want you to read the *New York Times* from cover to cover every Sunday, select an article on the world situation, and write a paper about it. I want another report every month on an article in the *Atlantic Monthly*. Here is a list of books. Go to the library and get busy."

At first I resented him. Who did this old man in that heavy tweed jacket think he was? But then as I began reading and discovering and taking it all in, I realized he was saving my life. From that moment on I stopped going to church on Sunday. I was after another kind of information now and spent the whole day immersed in the Sunday *Times*.

❧

Around the same time I started Music and Art, my sister Lydia was born. I adored her, and every day after school I would put her into her carriage and wheel her down to the park for an outing. When she was a year old (and I was fourteen), one of my pals took a snapshot of me sitting in her baby carriage. The picture was only a gag, but I thought I looked kind of happy and pretty, so on the spur of the moment I got an issue of *Ebony,* found out who the fashion editor was — a Freda DeKnight — and sent her the photo. I don't think I expected her to respond — after all, I was a far cry from the sophisticated young models I saw in every issue of *Ebony.* So, when she didn't answer I forgot all about it.

Six months later, there it was — a letter asking me to come to her office for an interview. I couldn't believe it, but I was in heaven, and in my normally organized and determined way, I set about preparing for this meeting.

I loved clothes but didn't actually know the first thing about fashion. If I had a deliberately set out to make myself look silly, I couldn't have done a better job. The interview was in the afternoon, and I wore my gray taffeta cocktail dress. I had no idea something like that was appropriate only for the evening. I only knew it was the best, the most grown-up dress in my wardrobe. To complete the picture, I wore black suede shoes with old-fashioned buckles that had to be buckled with a hook, a lavender straw hat with a veil left over from some bygone Easter, short cotton lavender gloves, and a black leather purse. Instead of stockings, I oiled my legs so that, God forbid, they wouldn't look "ashy." I looked, to put it mildly, ridiculous.

Freda DeKnight was expecting the simple, natural child she had seen in that photo. When she opened the door to the reception room and saw this overdressed disaster sitting there with her legs shining like beacons, she tried desperately not to laugh. But on the way back to her office I couldn't help noticing the amazement on her secretary's face. The way she arched her eyebrows seemed to ask, "Holy cow, where did you find *that* one?" Nevertheless, Freda must have seen past the silly outfit — I guess she saw a very thin, tall young girl with good cheekbones and hair that would photograph well, with a naïveté laced with sincerity — a gangly hopeful who wanted the job badly — and she hired me.

Freda sent me to a hairdresser named Frenchie, who styled my hair and urged me to pay attention to the makeup artists who worked with the photographers. And so began my education on how to take care of my looks. I learned about the hatbox, which was almost obligatory to carry to a photo session: in it were black pumps, preferably two pairs, one leather and one suede; gloves, both white cotton and black leather, in short, medium, and long, if possible; and naturally, my own makeup. For years I had this hatbox with me — either in the trunk of the car or under my arm.

My first job for Johnson Publications was a petticoat layout with three or four other teenage girls. When the picture was published, Dad hit the roof. No daughter of his was going to parade herself in public in just a bra and petticoat! He agreed to let me continue only after I promised never to pose that way again. He still wasn't happy about it, but gradually became somewhat more accepting when he saw that no one in the neighborhood seemed to disapprove. On the contrary, having my picture in *Ebony* had turned him into a bit of a celebrity. After church on Sunday people would come up to him and offer their congratulations. "Oh, I saw your daughter in the magazine. You must be so proud of her." And I guess he was — his only objection was to the clothes I wore . . . or didn't wear. And I think he was surprised that I was being paid the staggering sum of ten dollars an hour, which went straight into my bank account for my college education. Not bad for a fifteen-year-old kid — and Dad respected that. The whole thrust of his life had been to do, to achieve, to move ahead. And now, in my own way, I was following in his footsteps.

Since Music and Art was so demanding I couldn't work as a model very often. Not that the phone was exactly ringing off the hook for black models in those days. One could pose for *Ebony, Jet,* and *Sepia* and every great once in a while for an ad for some toothpaste or beer being touted to the black community, but that was about all. Yet I loved every minute of it. Once again a door had opened and shown me an unimaginable new world filled with possibilities. For the first time in my life I was working closely with sophisticated, well-educated, successful black businesswomen like Freda DeKnight — women with secretaries and expense accounts and limousines waiting outside to whisk them over to Sutton Place for a photo shoot — and that made quite an impression. As did the response of the successful photographers they hired. "Ah, she looks wonderful," they enthused as they snapped my picture. "She moves beautifully. Let's try to use her again." I began to sense that maybe I had something they liked. And maybe it could take me out into the larger world.

❧

The same year I started modeling I acquired my first boy friend. Tommy was eighteen, a full three years older than I was, and had already graduated from high school. He was the star boxer in our neighborhood, the winner of the Golden Gloves contest sponsored by the *Daily News*. I considered it quite a feather in my cap to have attracted his attention. Every Saturday night the two of us would go to a party in one of our friends' homes. The big thrill of the evening was slipping half a pint of whiskey into the punch bowl. Of course my folks would have killed me if they had known what we were up to, but that didn't matter. I suppose I was starting to push a little against the limits of parental authority, the way any adolescent does. But I still had to come home by the stroke of midnight, and Tommy made sure that I met my deadline.

He was such a caring, gentle young man, always so understanding and patient, even when it came to sex. One night while we were standing in the hallway grabbing at each other he smiled sweetly and then whispered, "I have to tell you something. You really don't know how to kiss. But that's all right. You'll learn." I couldn't imagine what he was talking about. Of course I knew how to kiss. I had seen all the movies. I held my head back at the proper angle and pushed. I'm surprised he didn't fall over, because I really pushed hard. I still don't understand how he had the patience to put up with me.

Tommy was every bit as gentle when, after two years of going together, we finally made love for the first time. I was terrified of sex and had put it off for as long as possible. (I can still hear my mother's voice: "Nice girls don't 'do it' until they're married"; "Remember, if you let yourself get swept away in the passion of the moment and become pregnant, your life will be ruined forever.") But for all his saintly patience, Tommy was persistent. "Listen, you're sweet and you're lovely, but let's face it, I can't keep going on like this. It's ridiculous . . ." And then he came up with a wonderful line: ". . . And, aah, um, I have to tell you, there's this other girl who wouldn't mind going all the way. It doesn't have to be anything more than that, and it won't change my feelings for you — but I'm just going to have to do it."

Those were the magic words. I've never been any good at sharing my men with other women. And I wanted to be wanted. So we made a plan. He would take care of the protection. I would tell my mother I'd be studying in the library after school. We would meet at his home, since both his parents would be away for the afternoon.

I walked to his house like a condemned murderer on her way to the electric chair. "You have got to go through with this, Carol Diann Johnson," I kept telling myself as I counted off the bars of the iron fence that ran along the children's park. Eventually there were no more bars, and I had to turn the corner and move on to my ultimate destination. I knew he was waiting for me, and I was frightened to death. He, on the other hand, was perfectly calm. Determined, but calm.

We struggled to make conversation for a while, but then it was time. I closed my eyes and blanked it all out. I remember nothing. When it was over I cried. "This is it?" I thought to myself. And then came the realization — "Oh, my God! What have I done!" Tommy, who must have thought I was crying for another reason, hugged me and said not to worry — he had taken the necessary precautions. Naturally, I went into the bathroom to look in the mirror and found that I really didn't look any different. I wanted to leave, but he asked me to stay. When his sister came home, she was attentive and kind (she knew what her brother had asked me to do). The three of us sat around talking, and I began to feel less strange. "Well, maybe this isn't the end of the world," I found myself thinking. "Maybe the next time it might be all right to open just one eye."

❧

Elissa Oppenheim — an auburn-haired, blue-eyed, freckle-faced joy of a person — was one of my best friends at Music and Art. She loved to play piano and I loved to sing, so it was only natural that we became a team. Once or twice a week we visited each other's homes after school to practice our act. Elissa was forever thinking about how we might break into show business. One day she came up with the bright idea of writing to *Arthur Godfrey's Talent Scouts* to ask for an audition.

Talent Scouts was a hugely popular television show in the early fifties. If chosen as a contestant, you were seen by millions of people. If you won the competition, you were asked to appear on Godfrey's equally popular daily radio program. When the letter arrived saying they would like to meet us, we were so thrilled we could hardly think about anything else. There was a week before the tryout, and we spent every afternoon rehearsing our big number, "Tenderly." We worked out quite a fancy arrangement. Elissa played the opening eight bars, then I came in, then she played the bridge without me, I came back in again and we finished together. We were very much a duo, billing ourselves as Oppenheim and Johnson.

The name almost finished us before we began. When we showed up for the audition, the production staff saw these two little sixteen-year-old high school girls in crinoline petticoats and couldn't help laughing.

"*You're* Oppenheim and Johnson? My God, with a name like that we thought you were an old vaudeville team!"

"Well, that's not who we are," I told them, not quite getting the joke. "She's Elissa Oppenheim, and I'm Carol Diann Johnson."

"Before we take this any further," the man in charge answered, "I'd like you to go home and try to find another name. There's no way in the world we can announce, 'Ladies and Gentlemen, Oppenheim and Johnson,' then have you two march out there. It's too ludicrous. Decide what you're going to call yourselves, then come back another day and we'll see what you can do."

I was crestfallen, but Elissa wouldn't let herself be discouraged. Late that night, a good hour after I finished struggling with my math homework and had gone to bed, she called with the solution to our problem.

"I've got it!" she proclaimed. "I'm changing my name to Lisa Collins and you're going to be Diahann Carroll! D-i-a-h-a-n-n C-a-r-r-o-l-l. How does that sound to you? Is it all right?"

"It's fine, Elissa. Just fine," I mumbled. (Actually, the spelling "Diahann" was on my birth certificate, but I didn't know that until I applied for my first job at Macy's, in the hat department, when I was fifteen.) I didn't really care — I thought it was for one time that I would use this name, and that would be that. So, with somewhat less deliberation than it would take to pick out a candy bar, Diahann Carroll is who I became.

The change to Collins and Carroll did the trick. We returned to the studio and got a date. We were incredibly nervous. It was the first time we ever performed with a real microphone. Elissa — Lisa — had rigged a fake mike in her living room to fortify us for this honest-to-God show business audition, but of course it was nothing like the real thing itself. Taking a deep breath, she sat down at the huge grand piano, ran her little fingers over the keys, then plunged ahead into the first part of our song. I tried to forget about the people watching us and managed to come in when I was supposed to. Three minutes later we were done.

We sat in the lobby waiting for the verdict. It seemed an eternity before the producer came out of the control booth to deliver the news. "All right, kids, here's the story," he told us, trying to smile. "We'd like to use the singer but not the piano player."

We were so shocked and disappointed that neither of us could speak. We were a team. Who would have dreamed they would want to split us up? We went to have a hamburger and a malt and sat there tense and depressed. Elissa, being the wonderful friend that she was, said all the right things.

"Of course you're going to do it."

"No, I wouldn't think of it."

"Don't be silly. This is your big chance. You can't give it up."

We walked down the street pretending nothing had changed, but both of us knew in our hearts that everything was different now and could never really be the same for us. A few weeks later I appeared on the show alone and won first prize.

Arthur Godfrey was an incredibly popular media personality in those days. He presented himself to his public as a relaxed, down-to-earth, average American kind of guy, but he had extraordinary power and didn't mind using it to intimidate. That's how he behaved with my mother when she came on the air with me. In keeping with the format of the program, she was the "talent scout" who had "discovered" me, and he flirted with her shamelessly throughout the little interview that preceded my performance. He could see how uncomfortable it made her, but that didn't prevent him from turning the screw tighter and tighter.

The next morning the two of us arrived at his office to discuss my going on his weekday radio show. Sitting behind his desk, lord and master of all he surveyed, he told us some awful racist joke about a slave who fell off a wagon, then studied us carefully to see how we reacted. Mom knew this was a terribly important moment for me, so she managed to muster up a nervous little laugh. But as far as I was concerned, he was insulting my mother, and his show wasn't the end of the world for me. If Godfrey didn't hire me, sooner or later someone else would. In my determined (and naïve) way I believed that, so I answered him just a shade too curtly, "I don't think my mother appreciates jokes like that. They are not funny." The moment I said it I was sorry. But five minutes later I was glad, because he leaned forward, pushed a buzzer signaling the end of the meeting, and when his secretary appeared, told her, "Well, I suppose Miss Smarty Pants here is going to be on our radio show next week." It was a good lesson for me — I had been right to stand up for what I believed and felt was right.

Despite the rocky beginning, Godfrey asked me to return for the next three weeks. I enjoyed every minute of it — getting up at the crack of dawn and driving down to the studio with my mother, sitting in that big dressing room with famous singers like the McGuire Sisters, putting on my makeup to look pretty for the live audience. (The staff makeup artist had never worked on a black person, so I did my makeup myself.) I loved the actual singing (I sang every love song I had ever heard on my dad's record player) and the way people in the neighborhood came up to me afterward. "I heard ya," they'd say, "I heard ya on the radio this morning." The whole experience was wonderful. Now different meant special.

ஒ&

When I graduated from Music and Art there was no question in my house that I would go on to college. Mom and Dad had their hearts set on sending me to Howard University in Washington, D.C. Howard was considered the best black college in the country, and they felt my northern upbringing needed the balance of a southern, predominantly black university. I went along with their dream all through my last years of high school, but when it was time to submit the application, I had to confront the fact that I really didn't want to go. I wasn't ready to leave home. I most certainly didn't want to give up my singing and modeling classes and my work at Johnson Publications.

My parents thought I should be a teacher or maybe a doctor. "The singing and modeling will always be there," they told me the evening we sat down for a family conference about my future. "They're not important right now. The most important thing is getting that piece of paper, that college degree." I conceded they might be right, so we worked out a compromise. I would stay in

New York but enter New York University in the fall to study psychology.

I tried to be a good student and give Mom and Dad what they wanted, but my real interests kept pulling at me. Early in my freshman year I entered another talent contest, a network TV show called *Chance of a Lifetime,* where I sang "Why Was I Born?," "The Man I Love," and "Someone to Watch Over Me," and won for three weeks in a row. My prize was three thousand dollars and a week's engagement at the Latin Quarter. What a thrill that was! I was in heaven!

Mom and Dad were impressed by the money, but weren't all that pleased with their seventeen-year-old daughter singing in a nightclub. The Latin Quarter served liquor, it had show girls, and, to make matters worse, the headline act the week I was scheduled to appear was Christine Jorgensen, the transsexual. But they knew how important this was to me, so once again, as long as I promised to keep up with schoolwork, they allowed me to do it. (They attended my opening night, but without any of their relatives and friends. I think they were too embarrassed to tell anyone.)

It was all so strange and new I didn't know what to make of it. The chorus girls wore such scanty costumes. They didn't seem to have any qualms at all about lounging around the dressing room practically naked. That frightened me a little, but I couldn't help being impressed by their professionalism and discipline. They were never late. They meticulously cared for their own makeup and hair. They dieted and exercised constantly to keep every part of their bodies in shape. From watching them go about their nightly routine, I began to understand that my skin, hair, and teeth were important tools of the trade and that I had to take good care of them. I'll always be grateful to those ladies for that experience. This is where I learned — this was my show business school. This was another beginning.

My costume was more along the lines of a high school prom queen. I wore a Florence Lustig gown with yards of tulle, white elbow-length gloves, and a little rhinestone tiara. As it happened, Christine Jorgensen dressed almost exactly the same way! The only place I topped her was with that silly tiara. One evening she waited for me backstage to tell me, in a deep, masculine voice, that since we both wore the same Florence Lustig gowns she'd like to teach me how to bow so all the tulle would float around me rather like a cloud.

"Thanks!" I answered, grateful that she would take the time to help me.

"All right, first bend your knees. Now, keeping your back straight, lower your body into the center of the skirt. That's right. No, hold your arms out and at your sides. Perfect. You look just like a little princess." I watched and listened. I was quiet, not volunteering opinions or thoughts, just taking it all in.

I remember that first night so well! The stage seemed enormous — absolutely cavernous. I wore a pale green silk tulle (as in net) Florence Lustig gown with a beaded bodice. (I think it cost $600, which was an enormous amount of money!) It wasn't the type of gown the audience was used to seeing at the Latin Quarter — instead of fitted and sexy, mine was pastel, full, and innocent. And I wore no jewelry — I figured that since I didn't have the real stuff, I would wear nothing at all.

And when the moment came to really do it, to sing, to perform on a stage in front of a live audience, I stood to the side and looked out at the audience and thought, "Here you go, Diahann Carroll. Here you go." I was scared — no, terrified — but not paralyzed. I handled this challenge as I usually do when I'm confronted with a new situation — I spent a few minutes by myself, blanked my mind, totally dismissed the fact that an audience was out there, and walked out onstage to work. I must have seemed distant even then — but what I was was determined to sing well. So I sang.

I sang all the old standards — "Where or When," "Why Was I Born?," "In The Still of the Night." And because I didn't know anything at all about singing in nightclubs, I just stood, straight as an arrow, and sang! There was no movement, no sexuality — I just sang my heart out. When I was done, I realized I didn't remember I'd even been out there.

The Latin Quarter was owned by Lou Walters, Barbara's father. When I finished the week, he called my parents and asked them to come to a meeting. He explained to us that he also owned a personal management office, and told us that he wanted to sign me as a client. Although he knew I had a lot to learn, he thought I had a future in the business and felt that his office could provide the grooming and guidance I needed. Dad mulled it over for a minute, then said, yes, that might be all right, as long as Mr. Walters understood that I was a full-time college student and my education came first.

I now had an agent, a personal manager, and a rehearsal pianist. Along with rehearsing and voice lessons and modeling, I also began to have some jobs as a singer. The one thing I didn't have was time for school. Starting a career turned out to be too consuming to allow room for anything else. I could barely manage to show up for class, and my absences overtook my attendances. A few weeks before finals, my adviser suggested I accept incompletes in all my subjects and not even try to take the exams.

Mom and Dad were bitterly disappointed when I brought home the news that evening. There was yet another big family conference around the dining table, and when all was said and done they agreed to let me take a leave of absence. I would have two years to try to establish myself in a career. If that didn't happen, I would go back to NYU and finish my degree. I accepted their conditions, but that was the end of my college education. I never returned to NYU, and the Johnson household remained without its first college graduate.

❧

If one kind of education was coming to an end, another was just beginning. My new teacher was a large, blond, fiercely dedicated young man of German descent named Chuck Wood. Chuck Wood worked for the Walters organization and had taken me on as his primary responsibility — he became my personal manager. But he turned out to be so much more than that. He was my mentor, my taskmaster, my second family, my friend.

Chuck Wood loved the theater, especially musical comedy, and that's what he wanted for me. "She belongs on Broadway," he told the Walters people, "not in those clubs. And I'm going to get her there." They thought he was slightly mad. How many black performers in the history of show business ever had a Broadway career? The Walters organization was used to booking nightclubs and hotels, but Chuck was so persistent he eventually wore them down. "Okay, okay," they told him. "Go ahead. Just don't spend too much time on it. And we'll still want her to play the Catskills."

Chuck found a pianist for me, a wonderful woman named Joyce Brown who went on to become one of the first (and few) female conductors on Broadway. He selected some classic show tunes by

Cole Porter, Harold Arlen, and Rodgers and Hart. He made out a schedule and booked the rehearsal hall. And we went to work. We would start on Monday and work without pause from morning to late afternoon. Even when we stopped for a quick sandwich, the work continued. Between bites Chuck would analyze, exhort, encourage, reprimand — do anything he felt was necessary to make me understand.

"My God, Diahann, what's the matter with you today? Come on, let's try this again. I want you to loosen up. You're stiff as a board. Look in the mirror. That's what the people are going to see. I know you can do better than that. . . . Joyce, you're not being strict enough. She's just singing the notes without paying any attention to the lyrics. She might as well be vocalizing. We don't want that! . . . All right, I'm leaving for an hour or so. When I return, I expect to see some real improvement."

I was exhausted by now but didn't dare stop. I never knew if Chuck wasn't crouched right behind the door with his ear to the keyhole. That happened more than once. "Jesus Christ!" I'd hear him yell. "I've been standing here for fifteen minutes, and you haven't sung a single note!"

My education didn't end when the sun went down. Very often after we finished working for the day Chuck took me home to his little apartment in Greenwich Village. He cooked dinner, introducing me to all sorts of new, exciting foods, then we moved to the couch in front of the fireplace and went on with the lessons.

Chuck told me what books to buy and the playwrights I should read. "Clifford Odets, Eugene O'Neill, Arthur Miller — if you're going to be in the theater you have to know their work." He played classical music and old Broadway shows for me, analyzing the fine points of the performance: "Listen to how Merman holds that high note. Listen to the sound when she comes off it. Do you hear that command and control?"

And if that was not enough, he carried on about my manners and clothes: "Cross your legs when you sit down. . . . Get rid of those rhinestones and sequins and all that shiny junk. . . . If I catch you chewing gum again I'll kill ya. Never forget you're a *lady*. . . . I want you in Peter Pan collars and lots of crinolines and pretty shoes. Let's see a little leg, but not too much. What perfume do you wear?"

Over and over again he held forth about what he thought I had going for me and how he saw my future in the business: "Never forget that you have a certain softness, a certain innate ladylike quality. Style and class. No matter where you go or how successful you become, you must never lose it. That's what sets you apart. That is the essence of what you are. You are not Lena Horne. You are going to suffer the comparison, but don't let that confuse you. Lena is marble. You are cashmere." He loved my naïveté, the softness, the vulnerability that he saw, and felt that these were my strong points — that these would help me find my niche. "Leave the sex, the raw emotions to the other singers," he would say. "I don't want you wearing tight gowns." And so Chuck was truly responsible for my first professional impression of myself.

Looking back now, I can see that Chuck was trying to give me a cram course in the entire history of the American theater so I would come to know it and understand it and find my place inside it. It was an incredible gift. He pushed so hard, though, that sometimes my head would start to pound and I would find myself screaming at him, "Enough, enough! God, leave me alone!" Often I was so exhausted by the end of the evening I didn't have strength to drag myself home and fell asleep on his sofa.

Margo Rebeil, my vocal coach, was just as loving and generous. "Put aside some time after your lesson tomorrow," she would tell me. "We're going to have tea. I want to show you how to serve. And then we'll take a ride in my car." She had a classic old Packard in mint condition, and when we finished the tea lesson the next afternoon she donned her large riding hat and whisked me off for a drive. "Do you like this car?" she asked.

"Yes, I do."

"Well, it's a very fine car," she continued, proceeding to explain all the reasons why. I knew that she wasn't just talking about cars. She was teaching me about quality. At Christmas she invited me to her annual cocktail party to expose me to her friends in the theater. "Be here at seven," she ordered. "Look pretty. Maybe you'll have a glass of champagne. Yes, let's try some champagne."

It was an extraordinary way to start in the business. I always felt cared for and protected just as I had at home. When I went into the rehearsal halls on Eighth and Ninth Avenues, even the winos on the sidewalk were parental.

"How you doin' there, Miss Diahann. Goin' to your practicin' today?"

"Yes, I am."

"Well, that's just fine. You work hard now."

❧

Through all this Chuck kept sending me out to audition for Broadway shows. No offers were forthcoming; very often the producers didn't even want to see me once they learned I was black. But Chuck protected me from this information. Not until years later did I know what had happened. Chuck had to let the Walters office book me into the clubs.

I began in the Catskill hotels for fifty dollars a night. I was usually sandwiched in between the apache dancers and the comic. The next step was going on the road to work at nightclubs in small towns. Here I traveled alone. This was the first time I had ever been out on my own, and there was no choice but to learn how to cope with the inevitable pressures. Some of these towns had never seen a black person before. When I walked down the street, I could feel everyone staring at me as though I were some kind of exotic animal.

I passed through some lonely places. The loneliest was Wilmerding, Pennsylvania. The main street ran about the length of a city block. At one end, there was an enormous coal mine and at the other the beer hall where I sang. When I got off the bus and checked in, the proprietor, a large, friendly woman in jeans and a leather jacket, took a look at me and laughed. "What have they sent me this time? How old are you, honey?" I told her I was eighteen. She shook her head, then guided me upstairs, unlocked these heavy wooden doors, and showed me my room. "You have to stay locked in here whenever you aren't singing," she explained. "If for some reason you need to go out, dial down to the bar and I'll come up with my keys. I don't want anything to happen to you."

The months out on the road gave me a huge advantage over most of my contemporaries. I was working, never mind where or how. I was not another one of the hundreds of young hopefuls who rent the rehearsal hall and hire the pianist for an hour but don't have the experience of standing in front of a live audience and hearing the applause (or lack of it) and learning from this experience. I began to understand the power of choice — that earning money gave me the chance to ask for more. Because I was earning good money, I could say to Chuck, "I heard a wonderful arranger. Maybe we could work with him. I heard a new song I like, one that really moved me. I feel the lyrics, and I think I can do it in a different style. What if I rehearse it and try it out on the road?" It was glorious to be able to do that — to have a say in what I was doing.

Eventually, the Walters office brought me in from the boondocks and booked me into Cafe Society Downtown in Greenwich Village. The club was about to go out of business; on the weekends we played to maybe half a house. But I was still being paid six hundred dollars a week, a serious amount of money for an eighteen-year-old.

Now that I was singing in a real New York City nightclub, it was time to get down to brass tacks. I put away my tulle and tiara and bought a couple of slinky new dresses to make myself appropriately seductive on stage. I was so skinny that the dressmaker had to pad almost every inch of my body to achieve the desired effect. There was so much padding around the hips and bust that the gowns literally stood up by themselves. But when I zipped myself in, presto, I was sexy — or so I thought. Chuck was furious when he saw what I had done to myself, but I was adamant. I was trying to make him understand that looking like a kid wasn't going to get me what I wanted.

But my new sophistication was only skin deep. Mom drove me to the club every night, parked the car in front of the entrance, and sat there, waiting. Her presence downstairs was very much with me even as I was giving my all to torrid torch songs.

No one could believe I was as naïve as I really was. The ladies room attendant was appalled when she offered me a reefer and I didn't know what she was talking about. I had never heard the word before in my life. "Let me get this straight now," she laughed. "You were brought up *where?*"

But I must have been doing something right, because one day Chuck called, wildly excited. The producer Saint Subber was casting a new show set in the West Indies, called *House of Flowers.* Chuck thought I'd be perfect for the ingenue and had arranged an audition. The Walters office was having some conversations with Hollywood about trying me out for a role in the movie of *Carmen Jones,* but this is what Chuck had been hoping and planning and preparing me for since our first meeting.

I auditioned on the bare stage of the Alvin Theatre. Saint Subber and the rest of the jury sat in the dark out in the audience, and I performed to their disembodied voices. As they asked questions and gave directions, I was able to make out the crisp British accent of the director, Peter Brook, the high southern tones of Truman Capote, who wrote the book and lyrics, and the warm, gentle voice of the composer, Harold Arlen. But I never saw their faces clearly. I don't remember how I got through it, but I must have, because a week or so later I was summoned to Saint Subber's apartment for a second meeting. After grilling me for an hour about my background and experience and just about everything else one could think of, they still seemed interested but couldn't quite make up their minds. The casting director, a young man named Monte Kay, clearly didn't think I was right for the part. Harold Arlen, though, seemed to be pulling for me. The meeting ended indecisively. Harold Arlen walked me to the elevator.

"I understand you might be going to California," he said.

"Yes, that's a possibility."

"Well, I think it would be very good for you. Go! Have a ball! Just meet people and go places and do everything you can. You know, try to live a little."

It wasn't until years later that I really understood what he meant. I was so protected, so immersed in the proprieties of my own background, that I could accept only what my parents approved of as correct, and that inhibited me both as a person and a performer. I was too stilted on stage. I couldn't bring myself to move in a way that wasn't ladylike. I was still living at home, constantly watched by my parents. I was still a child.

At the time, though, his words mystified me. Live a little? I was auditioning for the part of a fifteen-year-old. I was already eighteen. What was he trying to tell me?

But I took his advice, and when I was offered the opportunity to read for *Carmen Jones,* I grabbed it. No one seemed very pleased with my decision. Chuck thought I was wasting my time and talent. My boy friend, Tommy, didn't want me to leave New York. Mom and Dad were so apprehensive that they asked a family friend (whom I called Aunt Dorothy) to go with me to Hollywood to make sure I kept out of trouble.

And I had a few apprehensions of my own. I knew enough about the business to realize that just about the only black actress to achieve anything at all in Hollywood was Lena Horne, and she was usually seen in a separate segment that could be removed when the film toured the South. (I used to wonder, "How could anyone not want to look at Lena Horne?" But for many years films in Hollywood would be filmed one way for most of the country, and then would be totally recut to leave out the black faces for the South.) On the other hand, my determination and optimism made me feel that maybe time would change things. I guess that all performers are convinced they possess that special quality that will make them break through, and I believed it too.

Chapter Three

Otto Preminger was seated behind the longest desk I had ever seen. The light from the window shone down on his bald head, making him look absolutely formidable. To make matters worse, his office was the size of a hotel ballroom. So I didn't feel very big or important when I was whisked in for my audience and was introduced, "Mr. Preminger, here is Diahann Carroll." Without a word but with a slight nod he motioned to me, indicating where I was to sit while he interviewed me about a possible part in his upcoming movie, *Carmen Jones*.

Needless to say, I was overwhelmed by the place, by the man, by the fact that Diahann Carroll, age nineteen, the singer from New York, was sitting in front of this major studio mogul, waiting to hear about a part in one of his films. I had never before encountered power on such a grand scale. It made me so nervous that I found it almost impossible to answer Preminger's quite ordinary and impersonal questions. When the questions suddenly stopped, I was sure that the interview was over and began to leave, but Preminger had other plans. To my astonishment, he asked me to read from the *Carmen Jones* script with none other than James Edwards, and now he led me into the adjoining room to meet the famous actor.

If I was awed by Otto Preminger, I was totally bowled over by James Edwards. Like everyone else, I had marveled at his brilliant performance in *Home of the Brave* four or five years earlier. He was, at the time, the only really famous black actor. He was strong, sexy, and mysterious, and I was speechless — which is not too helpful for an actress. Preminger explained that he wanted me to read for the part of Carmen Jones and had selected one of her most sensuous, seductive scenes. He handed me the script and barked, "Take off your shoes and stockings — your boy friend is going to paint your nails." And then he left, quite ceremoniously, and we were alone.

Take off my shoes? Paint my nails? What was he talking about? Was he serious? I couldn't take off my shoes and stockings — my toes were so scarred from those cheap, tight shoes I had sneaked into my book bag as a kid that I was really ashamed of them. And polish my toes? Was he kidding? I had never had a pedicure. What was I going to do?

Before I could do anything James Edwards began to coach me on my lines. Now James was obviously a very worldly and experienced man, one of the most seductive men I have ever met, and I was more than a little frightened by his presence. He had a kind of animalistic awareness of himself that made me feel feminine yet somewhat on edge. He, on the other hand, thought it was terribly charming to be reading with an "actress" so young and fresh. He was very helpful, urging me to go over my lines with him.

Soon Preminger returned and asked us to begin reading. I started first, but all I could think about was the moment they would see my toes. I managed to stumble through my lines; I even managed to take off my shoes (although I think I had my eyes closed the whole time, figuring it was better not to see their horrified expressions when they finally got a look at my toes!). But then when we reached the place when Carmen's boy friend finishes applying the polish and blows on her toes to dry them, I almost shot through the roof. Nothing in my young life had prepared me for this kind of heavy sexuality, and I couldn't begin to handle it, even on the level of "let's pretend." I must have seemed ridiculous.

Finally, sensing my discomfort, Preminger asked, barking at me with his full force (but with a glint in his eyes), "Who ever told you you were sexy?"

"No one! No one! I swear!" I answered quickly, looking him straight in the eye, somehow recognizing that both of us knew this was outrageous, and that a friendship had just begun. And then Otto Preminger, the bully extraordinaire, threw back his head and roared with laughter.

I did not get the Carmen Jones part. That went to Dorothy Dandridge. But I never thought I would get it — I knew that I did not have the kind of sexuality needed to play Carmen. But I thought I did have the talent to be in films, and I wanted to have that chance, so I had come out to meet Preminger because I knew that if I did impress him in person, I would then be considered to play other roles.

I guess Preminger was quite amused by my audition, because he gave me a small role as one of Carmen's sidekicks. Wardrobe decked me out in a bright red fringed dress that had been designed for Bonita Granville (her name was in the label and I was thrilled — although I now remember that it was probably the ugliest dress I was ever to see!), big hoop earrings, and high-heeled shoes. They then sent me over to hair and makeup, where they slicked down my hair with a quart of Dixie Peach Pomade (a sort of Vaseline that was then used to straighten hair). When I was taken to the set for Preminger's approval, wobbling along on those high heels, looking like a puppy trying to find its right footing, he saw what they had done to me and started laughing.

Carmen Jones was the all-black version of Bizet's *Carmen*. The setting had been changed from Spain to the American South, and the original melodies were given new lyrics that reflected someone's misbegotten idea of how black people were supposed to speak. The plot and the characters and situations were every bit as ste-reotyped as the "dees," "dems," and "dats" that filled the dialogue. Preminger had assembled a wonderful cast of performers to try to breathe some life into this thing, including the beautiful Dorothy Dandridge, the incredibly beautiful Harry Belafonte, and the in-comparable Pearl Bailey, who immediately undertook the role of my adoptive mother.

But for all the movie-star fantasies I carried with me to Cali-fornia, it became clear as the weeks went by that none of us was likely to have much of a future here. We were the only black people on the lot. The producers, production staff, and crew were all quite polite and professional, but there was absolutely no ca-maraderie on or off the set, no sense of shared purpose. The un-spoken assumption seemed to be that we were outsiders, in town for only a short while to do our "black" feature film (there was a "black" film every few years), and when it was over we would go back to wherever we came from and no one would ever see us again.

I felt that the one possible exception would be Dorothy Dandridge. She had such presence and incredible beauty that it was difficult to believe she wasn't going to become a star. As I watched her dressing and undressing in the fitting room, I had to wonder why Preminger even bothered to have me read for her part.

Dorothy had done several low-budget films over the years, but *Carmen Jones* was her big break, the picture that was supposed to make her a star. There were rumors on the set that Preminger was involved with her and had made her success his personal goal. Dorothy wanted success desperately and worked hard to give him everything he asked for. He often screamed at her to force her to rise above her inexperience, and she always accepted his abuse. But for all her ambition and beauty she was a lonely, vulnerable woman with very little confidence in herself. On the set she seemed strained and uncomfortable. Off the set she was painfully shy and self-absorbed, concerned only with improving her performance. So much was riding on it that she seemed to be living in a constant state of anxiety. Her vulnerability touched me deeply.

Although she was years older and far more experienced, I found myself wanting to comfort her and take care of her. She had very few friends in the cast. Her looks made the other actresses jealous — she had the most beautiful face and the perfect body, and her smile and eyes were totally mesmerizing.

After the release of *Carmen Jones*, Dorothy was nominated for an Academy Award as best actress of the year. It was, I believe, the first time that honor had ever been bestowed upon a black woman. Her future seemed assured. But there were no offers of a long-term studio contract, no strong personal management to take advantage of the moment and consolidate her success. She made a few films, mostly in Europe, but her career never really developed. When I saw her again five years later on the set of *Porgy and Bess* — the next big all-black musical film — the early promise remained unfulfilled and she was wracked with uncertainty.

I remember one night Dorothy invited me to meet someone at her home in Hollywood. When we arrived I found a perfect little doll's house — everything in its place; white sofas and rugs, flowers on the piano; total Hollywood elegance everywhere. Dorothy explained that she wanted me to meet her fiancé, Jack Dennison. I thought that was sweet but asked, "Why me?" We weren't close friends, and I couldn't understand her interest in me. "I'm about to marry him and he's white and I thought you could give me some advice." Frankly, I was astounded. True, by this time I was married to Monte Kay, who was white, but I married him because he was a fascinating, wonderful man and I loved him, not because of his color. And Monte, a Jew from Brooklyn, could not have been more removed from Jack Dennison, who was Greek. I felt sorry for Dorothy — I tried to make her understand that she was marrying a man, a human being, not a color. That's always been my philosophy, and still is.

My own part in *Carmen Jones* was so insignificant I didn't have to contend with any of the pressures that caused Dorothy such anxiety. But I enjoyed this new kind of work. I was always prepared for the little I had to do and took advantage of the long waits between setups to try to learn something about filmmaking. Preminger enjoyed my enthusiasm and made me his mascot on the set. The only time I felt the weight of his famous temper was when I was being naughty and attempted to push myself into the spotlight. "Hold it, Stringbean!" he yelled. "Step back. Stand next to Pearl like you're supposed to. You're just trying to get into the camera."

He was right about that. I definitely wanted to be noticed. Not that I was. No one was fascinated by me when the picture was released. No one looked up at the screen and said, "Ah, I must have her for my next film." But it was fun while it lasted, especially being able to be on my own, to meet and have fun with people who interested me.

❧

During my Hollywood sojourn I stayed with Aunt Dorothy in a little hotel on Sunset Boulevard near Ciro's. Josh White, the folk singer, lived down at one end of the hall. At the other end was a large suite occupied by Sammy Davis, Jr. The two of them came from completely different worlds. Josh White often left his door open, and I heard him strumming his guitar and singing softly for his friends. They all had the same earnest, rather intellectual look about them and came and went very quietly. Sammy Davis's end of the corridor was a good bit more high-spirited from the uninterrupted merrymaking.

Sammy's record of "Hey There" had just become a big hit, and he was beginning to emerge as one of the genius talents of the day. Everyone was a bit awed by him. One evening I was sitting in the coffee shop downstairs having my usual overstuffed sandwich and thick malted in a vain effort to put some flesh on my bones when he strolled in with his retinue and the whole place fell silent. Sensing how uncomfortable we were, he yelled to the waitress, "Wine! Wine for all my friends!" The entire coffee shop exploded with laughter and immediately relaxed. I fell in love with him on the spot.

A few nights later, Sammy sent someone to invite me over to his suite to join a party. We chatted for a few minutes, then he pulled me aside and said, "There's someone here who'd very much like to meet you. He's a little shy. He's in the other room. I hope you won't mind saying hello to Marlon Brando." I couldn't believe what I was hearing! I had seen Brando give those incredible performances in *A Streetcar Named Desire, Viva Zapata,* and *The Wild One,* and like every other aspiring actor in this country, I was absolutely thrilled by the new depth and intensity he brought to American acting. Sammy introduced us, and then left us alone. We were both too withdrawn to have much to say to each other. I, naturally, was so nervous to be in the company of this great actor that I kept quiet. Brando, for his part, understood the mysterious power of silence and was perfectly content to sit there quietly without forcing himself to make any of the expected social conversation.

The following night a friend of Sammy's called to invite me to dinner with Brando and his date. I was expecting the Brown Derby or one of the other famous Hollywood glamour spots, but we drove to a tiny, out-of-the-way restaurant on La Cienega where Brando could keep a low profile. It was almost as if we were in hiding. Brando's date wore a blatantly sexy dress that looked like my bar girl costume in *Carmen Jones.* I was sure she was what my mother would describe as "loose," and that made me so uncomfortable I hardly spoke the whole evening. (Can you believe that? At nineteen, a continent away from my family, I was still aware of my mother's disapproving voice saying, "You're having dinner with that tramp!") Then, to make matters worse, as we were leaving the restaurant Brando came up behind me and gave me a little pat on the fanny. Before I realized what I was doing, I wheeled around and walloped him across the face. "How dare you!" I seethed. "Who do you think you are to touch me like that?" All those sentiments I had been raised with just came tumbling out of my mouth. He was astonished and I could not believe what I had done. I said *that* to *Marlon Brando* — and took a swing at him besides! I wanted to die.

When I returned from the set the next day, I found a large cardboard box waiting for me in my room. It was filled with books about acting, works like *An Actor Prepares* and many other texts that the serious actors of that time studied as their bibles. I was trying to figure out who sent it and why (there was no note enclosed, only the name of a movie studio on the outside) when the phone rang. It was Brando. "Did they get there?" he asked. "All right, you read them. Read every one of them from cover to cover. And the minute you finish this film you go home to New York and you work on your craft. Don't ever come back to Hollywood. It's not for you. You have no business here."

A night or so later he called again. "Oh, you're still here? When are you going home? Have you been doing your reading?" I had been reading a little, just enough to begin to appreciate the seriousness, dedication, and skill that the job of acting required. Up to now acting had been strictly secondary to my singing, but as I struggled my way through the pages of Stanislavski, I saw that it was a subject of enormous complexity that had to be undertaken by and for itself and that I had a long way to go before I could consider myself a real actress. Brando's gift planted the incentive that eventually led me to the Actors Studio, and I'll always be grateful to him.

Every week he called and asked the same questions. And every so often we would go out. Once we went to a party at Betty Comden's. I remember I wore a little taffeta skirt and white blouse because I felt I was too thin to wear any of those beautiful, tight-fitting dresses of the day. As usual, Brando placed me on a couch and went over to the other side of the room to watch what happened. That night Humphrey Bogart came over. The initial thrill of meeting Bogart didn't last more than a few seconds: because Brando was the new guy in town getting all the attention, Bogart saw him as some kind of threat that had to be challenged, and he wasn't a big boy about it. Instead of going after Brando himself, he attacked his date, me. Bogart had been one of my idols, and it was a huge disappointment to discover he could be so tedious and so rude.

"Why don't you tell us about him?" he asked me in a stage whisper that turned every head in the room. "We can't figure him out. He won't tell us anything. He's completely unapproachable. You're sleeping with him, so why don't you let us in on his secret?"

I was furious — my face flushed, and I clutched the side of the couch so hard I bent my newly polished nails. "How dare you!" I shot back, shaking with anger. (The line was getting to be a real habit!) "If you want to know anything about Brando, ask him. . . . And, not that it's any of your business, I am most certainly not sleeping with him!" (It's obvious my sense of humor had not yet developed — I was childishly furious!)

That happened to be true. The one evening Brando made a halfhearted play to take me up to his bedroom, all I had to say was, "Aw, please, Marlon," and he stopped. He wasn't really surprised. I don't know what he actually wanted from me. There was hardly an actress in Hollywood who wasn't throwing herself at his feet. Perhaps he found my feistiness refreshing. Maybe he just enjoyed appearing with me on his arm every now and then because he knew it would raise a few eyebrows.

I was flattered by Brando's attention, but the truth of the matter was I had become wildly infatuated with James Edwards. When he called later that week to ask me out for a drink, I was absolutely overwhelmed. To my nineteen-year-old way of thinking, James Edwards was practically a god. He was handsome. He was talented. He was famous. He was a successful movie star, someone who had done the undoable by creating an image of the black man as a sensitive, intelligent, articulate human being who had to be reckoned with.

I was so thrilled to be in his presence I couldn't begin to deal with the fact he was also married and an alcoholic and half crazy with frustration and rage from not being able to work. After the triumph of *Home of the Brave*, he had gone on to star in a few other low-budget movies, but there was really no place for him in the industry, and his career gradually ground to a standstill. Preminger had considered casting him as the male lead in *Carmen Jones* but finally gave the part to Harry Belafonte. James had an entirely different version of what happened: he had been offered the role but decided to reject it for something better. I believed him. Why not? I saw the nice house, the expensive clothes, the big convertible, and all the other accoutrements of success. I listened to him carry on about how he was meeting producers and developing projects and negotiating for the lead in this or that movie, and I bought every word of it, even though for one reason or another none of these prospects ever materialized. I thought he was wonderful.

I waited in my room night after night, hoping he might decide to call. When the phone finally rang and he told me to be downstairs in twenty minutes, I was there. He always smelled of alcohol. He drank constantly from morning until night. He was always full of anger, vengeance, and pain. "You know what I did yesterday?" he would ask, then tell me about how he screwed some producer's wife and, small world, would be seeing her husband tomorrow about a job. Then he'd go on to regale me with stories about the scandalous personal lives of all the powers in the business and how this s.o.b. owed him and this so-and-so better do what he wanted because. I had no idea how to respond. I could only say, "Oh, James, I don't know." "Don't be afraid," he would answer. "You must never be afraid."

We would drive around aimlessly for hours, eventually stopping at some Beverly Hills restaurant for dinner. There were very few places where he was still welcome. All the maître d's knew he was a time bomb just waiting to explode. Sometimes I saw it happen. He'd create a nasty scene, start a fight with the waiter or threaten the people at the next table. His behavior improved when we went to the bars in the black section of town. Everyone realized he drank too much and misbehaved, but they loved him and treated him like a king, allowing him to salvage some small shred of his tattered pride.

Through all this I kept on my blinders, never questioning his mad behavior or my own fascination for this strange, tortured soul. I was easy prey — I was the good little girl who had been brought up to believe that if a man wanted me, I should be grateful. I couldn't figure out why anyone could be attracted to me — I was skinny, devoid of sexuality, not really attractive. So when someone found me attractive, I didn't question, I didn't choose — I jumped. Just as I wanted the world's approval when I sang, so did I crave men's approval, and was grateful when it came. The fact that James

Edwards — successful, handsome, older black movie star — had chosen me for his companion was more than enough to quell any misgivings.

My Aunt Dorothy was every bit as dazzled as I. It was almost as though we had made a silent pact never to acknowledge he was married and drank too much and was very often dangerously out of control. Neither of us said a word that evening he came to our room with a bottle and became so drunk he fell asleep on the floor. On another drunken visit he tried to undress me right in front of her, and once again we both pretended it wasn't really happening. Aunt Dorothy had come to California to look after me. If it had been anyone else, she would have thrown him out of the room and headed straight for the telephone to inform my parents about the disgraceful company I was keeping. But because he was who he was, she just looked the other way.

I did the same thing, no matter how outrageous he became. One Saturday night I was sitting with him in a bar watching him grow more and more incoherent, when he looked up from his glass and muttered, "All right, come with me." He led me up the stairs to a little bedroom over the bar and shut the door behind him. "Take off your clothes," he ordered. I was totally confused, but did what he asked and stripped to my undergarments. I knew it didn't have anything to do with sex. For all his stories about his sexual conquests, there was no sex between us, no displays of affection — no hugging or kissing or tenderness. Maybe he was turned off by my naïveté and inexperience. Maybe the booze and the sense of failure and the years of using and abusing everyone including himself had finally taken their toll and burned him out. He just sat there staring at me for the next hour, and then he got up to leave.

"No, you stay here," he told me as I reached for my clothes. "I'll let you know when you can go." He turned off the light. I heard the door close and the key turn in the lock. I waited passively as the hours passed, without knowing why. It wasn't until the middle of the next day that he reappeared to take me back to my hotel. I did not cry or scream at him. I did not say, "How dare you!" I did not tell him I would never see him again. I just followed him meekly down the steps, and the next time he called to say he was picking me up I was downstairs waiting for him five minutes later.

One night, James dropped me off at the hotel, and when I walked into the lobby there was my old boy friend, Tommy, waiting for me. He was in the Air Force now and had used his leave to hitch a ride to California to pay me a surprise visit. We hadn't seen much of each other at all in at least six months. I had been too busy working in nightclubs and rehearsing with Chuck. When we had parted, I had promised to write him every week, and at first I did. But then, as the weeks went by, my letters became fewer and fewer and he began to fade from my thoughts. I was working in Hollywood and he seemed very far away. Now, as we stood there staring at each other, I had to face my true feelings.

Tommy suddenly looked so young in his uniform and short haircut, and so out of place. He rushed over to sweep me up in his arms, but I didn't want him to touch me. I felt terribly guilty, but there was nothing I could do about it. We sat there in the lobby for the rest of the night, talking together softly as I tried to explain what he already knew. No, we were not going to get married when I came back to New York. No, we would not be settling down in that nice little house with the white picket fence we had always dreamed about. I had a career now. I was traveling down a different road, and as wonderful as it had been between us, it was over.

And when I returned to New York, the "relationship" with Edwards, such as it was, was over, too. I didn't see him again until many years later when we ran into each other on Sunset Boulevard. I was quite successful and no longer a little girl. I had gone on to do a lot of the things he had wanted for himself. So when we met again he started to turn away, pretending not to recognize me. I suppose he was afraid I'd flaunt my success in his face. But I planted myself in his path, gave him a big hug, and insisted he stop to talk. I was devastated by his looks. The alcohol had ravaged him, and he seemed very sad and defeated. Yet he was still quite beautiful, and much more soft and gentle than the James I had known. I told him that I'd heard he had married a beautiful young girl who adored him. He said, yes, that was true. He was living on a farm and had stopped drinking and was taking care of his health. We were both late for our appointments, so we wished each other luck and went our separate ways. A few months later I read in the paper that he had died.

One afternoon shortly before *Carmen Jones* came to an end I received a telegram from Chuck Wood telling me to take the "Red Eye" back to New York the moment I finished shooting. The producers of *House of Flowers* wanted to see me again. There was a good chance I might get the part.

The plane touched down in New York just after sunrise. Chuck looked as though he had been pacing the airport for hours — he was as excited as I'd ever seen him. As we drove into the city I got a nonstop monologue: he told me what songs I should sing and what the producers wanted to see and all the other things I needed to know to be ready for this crucial meeting. Suddenly the cab stopped at a beauty salon where Chuck had set up an appointment for me. I was too tired to question. He instructed the stylist to cut my hair just a little shorter, then went on to his office to take care of the last-minute details. I dozed off in the chair while the stylist went to work with his scissors. Two hours later he nudged me awake. When I saw myself in the mirror, I screamed. I looked like a little boy. "My God," I sobbed. "I have an audition today. What am I going to do?" When Chuck returned to take me to the theater and saw what had happened, he was furious. But there was nothing to be done.

When I walked onstage the first thing I did was apologize for this bizarre haircut. There was a moment of silence. Then through the darkness I saw a small man in a white suit sort of floating slowly down the side aisle toward the stage. It was Truman Capote, the author of the play. "Oh, don't apologize," he said in that high southern drawl. "Your hai-yah is just mah-velous. It couldn't be mo-ah perfect. Now you look exactly lahk Ottilie."

I was hugely relieved but still very tired and nervous. Ending the film, then jumping on the plane, then the fiasco with the beauty parlor, and now the audition — it was all too much. I was hungry. I was scared. My whole body was shaking. Standing there under the glare of the naked light bulb hanging down from the center of the stage I felt a million miles away from those ominous voices somewhere out in the darkness who had come to pass judgment. I had just enough experience to know that the gap was too large to bridge in my present condition, so I decided to take a chance.

"Excuse me," I called out. "But would you mind if I sat down?"

Someone said, "Not at all. We'll get you a chair."

"No, that's okay," I answered, and then plopped myself down on the edge of the stage and dangled my legs over the side. It was a rather theatrical gesture, but it did the trick. The distance between us closed, and I knew I was ready for them.

This was one of those days that started out as a sure-fire disaster and became one where everything went right. I was in great voice. I knew the material backward, forward, and upside down. I started with "A Sleepin' Bee," which was the love song that Harold Arlen had written for the ingenue part. (Much later when we recorded the cast album, I had such a bad cold that Harold himself had to sing my high note for me!) I felt totally secure. All those many months of discipline and hard work and all the love and care Chuck Wood had devoted to me were finally paying off. I sang and I sang and I sang, and after about the third song I knew I had the part.

When I finished, the voices out front emerged from the darkness, took on their shapes and forms and became Saint Subber, Harold Arlen, and Truman Capote. Chuck followed close behind them, beaming with pride like a hovering father seeing his new baby for the first time. We all looked at each other and began to shake hands, and that was it — I was Ottilie. The role was mine.

The first few weeks of rehearsal were like walking through a dream. I couldn't believe that I deserved to be there, standing on the same stage with giant talents like Pearl Bailey, Geoffrey Holder, Josephine Premice, and Juanita Hall. Chuck always told me that anyone who could walk onstage and perform for an audience eight times a week was a truly extraordinary human being, and now I began to realize the kind of energy and commitment that required.

It was all so new. There was so much to take in that I couldn't begin to make sense of it. But by the time the rehearsal phase ended and we moved on to the tryouts in Philadelphia, even I could see we had some very real problems.

House of Flowers was based on a Capote short story about a young girl named Ottilie who grows up in a West Indian bordello, yet somehow manages to remain completely innocent and pure. To convert the story into a musical for Pearl Bailey, the emphasis had been shifted to the madam who raised Ottilie and her ongoing rivalry with the woman who runs the competing bordello across the street. In the adaptation process, a great deal of the original charm was lost. To try to recapture it, the show was being overhauled almost nightly. The book was in a constant state of revision; songs were added, dropped, and shifted about. Actors were fired and hired. The original choreographer, the great George Balanchine, was replaced by the almost unknown Herbert Ross. We rehearsed the changes during the day, then introduced them into the performance that night, doing our best to hold on to what was good about the old, while simultaneously trying to give birth to the new. It was difficult, and the result was pretty much of a mess.

All that might have been easier if Peter Brook, our English director, had any confidence in us. But, unfortunately, it seemed to me that because he had relatively little experience with black actors and seemed to think we were all charming and cute, rather than full-fledged professionals, he became patronizing. If he couldn't make the scene work, if he couldn't make us understand what he wanted, he let his confusion about how to give direction to these "naïve children" lead him to reduce his requirements so as not to put "too much pressure" on the poor little things. In his head, he wasn't dealing with actors — he was dealing with "Black People." And the result was that the show suffered badly from his compromising his standards. When we realized that he didn't believe in us, our spirits were totally deflated. By opening night in New York, Brook had thrown up his hands in despair, and so had the rest of us.

But if the show had some serious weaknesses, it also had more than its share of strengths. The brilliant Oliver Messel created costumes and sets that were absolutely beautiful. Some of the performances were wonderful. And Harold Arlen's music was, as always, simply exquisite, steeped in deep emotion that reflected both his Jewish background and lifelong fascination with the black community, and always completely true to the story line and characters. This was, after all, the man who wrote songs like "The Man That Got Away," and "Come Rain or Come Shine" — so it was an honor to sing his music.

We opened in New York the night before New Year's Eve, 1954. The reviews were mixed. Some of the critics raved about Pearl, the music and dancing, and the costumes and sets. Others felt these virtues were canceled out by the weak script. But despite the bad notices we were considered to be the hot show in town.

As for me, the critics were kind, but I didn't have time to be excited or impressed with myself. I was working too hard to think about anything else. And I did almost nothing else. Every once in a while Josephine Premice insisted on prying me from my dressing room for an hour or so. "You need to get out of this theater," she would tell me. "Come on, let's have a bite to eat." Josephine was, and is, a very sophisticated, warm, worldly woman. I was so flattered and so loved being in her company, I put down my script and followed her, hoping that Chuck wouldn't catch me.

In her own way, Josephine was as dedicated a teacher as Chuck was. She used our restaurant outings to instruct me in the proper European method of handling a knife and fork, the acceptable way to butter a piece of bread, and many other fine points of good table manners. When I dashed down the street to buy new clothes, she insisted I show her my purchases, then passed judgment on them. One afternoon I came back to the theater in a powder blue wool coat that had a tiny mink collar with little rhinestones.

"My dear," she exclaimed, reaching for the scissors. "One wears either a cloth coat or a fur coat. One does not wear a cloth coat with a tiny fur collar — and *never* a fur collar with rhinestones!" All of this was part of my education, and I ate it up like a starving child. But I have to tell you, it was a strange feeling to throw my pretty new mink collar in the trash.

House of Flowers was an enormous step up for me. Not many nineteen-year-olds have the opportunity to step on a Broadway stage and perform to the audience. And then, one day, lo and behold, Saint Subber called to tell me that I was nominated for a Tony Award. Shocked? Stunned! It was so unbelievable — my first Broadway play, and I had received the most coveted nomination in the theater. I was beside myself — and so was everyone around me. I didn't win — but I was so proud to have been nominated for my very first show.

❦

It wasn't until I started dating Monte Kay, the casting director of the show, that I began to realize there was more to life than just working and studying all night, grabbing a few hours of sleep, and rushing back to the theater. We had met the first time at my audition for *House of Flowers,* where he made it clear he didn't think I was right for the part. "She's too young. She's too inexperienced," he said. After we opened in Philadelphia, Monte came back to my dressing room to say how surprised he was that I had made the part work for me, and he then invited me out to supper.

We went to a wonderful seafood restaurant, where I had my first oysters and clams on the half shell. We talked. We laughed. There was no question that we were attracted to each other.

Later that week Monte returned to Philadelphia and we went out to dinner again. When I returned to my hotel, I found a message from Josephine. I went up to her room and sensed immediately that she seemed bothered. Never one to mince words, she came right to the point.

"Young lady," she asked, "how are your parents going to feel about your seeing this man?"

I didn't know what she was talking about. "How should they feel?" I asked her. "Is there something the matter with him?"

"No, not at all. Monte Kay is a very fine person. I've known him for years. I'm certainly not telling you I disapprove. I don't care what color he is. I just think you ought to tell your parents that you're starting to date a man who is not black."

I couldn't believe my ears. I thought she was kidding. It never occurred to me that Monte was white. He didn't *look* white. He had brown skin, and his hair was kind of curly-kinky. And, besides, I'd never given it any thought.

"No, I'm serious," Josephine insisted. "His real name is Fremont Kaplan."

I ran back to my room and dialed Monte's number. The phone rang and rang and rang, and finally I heard his voice.

"Hello?"

"Monte, I just left Josephine and we had a talk and she told me you're white, is that true?" I blurted out without taking a breath.

"Of course it is," he laughed. "I'm Jewish, too. Is that all right?"

I couldn't really think of any reason why it wasn't. The important thing was that I liked him, that he made me laugh and feel like a real, grown-up person. As for Mom and Dad, well, I would cross that bridge when and if I came to it.

"Well, yes, I guess it is all right," I answered. "I was about to ask you why you didn't tell me, but that is pretty ridiculous, isn't it?"

"Yeah, it is," he agreed.

"But why are you so brown?" I asked.

"Well, I guess it's because I love the sun and my sunlamp. I like to be tan."

That's about all Monte would say about it, but as we came to know each other better and he began telling me about his earlier life, I saw that he had been attracted to the black music world from the time he was a young teenager, when he used to sneak off to Greenwich Village to listen to jazz. Monte grew up in a financially comfortable, very conventional Jewish family in Brooklyn. There wasn't much affection at home, and the music provided the kind of solace and joy he needed. When he was fifteen years old, he rebelled against his parents' values by moving out of the house and taking a small apartment in the Village with a couple of pals. They spent their time going to hear gospel singers in the black churches of New Jersey, and haunting the New York jazz clubs.

Eventually, Monte began involving himself in the business end of the music. While still in his teens he produced concerts featuring talents like Charlie Parker and Dizzy Gillespie, then went on to open Birdland, one of the great jazz clubs, and to manage artists like Chris Connor and the Modern Jazz Quartet.

Once *House of Flowers* settled down on Broadway, we began seeing each other fairly often. "You have to have something in your life other than just rehearsing and performing," Monte would argue when I tried to explain I was too busy to go out. "Come on, we'll go to the movies on Sunday. It'll be good for you." And he was right — it was great for me. I had forgotten what it was like to do anything but work.

But while Monte wanted to introduce me to a little freedom and an exciting new world, Chuck wanted me to concentrate on work, and he was threatened by Monte's presence. "If you aren't striving and accomplishing, if you're not totally committed to your career twenty-four hours a day," he would lecture, "you're just wasting your time." He began sounding like my mother, and I resented it. It was a touchy situation, and he and Monte fought constantly, despite my efforts to keep them apart.

But I wanted Monte. I was now twenty years old and needed a man like Monte — eleven years older, wise, kind, and full of fun. I guess I wasn't ready for an all-out break from being a protected young woman and artist, and Monte represented the halfway mark between being a total rebel (which I wasn't) and the enveloping control of my parents.

And I loved being with Monte — I was finally in love. He was proud of me and enjoyed showing me off to his friends. But I was so totally different from the more sophisticated ladies he had dated before that many of his friends didn't know what to make of me. At first I think I was a bit of a joke. "Oh, Lady Diahann is with you tonight," they would tease when he took me down to his club, Birdland. "I see you brought your princess." I was such an alien presence, and felt so shy and different and somehow inadequate, that I receded into an attitude which people have often called "aloof."

But I didn't care. I loved him. He opened up the world to me. I had never before dated anyone who operated with that sort of knowledge and style and willingness to share, and I found it all quite exciting. In return, I brought to his life some qualities he hadn't experienced. My values were very clear, and nothing was going to pull me away from them. For example, when it came time to confront that inevitable issue, whether or not we would go to bed with each other, I faced it with my usual understated, well-thought-out aplomb.

"All right, Monte," said I. "If we have sex then that means I'm your girl and you're my fella. Are we going to get engaged? When are we going to get married?" Monte just loved it.

But there were troubles ahead. Josephine had been right about my parents — especially my father. When I finally told him about this wonderful man I was seeing, he was visibly shaken. It was bad enough that Monte was so much older — it was even worse that he owned a nightclub. But the fact that he was also white — well, that made our relationship totally out of the question. Whenever Monte telephoned the house, my father hung up without speaking to him and never gave me the messages. When I found out what he was doing, I packed my clothes, took a cab into midtown Manhattan, and checked into a little five-dollar-a-night room in the Wellington Hotel. It wasn't an easy thing for me to do. I thought the world revolved around my parents. Our relationship was strong, bonded; but it was also becoming stifling. And the simple truth of it was — I loved my parents, and I was in love with Monte. And I didn't see any other way to handle my father's opposition. I suppose the move was inevitable. I was twenty — it was time to move on.

A few weeks later Mom came to visit me at the hotel. She looked at the daughter she had brought up to be so good and proper, saw my living circumstances, and promptly burst into tears.

"I can't believe this," she sobbed. "All your things cramped into this tiny, ugly place — how can this be acceptable to you? We have such a lovely home, and your beautiful room is just sitting there empty. Where have we gone wrong? Where have we failed?"

I was prepared for some of this martyrdom, and I knew she was sad and in pain. But that beautiful room I had loved so much just wasn't mine anymore. It was behind me now. My clothes were hanging in this closet. My rehearsal materials were neatly stacked in this desk. Nothing about this awful hotel room seemed foreign or impermanent to me. I was trying to move on to the next step in my life, and I had to do it alone.

My mother asked me to come back with her. I told her I couldn't. She said she couldn't leave me there. I told her she had to. And I reassured her that I would be just fine.

And I was. Every morning I ate breakfast at the little coffee shop on the corner, where I saw other people in my profession having their English muffins and coffee, and felt like I belonged there. They were reading the trades and telling each other how they were afraid they'd blown the audition because of a cramp and how this voice teacher's class was taking every dime they made and how they were going home to visit their parents for a while but would return in time to try out for the new shows next season — and it was all delicious dialogue that I needed to hear. It made me feel comfortable, connected with something. If Monte was away on business checking out some new group, I would have dinner by myself at the big, impersonal restaurant in the lobby of the Wellington, browse through the trades or study a song, then take a bath and go to bed.

I loved the privacy; I loved being in my own "home" doing what I wanted. It was a fine way to live for a young performer. And when I saw Monte it was even better. If it weren't for the occasional stabs of guilt about my parents, I couldn't have been happier.

My mother, who had always deferred to my father, found that she couldn't stay away. She also thought Monte was too old for me, and she didn't like the fact that he was in the nightclub business. But she had absolutely no respect for any form of racism and couldn't bring herself to reject him because of his color. So, after a while, as Monte became more and more a part of my life, she defied my father and came to see us at Aunt Dorothy's, which was neutral territory. She saw that we were seriously in love. She also saw that Monte was a kind, considerate, gentle man who was very good to me. By the time she left, she promised to do what she could to soften my father's resistance.

About a year after we started dating, we decided it was time to get married. When I broke the news to my parents, my dad said, with forceful determination, "Never!" and stormed out of the house. Monte's family was almost as adamant: "My God — a black woman, an actress — what are you doing?" Monte just smiled and answered, "Well, maybe you ought to meet her."

Now it was my turn on the witness stand as he gradually began to bring the Kaplans around to cross-examine me. Eventually I met his older brother Solomon, who managed the family estate.

I remember our conversation so clearly even today.

"Have you thought about having children?" Solomon asked.

"Of course we've thought about having children," I replied with some amusement. What couple in love doesn't?

"Well, what will they be?"

"They'll be part of Monte and myself."

"Yes, but don't you think a child who is half black and half white is going to have an awfully hard time fitting in?"

In my naïveté, I found this to be a rather strange question. I had been exposed to so many biracial children in this business that I really didn't take the question seriously. I had this image of a human being with a line drawn down the middle of its body: black on one side and white on the other.

"Well, as long as it's loved and cared for, I think it should be fine," I answered to reassure him. I really believed that if we set our minds to succeeding, we would.

Solomon returned to Ocean Parkway and assembled the Kaplan clan for a family conference. A few days later Monte's sister-in-law Edith met me for a drink to give me the verdict.

"I told them we should stop interfering," she said. "I told them all that this is probably the healthiest, most positive relationship Monte has ever had, and if we don't stop this foolishness we may lose you." I liked Edith, and I really appreciated her kind words that day.

Mom still had some doubts about the marriage, so she asked Adam Clayton Powell, who by now had become a U.S. congressman, to speak to me. He called at the theater and suggested we meet for dinner at Sardi's. I told him that my fiancé would join us. When I arrived, I received a mini-lecture on my neglect of the Church. As we sat there debating the pros and cons of organized religion, Monte joined us and Adam's whole demeanor changed. It turned out they were old pals. Adam loved jazz and knew Monte from Birdland.

Adam then asked us many questions to reassure himself that we were serious about our relationship. Finally, he said, "The two of you obviously love each other and are of your own mind about this. If it's a mistake — and I'm not saying it is — no one is going to stop you from making it. Now let's relax and have a good time." Before the evening was over, Adam had offered to perform the wedding ceremony for us at his own home.

Now that it was settled, Mom threw herself into all the details that had to be looked after to give me the kind of wedding she always wanted. She helped me choose the fabric for the bridal gown, selected the place for the wedding supper, worked out the menu, ordered the flowers and the flower girl dress for Lydia (who was now seven), and rode herd over the thousand and one other preparations that had to be attended to.

My father would have nothing to do with any of it. I kept praying he would change his mind, but he didn't give an inch. The same white community he hated and mistrusted, that had always held him back and tried to take away his manhood, was now laying claim to his precious older daughter. I knew my father worshipped me and felt I had betrayed him by going over to the enemy camp.

We were married in September 1956. As I was leaving my parents' home in my bridal gown the afternoon of the wedding, I stopped to speak to my father and begged him to come with me. I'll never forget the look on his face. He stared up at me with a mixture of disappointment and hate, slowly rose from his chair, and stalked out of the house without saying even one word.

After the wedding supper, we returned to my parents' home so I could change into my traveling clothes. Monte's brothers and their wives tagged along with us so they could see us off. Dad must have miscalculated his timing. A few minutes after we arrived he came walking through the front door. When I introduced him to Solomon and Joe, he shook hands with them, but when Monte put out his hand he turned away and disappeared upstairs. Monte and I were both hurt and embarrassed for my father. But I understood his feelings. I understood how they hampered him and how he couldn't move beyond them. It was as if he had no love left in his heart for me anymore, as if I didn't even exist. And that hurt me beyond measure. I wanted his blessings so badly, so I followed him up the stairs to make one last effort. "I love you, Daddy," I told him. "I'll always be your daughter. If I'm ever in trouble, I'll always call you." There was a long awkward silence filled with pain. Finally he nodded. But he wouldn't look at me, he wouldn't smile. It was, to him, as if I had died. It was so tragic, but there was nothing I could do. I stood there waiting for something more to happen and then he asked me to leave. "Just go," he said.

But, sometimes, time really can heal the most serious wounds. Late one afternoon about a year after the wedding, I returned from the rehearsal hall to find Monte playing on the floor with Lydia. "Guess who stopped by?" he asked, grinning from ear to ear. "Your father." Dad and Lydia had been in town for the day, and she had persuaded him to drop her off at our apartment to visit for a while. When Monte opened the door, there was nothing my dad could do but step inside to say hello. He saw our apartment, and saw Lydia's joy at the prospect of having Monte to herself for the afternoon. Talking to Monte, he began to realize that he was a smart and warm man. In spite of himself, he liked him. When he returned to take Lydia home later that evening, I was so happy to see him I almost burst into tears.

"You didn't really have to leave," I told him. "We could have all had dinner together."

"All right," he answered. "Next time we will." And we did.

❧

When Monte and I returned from our honeymoon in California, we moved into our new apartment on Tenth Avenue, and I threw myself into the business of becoming a wife. It was second nature to me. I had seen it my whole life. (I still rehearsed new material regularly, still worked the nightclubs; but the career was no longer so all-consuming, and I let the success of *House of Flowers* lie dormant, at least for a while.)

My primary concern now became making a home for us. So I

immediately moved into Macy's (you know — 34th Street — the "World's Largest Department Store"). Macy's had always been a second home to us — it was, indeed, a very integral part of our lives. My mother believed that if Macy's didn't have it, it had not yet been made. So the ninth floor — Home Furnishings, if you please — became my hangout. That's where I found the perfect coffee table and sofa, the carpets and drapes, all the pots and pans and the cookbooks I would need to learn how to use them. It was a lot of fun, and when the dust finally settled and everything came together, I was so proud of myself! I loved the look of astonishment on Mom's face the first time she paid us a visit and saw what I had accomplished. Before the wedding, she would tease Monte, "Don't forget, Diahann only knows how to hang up her clothes," and that was perfectly true. I was very much the spoiled, pampered child when I lived with her. But now that I had taken a step into the world, another, more grown-up, human being was beginning to emerge.

For Monte, this new person was somewhat of a surprise. If part of Monte adored the middle-class homemaker in me, another part was frightened by it. It smacked too much of the same bourgeois values and attitudes he had been running away from all his life. Once, when we met at Macy's, I chattered on and on about how I thought the bedroom set was light and pretty but not too feminine and wasn't it elegant and wouldn't it suit us both perfectly, while Monte stared at me in disbelief. "Oh my God," he seemed to be thinking. "She really means it. She's really serious about this stuff."

"You better watch her," his partner and sidekick Pete Kameron warned him, teasing yet perfectly serious. "If you're not careful, she's going to spend every cent you've got putting you on the cover of *House Beautiful*."

"Holy smoke! She's a Jewish girl!" Nat Hentoff ribbed him. "A Jewish princess with a suntan. She's exactly what you tried to avoid your whole life, the very thing you always said you didn't want."

I was too caught up in my own little fairy-tale fantasy of wedded bliss to appreciate how Monte was being torn apart by the dilemma of wanting it both ways. On the one hand, he liked the nice, comfortable home I made for him. He enjoyed entertaining his close friends with sit-down dinners followed by brandy in the living room. He liked me this square. Square seemed to work for me, and it gave him a sense of solidity and clarity that some part of him needed. On the other hand, he also liked the open-ended sort of jazz life he had lived before he met me and wasn't about to give it all up just because his new bride didn't want to sit in Birdland till three in the morning every night of the week and expected him to come home for dinner when he said he would be there.

The problems started on our honeymoon. We went to the West Coast so Monte could see some of his clients. One morning when I woke up in our room in the Beverly Hilton, he was sitting on the terrace reading a book, and when I called out to him, he simply ignored me. I knew he had a habit of getting absorbed in what he was doing, but this time it frightened me. I had never been away with a man before and suddenly realized that it was just the two of us now and we had made this decision and here we were, partners for life.

I went out to the terrace and begged Monte to answer me. He continued reading as if I wasn't there. When I pressed him again, he glared up in irritation, then returned to his book. I was supposed to know that I was expected to remain quiet until he finished. But I couldn't do that. My insecurities got the best of me, and I ran back to the room, jumped on the bed, and began attacking the wall with my fists. "Why don't you like me?" I screamed. "Why did you marry me if you didn't like me? Why won't you speak to me?"

Monte was totally baffled by the explosion. He was accustomed to being alone and withdrawing into his privacy. He had always behaved that way with women, and they had always accepted it.

"My God, Diahann, what's the matter with you? What do you want from me?"

"Anything," I sobbed. "I'll take anything, any kind of exchange. Talk to me about the weather, the laundry, whatever you're thinking. Tell me my shoes are dirty. I don't care. Just answer me when I talk to you!" By this time I was shouting.

"Oh, for crying out loud, is that all? You know I was busy. You know I'll answer you later. What are you so excited about?"

"No, you can't do that. Tell me you're busy and you'll talk to me later, but you can't just ignore me."

Suddenly the police were banging on the door. Monte and I looked at each other, realized the absurdity of the situation, and fell into each other's arms, laughing. We had come through our first marital crisis. But it wouldn't be the last.

We loved one another. We wanted to make this thing work. Each of us tried bending a little to keep our differences from getting in the way. I tried to be less demanding. He tried to be more attentive. We bought a convertible and ran off to the country on weekends so we could be alone. But our expectations about marriage were so different that the problems wouldn't just go away.

There were other flareups that are common to many marriages. One night after I had cooked Monte a special dinner and watched it spoil as I waited and waited for him to return from the office, I became so angry I threw on my best bib-and-tucker and went off to the theater to see *Golden Boy*. By the time I returned home, Monte had telephoned everyone we knew and was ready to call the police.

"Jesus Christ! What happened?" he fumed. "Where have you been?"

"Well, I was tired of waiting for you," I answered, matching his anger with my own icy cold rage. "I thought it was rude of you not to call when you knew you were running so late."

Another crisis solved. And there were to be more personal problems along the way. But the thing we always shared was my career. Unlike a lot of performers' husbands, Monte was happy that I had my career. The fact that we were both in the business and shared the same intense love of music was a great bond between us.

Chuck had absolutely no respect for jazz. "You don't have any business being around that kind of music," he would tell me, throwing up his hands in despair. "Doesn't Monte realize that's not what you've been working and training for all these years?"

Monte's response was, "All right, I do understand that Chuck is the one who handles your career, but why don't you try stretching out a little to see what happens?"

"She belongs on Broadway," Chuck would argue.

"But there's no show for her, so where do we go from here?"

"Well, we stay prepared. We rehearse and work every day so we're always prepared for the next role that comes along."

"What next role? What is she going to be up for? She needs another outlet, someplace else to go with her talent."

Chuck was even more unhappy when I decided to seek out Phil

Moore to work with me. There was no arguing about Phil's ability to put the best act together — everyone knew he was the best in the business. He had coached Lena Horne, Dorothy Dandridge, Marilyn Monroe, Ava Gardner, and a host of other performers. But Chuck was afraid he would try to cast me in Lena's likeness. When I raised the question with Phil, he dismissed it with a flick of his pipe. Lena was Lena, and it would become clear in time that I was me. Phil came up with some perfect material for me — I remember a song called "Shopping Around" that fit my personality like a glove — and gave me a kind of young, pouting, kittenish sexuality, which was about the only sexuality I could handle.

For all Phil's efforts, my singing was still very cold, very Broadway perfectionist. I was in such awe of masters like Cole Porter and Harold Arlen that I was afraid to take any liberties with their songs and sang them exactly the way they were written. But something — I didn't yet know what — was beginning to brew just below the surface. It became clearer when I became friendly with my next-door neighbor, Miles Davis.

Miles Davis was such an overpowering presence that whenever I passed him in the hall I averted my eyes and pretended not to see him. I worshipped Miles — his music, his talent, his great gift. And then, one afternoon, he knocked on my door and asked to borrow a cup of sugar. When I returned from the kitchen, he looked down at the cup, looked up at me, and laughed.

"You really are what they say you are!"

I may be slow, but not that slow. "You mean you don't want a cup of sugar?" I asked.

"Hell, no!" he answered, laughing. "I don't want no damn cup of sugar."

I laughed, too. And a few minutes turned into a few hours. For the rest of the afternoon we sat on the steps leading down to the living room and talked about music. I told him how much I loved singing and how, when I was still a kid, I rolled my hair into a "Gibson" do, put on my wedgies to make myself look older, and then sneaked into a club called the Down Beat to hear him. He asked me endless questions about what songs I sang, why I had selected them, and what kind of music I listened to. By the time he left we had become friends. "Nobody — not Monte, not anyone — is gonna believe we've just been sittin' here talkin' all day!" he said on the way out.

Miles could swear like a truckdriver, but he was one of the most sensitive, intuitive, finely tuned human beings I have ever met. His whole life was about quality. One could see it in the elegant, finely tailored clothes that he wore. His taste responded to clean, uncluttered lines and the finest fabrics — silk, vicuña, cashmere, wool, beautiful cottons. One could see it in the delicious gourmet meals he created in his kitchen, the exquisite Italian leather chairs he bought, and the pleasure he took in the design and craftsmanship of his Ferrari. Most of all, one could hear it in his music.

Miles worked hard at his craft, always evolving and changing and asking more of himself as he dug deeper and deeper into his feelings. When he invited me over to listen to the tapes he had just brought home from the recording studio, I heard the profound emotion with which he explored songs like Cole Porter's "All of You" that I'd heard a thousand times and thought I knew backward and forward, and I was so overwhelmed I couldn't speak. The same thing happened when his wife, Frances, and I went down to the Village Vanguard to hear him play. Sometimes I was so moved by his genius I cried. I couldn't find the words to express what I was feeling but was overjoyed that I could feel it. I was also a little saddened. Why couldn't *I* express some of that emotion?

Part of me was beginning to crave deeper emotions and greater freedom in my work. Another part was deathly afraid of these feelings and held me back. I was still intimidated by the great jazz and blues artists, still too confined by the standards of propriety and acceptability I inherited from my parents. Many years would pass before I could finally bring myself to change. But Miles Davis was the beginning of the search.

❧

For some time now, Chuck Wood and I had been gradually drifting apart. I was growing up, starting to have some confidence in my own opinions, and his almost Svengali-like overprotectiveness and control were becoming harder and harder to live with. He was wonderful and needed in the beginning, but now I had outgrown this kind of control. Then, quite abruptly, our relationship came to an end.

Chuck had left the Lou Walters office to open his own personal management firm and wanted me to come with him as his first client. I couldn't decide what to do. He had given so much to me and I knew that I owed him. Yet as Monte and some other people I trusted pointed out, although Chuck was a marvelous teacher and a devoted friend, he did not have the experience or the clout to be an effective personal manager for me. That was becoming painfully clear. I was beginning to move in circles that frightened him. Other agents could often outtalk and outplan and outdeal him. Many people in the business preferred negotiating with someone who was not so emotionally charged.

Chuck had secured the promise of a bank loan on the basis of my signing with him and opened his own office near Sardi's. The afternoon I was due to put my signature to the agreement, I still hadn't made up my mind. I was running late and it was pouring, but I kept wandering around the theater district while I wrestled with the decision. I was terrified of losing him — we had been together for such a long time. It had been so marvelous having this loving mentor who pushed me and taught me and helped mold me into shape.

Finally, after endlessly weighing what I would gain or lose by signing that piece of paper, and what my decision would mean to Chuck, I came to the conclusion that I couldn't do it. Instead, I would give him the ten thousand dollars he needed to start his own business. I had enough only to make a down payment and would have to pay off the rest from future jobs. But I knew he deserved every cent of it.

He was pacing the floor waiting for me.

"You're late. The bank will close in fifteen minutes. . . . What's the matter with you? What's wrong?"

I think he knew what I had to tell him before the words left my mouth. And then he said, "You realize this means I can't be there for you anymore — I'll have other clients."

"Of course," I answered quietly.

We wished each other good luck and said a painful goodbye. I walked downstairs and out into the rain, tears in my eyes, and knew that an important chapter of my life had just closed. I walked all over the city, thinking about what I had done. Now I would have to take responsibility for myself. The prospect was frightening, but it was what I wanted. It was time to take charge of my own career.

Monte offered to take over as my manager, but I decided against it. We already had enough problems without arguing about replacing the third trumpet player or trying out this material or accepting or rejecting this or that job.

Then, in 1959, after I had been married for three years, I received an offer to play the part of Clara in Sam Goldwyn's movie version of *Porgy and Bess*. I didn't want to do it, for many reasons. First of all, I had decided after *Carmen Jones* that there was no real benefit for me to do bit parts in movies when I had center stage as a singer. If I were the star of the film — like Dorothy and Harry — that would be wonderful, because then I would get the experience, the press, and the money. But to be just another "extra" in a film — that didn't seem to me to be the right step in my career.

Second, the racial stereotypes of Catfish Row held absolutely no attraction for me, and I was offended by the story. Third, even though George Gershwin's music was glorious (the score was every artist's dream!), the producers had hired opera singers to dub the songs, so my voice wouldn't even be on the soundtrack. So, it seemed to me that I really had nothing to gain, and I decided to turn the job down.

Monte thought I was making a very big mistake and flew to Chicago where I was working at the Black Orchid to persuade me to change my mind. "You need film," he argued. "This is an excellent opportunity." So much for resolve. He persuaded me that he was right, and I called my agent and accepted the role.

Sometimes we look at each other now and wonder what our lives together would have been if I hadn't.

Chapter Four

The door opened. He stepped inside. My life changed.

The first thing I saw was a man who moved like an animal, an incredibly beautiful, self-confident, jet-black man with the satin skin of a panther. His eyes swept the terrain, seeing and measuring everything in sight. I'm sure he saw, maybe even smelled, my sudden discomfort, my self-conscious uneasinesss. His presence was so mesmerizing, his whole bearing so unashamedly sexual, that I was totally overtaken by the moment. Not knowing where to look or what to do, I must have crossed and uncrossed my legs a hundred times as he went around the room saying hello. Finally it was my turn.

"Well, how are you?" he asked, all charm and poise and unassailable self-assurance. "I'm Sidney Poitier. I've looked forward to working with you." He flashed that wonderful smile, then from inside his gut came a deep, masculine laugh of delight. To have evoked that from this glorious man was an overpowering thrill, and he knew it. But just to make sure the capture was complete, he stretched out those enormous arms and pulled me to him for a second, not long enough to be out of line, but just long enough to make the point that he had control. Then he held me at arm's length to complete his appraisal before engulfing me in another roar of laughter.

"Nice to see you," he concluded. "We must talk."

I was too unnerved to answer. I just sat there in a daze, trying to mask my confusion behind small talk with the other members of the cast. I couldn't take my eyes off him. We had been summoned to Sam Goldwyn's office to receive the new production schedule for *Porgy and Bess,* but all I could do was stare at Sidney.

The intensity of my response shocked and terrified me. My God, I was a married woman. Monte and I may have had our problems, but we both took those wedding vows seriously. The last thing I was looking for was a little on-location romance. Besides, Sidney was also married, and he had children. A casual extramarital fling was one thing to Sidney. A serious love affair that threatened the stability of his family and home was quite another.

Although he was hugely successful by now and had become accustomed to being pursued by all sorts of women, the fact that I wasn't so overtly sexual or experienced intrigued him at first, then finally disarmed him, and once his defenses began to crumble he knew he was headed for trouble.

As for me, well, the attraction was most certainly there, but I was raised to remember that if you aren't careful and sex becomes too important, it can disrupt your life. I was a traditional wife. I had my self-respect. Casual sex was out of the question for me.

But what to do? I decided to deal with the situation by avoiding Sidney. It seemed that he had come to the same conclusion. We did our best to keep out of each other's way, but it wasn't easy. We saw each other on the set every day. We were both staying at the Chateau Marmont, the wonderful old hotel off Sunset Boulevard favored by New York actors. (It was really like living in a college dormitory — everyone took turns cooking and playing together.) So, for us, even though the germ of romance was there, it was innocent, and being surrounded by so many friends seemed to insure that it would remain that way. I suppose that out of precaution one of us might have moved, but the danger was much too seductive.

I wanted to avoid him at all costs.

I prayed to God I'd run into him each time I turned a corner.

I was so transparent everyone could see what was happening, even the hotel garage attendant. "Oh, Mr. Poitier pulled in five minutes ago," he would tell me. "You just missed each other." I shrugged off the news as if I couldn't care less, but my whole body was trembling as I walked upstairs to the front desk, hoping maybe

I would find him there. When I did, I just nodded hello and kept on walking.

The hide-and-seek continued for a while. Then, inevitably, the game moved on to the next phase.

One afternoon Sidney stopped by my dressing room to say that Ruby Dee and some of his other New York friends were in town and would be having dinner together that evening. Would I care to join them? That seemed innocent enough — as long as I didn't stop to examine it too closely — so I accepted the invitation.

"It sounds like fun," I told him. "Shall I meet you at the restaurant?"

I wasn't at all surprised when he answered, "Well, it doesn't really make sense to take two cars. We'll both leave from the hotel, so why don't I drive you?"

Despite our efforts to keep up the pretense we weren't doing anything wrong — and in truth nothing had happened, not even an overt acknowledgment of the attraction — we were both overcome with embarrassment the moment we stepped inside the restaurant. No matter how much we tried to be understated and casual, our entrance was anything but. First of all, this was my first "date" with Sidney, so you can be sure I prepared for it. I bathed in my usual Mary Sherman's Bath Oil, which smelled divine. I just had my long, black, shiny hair washed, and it looked great. When we walked through the doorway, trying to maintain our coolness, our attitude that we were totally innocent (which, of course, was true), we looked fabulous! And yet there was something in the air — a sense of illicitness — that was so heavy that everyone in the room turned and stared.

Ruby Dee looked at Sidney, looked at this young thing walking along with him, and knew the whole story. Ruby and her husband, Ossie Davis, were very close to Sidney and his wife, and I knew she wasn't at all comfortable with what she saw. Her discomfort was nothing compared to my own. It was as if I were bleeding all over the tablecloth but couldn't even admit I had cut myself.

The evening was awful, but it broke the ice. We began seeing each other after work several times a week. Both of us always made sure there were other people around. I would drag along my pal Diane, a friend from New York who was staying with me at the Chateau. Sidney would bring his sidekick Frank London and, once in a while, the actor Ivan Dixon. That relieved some of the pressure, and we were able to relax a little while getting to know each other. We would all have dinner at his apartment or jump in the car and drive over to a little restaurant Sidney liked. We all sat there for hours and talked about everything — my God, we were opinionated! But that atmosphere of back-and-forth was wonderful! And when we had the day off, I tagged along with him to the nearby ranch where he was taking riding lessons or kept him company while he practiced his golf swing on the driving range.

The more time we spent together, the more dazzled I became. The sexual attraction became stronger and stronger. It was never verbally acknowledged, but nevertheless there was no denying it. And, the more I knew Sidney, the more I found him to be the most fascinating of men. He read voraciously. (He read the *New York Times* from cover to cover every day, even when we were in L.A., and the books in his room resembled a full library.) He thought about everything — he was the most political human being I had ever met. Moreover, he expressed his opinions with enormous clarity and conviction.

We talked for hours on end. He told me about the poverty he had been raised in — poverty so excruciating that at one point in his life he had been forced to sleep on the rooftops around Times Square, warming his body in the heat of the light bulbs of the electric signs. And we talked about his work — I was inspired by the standards he set for himself as an actor and by his talent and determination. I was awed by the way he took charge of his career. I had never seen my father or, for that matter, any black man deal with the white world with his kind of self-assurance and strength.

I remember how Sidney dealt with some of the problems with *Porgy and Bess*. The film generated a huge amount of controversy, and as the star of the film Sidney was subjected to tremendous pressure from all quarters. On one side, people like his longtime pal Ossie Davis criticized him harshly for his involvement with a picture that was so stereotyped and insulting to blacks, and wanted him to disown it. On the other side, the Goldwyn studio pressed Sidney for public statements endorsing the project. But once he made the decision to do the film, Sidney wouldn't allow anyone to bully or influence him. When the studio set up an important interview with the *L.A. Times*, he very carefully considered the point of view he wanted to express and how he wanted it presented, then made it clear he would talk to the journalist only if he agreed to those conditions. When I asked him why he had not allowed his press agent to handle it, he answered, "I don't have a press agent. I'll handle it myself. I make my own decisions about my life and career." He went on to explain that the statements one puts in print aren't just for the moment — they stay with you forever, so you must take complete responsibility for them.

I was floored. This was completely new to me. All performers had press agents. I had one myself, and like a good little girl went along with almost every dumb thing he suggested. If you were an entertainer, how could you possibly dare defy the press, much less the people in power who control the business? Sam Goldwyn and the head of his publicity department were just as amazed, and pressed Sidney to give up his demands. But he held his ground, and they eventually backed down. When the interview was published, it was exactly the way Sidney wanted it.

As long as Sidney and I played it light and bright and made sure our friends were always around to protect us, I was able to go along mindlessly pretending I wasn't involved in anything that might jeopardize my marriage. As the weeks went by (it took us approximately three months to shoot the film), it became more and more difficult to ignore that small voice inside that kept insisting I had fallen head over heels in love with this man.

One night a group of us were together in my small apartment at the hotel. After a while everyone left, and then it was just Sidney and me. I was so frightened that I went into the bathroom, locked the door, and turned on the bath.

Sidney called out, "What are you doing?" (a natural enough question).

"I'm taking a bath. Good night!" I answered as nonchalantly as I could, making sure he heard the water running.

Sidney must have thought I was nuts, but he left. I sat in the bath for a long time, thinking about this extraordinary man and my feelings for him. And then I called Monte in New York.

"I've just had a marvelous idea," I told him. "Why don't you fly out for the weekend? I'll book us a suite at the Beverly Hills Hotel. Doesn't that sound wonderful? Just the two of us and room service."

I hadn't really thought it through, but I knew if there was any chance of getting Sidney out of my system I had better grab it now, before it was too late. I also knew that I better keep Monte and Sidney away from each other. If the garage attendant could sense the attraction, how could Monte not see it?

I met Monte at the airport, dropped him off at the Beverly Hills Hotel, and then drove back to the Chateau Marmont for my things. As I was packing my suitcase, the doorbell rang. I looked at my roommate and, panic-stricken, ran into the closet and slammed the door behind me. I knew it was Sidney at the door. And, sure enough, he came striding into the room looking for me. While he searched through the apartment I cowered behind my dresses like a frightened child. One part of me had been expecting him and was happy he had come to look for me. Another part was frightened he was going to ruin my life and prayed he would stay away. Finally he found me.

"Diahann, what are you doing in there? What's going on?"

"Monte's here," I gasped. "He's waiting for me at the Beverly Hills Hotel."

"Oh? . . . Why is Monte here?"

"I asked him to come."

Sidney immediately realized why I had called Monte, and it surprised him. I don't think it ever occurred to him that I felt so strongly about my marriage that I would reach out to my husband to try to save it.

Sidney and I stood there in front of the closet staring at each other, not really knowing what to do. I saw that he was angry. I saw that he was jealous. I saw that he wanted to be possessive and lay down the law but realized he didn't have the right. We said very little, but for the first time I knew for certain that I wasn't going through this emotional havoc alone.

Until this moment I wasn't entirely sure. Obviously, the attraction was very mutual, but I had wondered if all that disquiet and confusion were only on my side of the fence. Maybe Sidney didn't feel that way at all, and I had better try to force myself into a lighter frame of mind. But clearly that wasn't so. His feelings mirrored my own. We were both caught in the same dangerous undertow.

The weekend with Monte was miserable for both us. Now that he was here sharing my bed, I was hit by the full impact of my longing for another man. Monte and I were so lonely and disconnected. I couldn't talk to him, couldn't even bring myself to look him fully in the face. I just sat there in the room the whole two days lost in my own private thoughts. Finally it was time for him to leave.

"This has been the most horrible weekend of my life," he told me. "I don't know what's wrong with you."

And I wasn't able to give him an answer. I was appalled at myself for behaving so badly. Monte was the last person in the world to deserve that kind of treatment.

In the week that followed I tried keeping myself busy after work so I wouldn't have to see Sidney at all. When Diane asked me to come with her to a dinner party Saturday night at the home of a writer friend, I quickly accepted the invitation.

It turned out to be a lovely evening. The writer was a warm, funny man and a gracious host. The guests included Red Buttons and the young genius Mike Nichols, who had just arrived in California to try his hand at film. I almost managed to forget the heaviness around my heart. But when everyone moved into the television room after dinner, for some reason the pain of being without Sidney became overwhelming, and I had to get out of there. I excused myself and wandered out into the courtyard. It was a beautiful night — the moon was shining through the trees; the scent of tropical flowers hung heavily in the air. The romanticism of the setting only heightened my longing, so I decided to go home. I said my goodbyes, got into my car, and drove back to the hotel.

A message was waiting for me at the front desk. It was from Sidney. "Where are you?" he wrote. "I've been looking for you everywhere. I'm at the little club down the hill. Come at once." Everything in me told me not to go. Sidney sounded too urgent, too desperate, too out of control — too much like myself. But before I realized what I was doing, I was running down the hill.

Sidney was sitting near the piano bar watching the front door. He knew I would come to him. When he saw me, he got up and came toward me, quickly. He took my hand and led me back to his table. We didn't speak — we just sat there looking at each other for what seemed to be a very, very long time. The antics of comedian Slim Gaillard had the audience in stitches, but we didn't hear anything. Finally, Sidney got up and said, "Let's go!"

Very slowly we walked back to the Chateau Marmont together, then rambled around the hills for a while so we wouldn't have to say good night.

And then Sidney grabbed me.

"All right, I love you," he said quickly.

"And I love you too," I told him.

So there it was — the truth was finally out in the open.

We kissed. We held each other. We cried.

"Oh God, what are we going to do?" Sidney asked.

"I don't know," I answered. "I just don't know."

Sidney paced back and forth, his long legs carrying him like a panther stalking his prey. He said he couldn't possibly leave his wife. Yes, he loved me. *But . . . But* she was a good mother. *But* she was a good Catholic. *But* she had stuck with him through all those long, lean years when he was a struggling, out-of-work actor. *But* she would take him for every dime he had. *But* he would lose his beloved children.

I said that I couldn't possibly be unfaithful to Monte. I would have to leave him first. But then Sidney would have to leave his wife. That was the only way we could be together: our spouses would have to be told. I couldn't bear to have my life and my relationship with my husband ripped apart by some sneaky little affair with a married man — no matter how much I loved him and ached to hold him in my arms.

We walked back to the hotel. Sidney returned to his apartment, and I returned to mine. We both had a lot to think about.

Porgy and Bess was coming to an end. Sidney's next project was *A Raisin in the Sun,* the wonderful play by Lorraine Hansberry about a black family's struggle to achieve their share of the American Dream. Rehearsals would be starting shortly after Sidney returned to New York. When I read the script, I thought it was superb — a work of substance that dealt with real people and real relationships and real issues. The producer was considering several actresses for the part of the sister but hadn't yet reached a final decision. When I heard he was coming to Los Angeles, I begged Sidney to let me read for the role. I recognized the risk of being in such close contact with him if we worked together again, and that was a strong reason *not* to audition. But the part was one of those rare opportunities that comes along once in a lifetime, and I was sure I could do it justice.

It turned out to be a very bad idea.

Sidney had met me as an actress and knew I was gaining some reputation as a singer, but he couldn't bring himself to acknowledge that my work really mattered to me. He enjoyed being with a woman he could talk to about the business, and as long as the conversation centered on his career, that was fine. But as far as he was concerned my work was neither important nor necessary. He was visualizing someone who wanted to share his life with him, not someone who had a career of her own. I didn't realize that then, though I certainly should have. From the very beginning he always discouraged me. During *Porgy and Bess,* whenever I asked him for advice, his lack of enthusiasm seemed to imply, "I want you to forget about a career." The one time he responded strongly was when I showed him some publicity photos I recently had taken, and then he became furious.

"Who is this?" he growled.

"It's me."

"Why do you let them do that to you? What is all this makeup? They look ridiculous. Throw them away."

I was mystified.

"Sidney, please." I tried to explain. "You've been to nightclubs. You've seen the glamour shots of the entertainers. They have to look like that."

"Well, you don't have to look like that. You look fine without makeup."

"But, Sidney, you know that doesn't make sense."

I suppose I couldn't hear what he was trying to tell me because I didn't want to hear it.

Nor did I want to hear his disapproval when I asked to try out for *A Raisin in the Sun.* I assumed that because I had so little to do in *Porgy and Bess* he simply didn't believe I had the necessary talent. There was no question in my mind that I did, and I pressed him until he relented.

The reading took place in Sidney's apartment at the Chateau Marmont. It was disastrous. I was so flustered by his presence I couldn't begin to focus my attention on the script. I was dreadful, and there he was sitting across the room watching me make a total fool of myself. I don't know which of us was more embarrassed. Needless to say, I didn't get the job. The part went to Diana Sands, and, of course, she was brilliant.

The shooting of *Porgy and Bess* was finished. For months Sidney and I had seen each other practically every day. We lived one floor apart in the same hotel. He was only a phone call or a knock on the door away. Our friends were always there to keep us safe, and we never had to be separated from each other. Suddenly, time was running short — it was almost over. That scared me — and I took advantage of every moment I could to see him. Toward the end I even stopped by the set after work to say goodbye to everyone.

"Oh, is it *me* you've come to see?" Preminger would tease.

Sidney and I agreed that it would be best to leave California separately. But at the last minute we couldn't bear to be separated and decided to fly back together on the "Red Eye." Both of us were completely exhausted from the pressure, but we stayed awake the entire night, holding hands and talking quietly. Sidney kept the light on for most of the trip. "I want to look at you," he said. Some of the cast members on the plane made insinuating little jokes about on-location romances when they passed by our seats. Others were sensitive enough to realize that we were truly in trouble.

Reality was waiting for us when we touched down at the airport. A group of Sidney's friends had come to take him home and were standing at the arrival gate. There was no way for me to disappear into the crowd. I had to say hello to them. It was a very ugly and uncomfortable moment for me and for them. The knowing looks on their faces told me immediately that I had been cast as the Other Woman, the bad lady who was trying to steal this man away from his wonderful family. We waited for our luggage without speaking. When it finally arrived, we parted like strangers. Nothing had been resolved.

❧

Sidney went back to his wife. I went back to Monte. The gossip about us circulated through the streets. One day one of Monte's dearest friends, the disk jockey Symphony Sid Torin, stopped by the apartment for a private chat. After a stab or two at social conversation he cleared his throat and got to the point.

"Okay, I'm going to ask you," he said. "Are you screwing Sidney Poitier?"

"I know there's gossip about it," I told him, trying to ignore the sinking feeling in the pit of my stomach, "but, no, Sid, I'm not."

He didn't seem to hear me and kept repeating the question over and over again. "Are you sure you're not sleeping with him? Are you really telling me the truth? Everyone says that you are, and I don't want to believe them. It would kill Monte, just kill him."

The truth really was that Sidney and I were not having an affair. In fact, it would take three years of this erratic and complicated relationship before we finally consummated our love.

I returned to singing in clubs and hoped that by working hard I would forget Sidney. This was my usual plan of action — even today, whenever I am in trouble, whenever there is emotional difficulty in my life, I always find solace in my work. At these times I find it very easy to make career decisions. I go back to the basics. I study voice, I practice my music, and I sing.

This time I went back to one of my favorite nightclubs in New York — the Persian Room at the Plaza Hotel. The Persian Room was a beautiful, intimate little nightclub that attracted an audience that came to listen, not just to talk and drink. I was lucky that Monte had taken me to Dave Baumgarten, who had agreed to prepare the Persian Room contracts. I loved every minute of my time there. And each time I played that room I became a little more successful, a little more of a New York event. And I continued to learn — from my musicians, from my audience, and from my songs.

After a while I became a regular at the Persian Room, and I was more than happy to be able to return there time after time. Whenever I appeared there, I put together a special act designed to bring the feeling of theater to the nightclub stage. With the help of my two coaches, Phil Moore and Peter Matz, I hunted through all the recent Broadway musicals for the pieces that would best suit my personality, then presented them in such a way as to recreate the dramatic moments from the original productions. I did a great deal of dramatic interpretation over the course of the evening, often taking on a different character for each song.

Creatively, this was one of my happiest, most satisfying and productive periods. I used musicians of the highest caliber and hired the most gifted people I could find to do my sets, lighting, and choreography. My costumes were simple but elegant — in the beginning, I wore nothing but a white silk chiffon shirt and a black satin skirt to give myself the feeling of being "in concert." Then I discovered simple, elegant, beautiful haute couture gowns with very uncomplicated lines that enabled me to create a particular mood, the mood of a chanteuse, which is what I was. The gowns were designed by such extraordinary talents as Ben Zuckerman, Jimmy Galanos, Arnold Scaasi, Stravapolous, Norman Norell, and Bill Blass, all of whom made an indelible impression on my life. (I would walk into Martha's — that elegant couture dress shop — and almost stop breathing at the sight of all those gorgeous gowns!)

I remember the first time Norman Norell invited me to see the show of one of his collections. Now, in the late 1950s, I was an absolute novelty at these places. The people who came to these shows were the buyers and the rich socialites of New York — not a black singer and actress!

But, fortunately, the designers loved me. And so they invited me. They said I had a body that was made for these clothes. This was a great surprise to me. I had always hated my body. I thought I had a boy's body with these two "things" sticking straight out. I was teased constantly: "You're so skinny! Look at that string-bean!" But the fashion world made me fall in love with my body. It was the first time anyone had ever looked at me and said, "Ohhh! You're great! You're marvelous! Look at that body! Look at it move — look how the clothes love her!" And I thought to myself, "Yes — I'm all right." And I would look in the mirror with new eyes, and see what they meant — an outfit hung right, it moved well. I wore the clothes — they didn't wear me.

And I decided never ever to wear any jewelry. These gowns could stand on their own. Besides, I never owned any great jewelry, and if you can't wear the real thing, why wear anything at all? From then on, it was me, the gown, and a song.

The critics were happy to see me back in New York, and I was ecstatic to be playing the Persian Room again. (I actually played there twice a year for nine years!)

꧁ꕥ꧂

My thoughts about Sidney faded in and out of my mind. Because he felt that he couldn't end his marriage, and I couldn't go on with this craziness, we promised not to see each other. That was, we agreed, the only mature way to handle it.

But then we began behaving like silly children. Sidney would call during the day when he thought Monte was at his office. (Several times Monte was at home, and there was an abrupt hangup on the other end of the line when he picked up the phone. Monte may well have suspected something, but he wasn't one to pry, and let it pass without comment.) We would meet at a sleazy movie house on 42nd Street, near the theater where Sidney was rehearsing *A Raisin in the Sun*. We talked, we argued, and we came to no conclusions.

Finally, after God knows how many whispered phone conversations filled with we-have-to's and I-can't's, we reached a series of decisions:

Sidney would leave his wife.

I would leave my husband.

I would check into the Waldorf Astoria.

He would establish residence at some other hotel.

Thus, finally, we would be together.

On the morning set for my departure, I woke up in my bedroom, saw Monte lying next to me and just blurted it out.

"I've fallen in love with Sidney Poitier," I told him. "I'm leaving you."

There was a long moment of silence while he absorbed what I told him. Then he suddenly kicked me, and I found myself on the floor. I had never seen him so angry. Monte is a very gentle, sensitive man. It had taken him many years to decide to marry. He placed a great deal of trust in me, and I had betrayed him.

I picked myself up and moved over to the chair on the other side of the room. We stared at each other, not knowing what to say. Then he began to cry. We both cried. It was done. There was nothing left to do but throw some things into a suitcase and leave. Packing was torture. I felt just terrible.

I called Sidney at the theater.

"All right, I've told Monte. I've left him. I'm at the Waldorf."

He couldn't have sounded happier.

"Great. Wonderful. I'll be there the second I finish rehearsal."

For the rest of the afternoon I sat in the hotel room counting the minutes until he arrived. Finally, toward evening, there was a knock on the door. It was Sidney. We fell into each other's arms and held on for dear life. He said he was proud of me for doing as we planned.

And then a most peculiar thing happened. He looked over at

the small suitcase I had taken with me and suddenly turned icy cold.

"Is that it?" he asked. "Is that *all* you brought?"

"Well, yes."

"I see. Well, you don't plan to stay very long, do you?"

I couldn't imagine what he meant, but as he went on, working himself into a frenzy, he started attacking me for not living up to my end of the bargain.

"I knew it! I knew you didn't really intend to do it! I knew you were going to go back to your husband!"

I was totally confused. What was he talking about? I had packed, I had moved out of my home — what more did he want?

Trying to find some solid footing, I asked him for the name of his hotel. At first he was very evasive, but I pressed him for an answer and he eventually admitted he hadn't moved into a hotel.

So that was it! He was still living at home. He had not left his wife. He hadn't done any of the things he promised. At the last minute he had lost his nerve.

By now I was furious. It was clear to me that Sidney was looking for a way out. He was frightened. He resented me terribly for the demands I had placed on him. And for Sidney, the best defense was an attack.

I was too devastated — too frightened and angry and hurt — to say anything. We sat there for an eternity, unable to reach out to each other. Finally Sidney looked at his watch, raised himself from his chair, and said that if he hurried he could be home before his children went to bed.

The door shut and I couldn't move. I sat there, staring into space, trying to comprehend what had just happened, what I had gotten myself into. I must have sat there for hours, because it was three in the morning when I called home. Monte hadn't been able to sleep either. He asked me to come back to talk. So many things had been left unsaid, things we needed to get out in the open, that I said that I would and hurried downstairs for a cab.

Monte and I talked through the rest of the night. I told him the entire story — how I hadn't intended to fall in love with Sidney, that I didn't really know why it had happened or what I was going to do. I was as astonished as he and every bit as lost.

I certainly wasn't proud of anything I had done, but I tried to make Monte understand that I hadn't gone to bed with Sidney.

Monte was, of course, still terribly hurt, but now that he had the details of my behavior it didn't appear quite so ugly. He said that he was willing to try a reconciliation.

By now the sky was turning light. Both of us were exhausted. I felt uncomfortable staying at my own home, so I said good night and went back to the hotel. And, lo and behold, there was a message in my mailbox. Sidney had called. A few hours later the telephone roused me from my sleep.

"Of course you went home, didn't you?" he accused me, with tremendous anger. "Of course you never intended to leave your husband!"

"Oh, Sidney! You can't be serious!" I shouted back at him. "How can you possibly say that? I did what I was supposed to do, Sidney. You're the one who didn't, remember? Look, there's something we haven't dealt with here. If you're not ready to leave your wife, that's fine. Then you shouldn't. But you are not going to have your cake and eat it too. You're just not. We have to make decisions and move toward a conclusion, or else we have to part. That's it."

I don't remember which one of us slammed down the telephone first.

I stayed at the Waldorf two or three days, then came home again dragging my tail between my legs. Monte was hurt. I felt guilty. We did what we could to put the marriage back together.

But Sidney and I certainly weren't finished with each other yet. He still called. I still met him. We continued playing out the same accusatory routine.

I was being unreasonable, he would remind me. He had children; I didn't. I couldn't understand how difficult that made it for him. I couldn't understand that if he left his wife he would lose everything. He would have to tear apart his entire life. He needed more time to resolve his problems. Meanwhile, why couldn't I move out and take my own apartment so we could be together?

He was being unfair, I would answer. If he had problems, why couldn't we solve them together? Why couldn't we make our relationship a reality and then deal with his marriage and children? Don't ask me to leave my home in order to be available to you, and in your own good time you will do whatever you feel is appropriate. Don't ask me to be your woman on the side. For me, that's absolutely out of the question.

We went around in circles, getting nowhere. After a while there was nothing more to talk about. Every time I agreed to meet him I found myself asking the same questions: "Have you left home? You haven't? Then why are we here?"

I decided to tell my mother that my marriage was in trouble. She was shocked "beyond belief," and immediately reminded me that there had never been a divorce in our family. That wasn't exactly my concern. I just wanted to talk it out.

Monte, too, talked to his family. The Kaplans held a family conference and appointed my sister-in-law Edith official spokeswoman. Edith was a warm, caring, goodhearted woman, and I trusted her. She was also a bit of a character. We met for lunch to discuss the future of my marriage, and, in her usual madcap manner, Edith first showed me her new Bergdorf Goodman suit and her new Saks Fifth Avenue shoes. But then she knuckled down to business.

"You do understand, don't you, that the Kaplans have a great deal of money? You can be taken care of the rest of your life, Diahann. So how can you even think about running off with an actor who may never work again? Sure, Sidney Poitier is an attractive man, but, my God, what do you expect him to earn? What can he earn?"

"I don't know, Edith. I haven't thought about money."

She said that I should think about it — after all, wasn't I twenty-three years old? It was time for me to stop behaving like an irresponsible child. It was time to start being serious about the important things in life. I should open more charge accounts. I should spend more time shopping. Monte and I should have a baby.

A baby?

"I wasn't thinking about having a baby, Edith — my marriage is in trouble." It wasn't that we hadn't tried to have a child. I had had two miscarriages, then put the thought of having a child out of my mind. Edith, however, was adamant that a baby would save my marriage, and would not let up until I agreed to make an appointment with a doctor.

I called my mother (I seemed to be consulting everyone!) and she agreed with my in-laws. Everyone thought that a baby was the answer, and would put the relationship with Sidney in a more realistic perspective. Monte and I talked it through. He was skeptical at first about seeing the doctor, but finally decided we might as well give it a try. Edith made the appointment and took me for the consultation.

Doctor Wittner turned out to be a rosy-cheeked female Santa Claus who just loved helping couples make babies. She examined me, discovered that I had blocked tubes, then proceeded to open them by turning me upside down on a table and injecting me with an oil. The entire process took only two sessions and was completely painless. As I left her office the second day, she handed me a card listing the dates when Monte and I were required to have sexual intercourse. It was such an embarrassing thing to live through — just awful! When Monte came home from the office I would be waiting for him in my peignoir. "Oh, this is the night," he would laugh. "This is the night I have to perform my obligation."

Doctor Wittner's treatment proved successful — I became pregnant. I was terribly excited. I wanted to be pregnant, and, in some strange way, I really wanted Monte's baby. I still loved him and was very secure with him. And now we would be a family.

I loved feeling the baby inside me. I loved going to the natural childbirth classes with Monte and practicing the breathing exercises with the other couples. I loved sitting at home in my rocking chair while Mom and Dad and the whole Kaplan family floated in and out of the apartment to visit this prize in my enormous belly. I felt protected and safe. It was such a joyful, fulfilling time.

I was reminded just how special it was when I flew out to California to work the Mocambo, a plush nightclub of that period, and the movie executive Max Youngstein brought Marilyn Monroe to see my show. When I sat down with them afterward, Marilyn, who wanted a baby so badly, looked at me wistfully with that sweet face and put out her hand and placed it on my stomach. "You must be so happy," she sighed. I still remember the sight of her white hand on my black silk organza evening gown and how she kept touching and staring down at my tummy. "Oh, you'll have a baby," I assured her, trying to share my happiness. "I'm sure that you will."

Monte was wonderful during the pregnancy, even though the prospect of fatherhood frightened him at first. His relationship with his own parents had been less than ideal, and most of his pals weren't especially interested in becoming fathers and had put off having children. But as the months went by, he looked forward to the natural childbirth classes as much as I did, and took just as much pleasure picking out the crib and layette and deciding what color to paint the nursery.

The morning I placed his hand on my stomach and he felt the baby move for the first time, he was ecstatic. "I think that's a fist! No, maybe a foot!" he whooped, overjoyed that there was a living, breathing person inside me and he had put it there. We became closer than we had ever been. Yet there was always that nagging feeling somewhere in the back of my mind that we still weren't out of trouble.

I'm not sure how much of that feeling had to do with Sidney. I was so caught up in the experience of carrying another human being in my body that I hardly thought about anything else. Sidney and I hadn't spoken for months now, not since the day he called and I told him I was seeing a doctor to help me conceive a child. The news made him very angry. Every now and then he would telephone me and hang up or linger on the line for a moment without speaking while I talked to him, knowing he was there. But that was the extent of our communication.

Then one afternoon shortly before I was due to give birth I was strolling across 57th Street near Carnegie Hall and suddenly there he was, coming from the opposite direction. He strode up to me, planted himself in front of me, looked down at my bulging stomach, and hissed: "You were never supposed to have anyone's child but mine!" And before I could answer, he was gone. A few weeks later I found out that Sidney was going to be a father, again.

When my labor pains began, it was obvious that this was not going to be an easy delivery. My pelvic area was very narrow, and natural childbirth proved extremely difficult. Dr. Wittner prepared me for the possibility of a cesarean. But the baby didn't want to come out, and my labor stopped. Dr. Wittner suggested that my parents take me out for dinner. So we went to a Chinese restaurant, and then in my lunacy I decided I had to be pretty and made them take me to a beauty salon to have my hair set. Then they brought me home.

I was stretched out on the bed with Monte watching the old Bogart-Hepburn movie *The African Queen* when the first serious contraction ripped the top of my head off. "We better get back to the hospital right away," I gasped. "We're about to have a little African Queen of our own."

The contractions went on for hours. They say you never forget the pain, and they don't lie. I was delirious from all the shots they had pumped into me, and when the anesthetist tried placing the mask on my face, I bit her. After that, I guess they had no choice but to tie me down. Doctor Wittner decided it would be better to hypnotize me in order to help me deliver the baby.

And then, on September 9, 1960, there she was, a miniature Monte Kay, eight pounds, two ounces, a full twenty-one and a half inches of beautiful baby girl. Suzanne Patricia Ottilie (can you believe I did that to my own child?) Kay. But I loved each name for a special reason.

I was a mother. I wanted to laugh. I wanted to cry. I felt such pride, such an incredible sense of wholeness. But the peace didn't last long. Having Suzanne had brought Monte and me closer, but not close enough. Nothing had really changed. For some strange reason, I finally knew and accepted the fact that the marriage was not going to work.

We were standing in the hospital lobby when I broke the news to my mother.

"I'm going to leave Monte," I told her. "Not today. Not to-morrow. But soon."

She was shocked, as I knew she would be.

"Oh, no. My God, I thought all that was over by now."

"No, Mom, I'm afraid it isn't."

"But how is that possible?"

"I don't know. I love this baby. I care about Monte. But I cannot stay married to him."

She found it so strange, so difficult to accept.

"I don't understand you, Diahann. I don't really know you at all. I thought you were so happy."

"I was happy, Mom. I was happy about carrying the baby. I was happy that Monte is the father. But that doesn't mean the marriage is right."

"Have you seen Sidney?"

"No, I haven't."

"Have you talked to him?"

"Months ago."

"Are you leaving because of him?"

"I don't know. But I have to move on."

I nevertheless went back home, knowing that I was living with a time bomb. And I went back to work.

By now I was quite well known and the newspaper and magazine interviewers were constantly around. I gave a lot of interviews about the baby, about being a mother, about my newly decorated apartment, and about my life. The baby took up all my time, and when I wasn't with her I worked — I sang, I sang, I sang.

❧

Suzanne was four months old when I received the screenplay for *Paris Blues,* a movie about the romance between two expatriate jazz musicians and a pair of small-town schoolteachers who visit Paris on a brief vacation fling. As soon as I finished the script I knew I had to do it. Unlike *Carmen Jones* and *Porgy and Bess,* the only other films I had made, it was a contemporary love story that showed some social and political awareness and presented black people as normal human beings. One of the couples was white and one was black, but the relationships were similar and all four characters dealt with each other on an equal footing.

When I told the producer, Sam Shaw, I was very interested in the part, I learned that the other leads were to be played by Paul Newman, Joanne Woodward — and Sidney Poitier. I was apprehensive, but inside I was also excited. Since the picture was to be shot on location, it meant Sidney and I would be thrown together again for several months thousands of miles away from the safety of our families and homes. True, Sidney and I still hadn't resolved our emotional entanglement, but I felt I had done some growing up since *Porgy and Bess.* I was a mother now. Sidney also had a new baby. Perhaps we could just do the work and leave each other alone.

Obviously, Monte wasn't at all happy with my decision to do the film. We were already in terrible trouble without my flying off to Paris to play opposite Sidney Poitier. But Sidney or no Sidney, I felt I couldn't pass up the opportunity — offers like this didn't come along very often, especially not for a black actress. Monte knew that too and, unselfishly overcoming his reluctance, didn't try to pressure me out of it once I made up my mind.

Leaving was difficult — I was leaving an uncertain marriage, and I was also leaving my baby, Suzanne, for the first time. My stomach was in knots as we drove to the airport together without talking about what might or might not happen. The silence was awful. As the plane taxied down the runway I saw Monte standing alone behind the window of the observation deck watching me disappear out of view.

I didn't realize how frightened I was until the plane lifted off the ground, circled the airport, and headed out over the Atlantic. My God, what had I gotten myself into? I had left my husband and my beautiful baby. Now that Suzanne had come into my life, my sense of responsibility had grown. I missed her already! The pediatrician felt she was still too young to travel, but she was never out of my mind. I knew I would spend a fortune calling her every night just to hear her gurgle and coo.

And here I was, on an airplane, and in a few more hours I would be in the presence of the married man who, in spite of everything, I had to admit I still loved.

I knew Sidney was staying at the Georges V, so to be on the safe side I had taken an apartment at the Hotel de la Tremoille. We didn't see each other until we met to read through the script with Paul, Joanne, and the director, Marty Ritt. I had been taking lessons with Lee Strasberg by now and was much more serious about acting than the last time Sidney and I worked together. Not that I forgot for a second that he was sitting there right across the table, but most of my attention was focused on how the actors were approaching their parts. I was fascinated by the deliberate blandness of Paul's reading. He had already mastered the principle of preparation I was just beginning to learn: that before you can supply emotions to your lines you have to discover your character, then build from there.

Luckily, Sidney's presence didn't overwhelm me nearly as much as I had feared. When the rehearsal ended, Sidney and I talked for a few minutes while we waited for the car to drive us back to our hotels. He said that his life was just fine and he was enjoying his new baby. I told him Monte and I were probably going to be divorced, but it had nothing to do with him. We made a pact that we would not renew our relationship (even as I think of it now, I can't believe that we still hadn't had an affair!), and both of us agreed that was for the best.

I went about my merry way. I accepted a few dinner invitations, and showed up at a few parties. At one party I met the director Anatole Litvak, who was shooting *Goodbye Again*. He asked if I would sing two songs by Dore Previn in his film. I was flattered beyond words — here was a respected director who was doing a film starring Ingrid Bergman, Yves Montand, and Tony Perkins, and he wanted me! I said yes immediately, and fortunately was able to work out my schedule so I could shoot both films at the same time! (It was a lot of fun — one was a dramatic role with no singing, and the other was a singing role. What a treat that was!)

There was not much time left in the day, but, somehow, Sidney was beginning to take hold of my subconscious, and there was no denying it. As much as we laughed and joked on the set, it was beginning to happen again. It was hard not to fall in love once more. After all, we played the parts of newfound lovers in the film. And in this case it was becoming difficult to separate our lives and our roles. I remember one line in the movie when Sidney and I first declare our love for one another — I put my head on his shoulder and say, "You make me feel beautiful. I don't feel average when I'm with you. I feel very, very special." At that time, at least, that was so true.

Several weeks into the shooting we met after work for a drink. Both of us were on our best behavior, and on the surface it was all quite lighthearted and relaxed. As the evening wore on, we were even able to look back at the ups and downs we had gone through without any of the usual recriminations. Sidney seemed to feel our biggest mistake was not coming to terms with the sexual attraction we had felt — that, let's face it, we still felt — for each other. He kept saying that if we could only get that out of the way we could finally put the relationship to rest and move on with our lives. Even though I knew this was total bullshit, I wanted him and agreed with his somewhat ludicrous philosophy. Both of us had the next day off, and we agreed to spend the afternoon together at his hotel.

I spent hours the next morning preparing for this momentous occasion. I took my milk bath, did my hair, tried on ten different outfits, finally settling on a simple, subtle black wool dress (perfect for a funeral!). When the time came, I was petrified. I wanted Sidney, but I felt funny. After all, here we were, setting a date to make love. There was nothing spontaneous about it.

The day turned out to be a total disaster.

We laughed and talked easily for a while, but then when we moved to the bed I tightened up the moment he reached over to touch me and pulled away from him. I was just too guilty to go through with it. So there we were again, back to the same old heavyhearted dialogue:

"Diahann, what's the matter with you?"

"I don't know, Sidney. But being with you like this makes me feel like trash, like absolute trash. I don't know if I can change that, Sidney. I don't know if I even want to. And since you're not about to change, I guess that puts us right back where we started."

"Well, if you need to have me give up my wife and kids and everything I've worked for, then I'm not enough for you. You want too much."

Again, we were getting nowhere. I left his hotel room, making yet another vow not to get into this position again. I *did* want too much.

I backed away from Sidney and threw myself into my work. Being on the same soundstage every day with an actress as gifted as Joanne Woodward was a constant reminder of just how fine film acting can be. As I watched the rushes of one of her scenes, I heard Marty Ritt marvel, "Oh, the things she can do in front of that camera!" and thought to myself, "Yes, I want to be able to do that too. Look how she stands there and triggers in herself exactly what she needs to make the scene play. You can see it in her expression, in her eyes." I learned so much from watching and working with Joanne. The experience was tremendously important to my own development as an actress.

The work was all-consuming, even when Sidney and I found ourselves alone with each other. The times we rehearsed together I was able to say to him, "There's something wrong with this scene, Sidney; it's not happening. Let's try it another way." I had a point of view now, and I wasn't afraid to express it. I'm sure Sidney was drawn to that; at the same time, it repelled him. I was starting to grow, and in spite of himself, he had a new respect for me.

The new glimmers of self-confidence stayed with me when the day's work was over. I no longer felt quite so helpless and inadequate because I was alone. "Don't mope around the hotel hoping the phone will ring," I told myself. "You're in Paris. Take advantage of it. Walk through the streets. Go to the cafés. Look at the people. Listen to the language. Go out. You don't have to wait for a man to shepherd you around."

One evening as I was leaving the hotel I ran into Duke Ellington, who was composing the score for *Paris Blues*. "Come on," he said, taking me grandly by the arm and escorting me through the lobby as though I were some kind of treasure. "I'm about to have dinner. Why don't you join me?" Oh, what a warm, lovely night it was, such a relief from the pain and heaviness that were there all the time with Sidney. Duke was proud of me and enjoyed being in my company and delighted in showering me with his attention. He saw a floundering young woman who wasn't being given the emotional nourishment she needed, and in order to help me grow, he became my teacher for the evening.

"Allow me to order this for you," he repeated in his quietly grand manner as he selected his favorite items from the menu. "Please taste this caviar. If you don't care for it, we'll try something else." It was as if he were reminding me I had something special of my own to offer, my own value and charm, and I needed to know that. I loved him for it. With Sidney, I always felt that he was so much more than I, so much more important and valuable as an artist and human being. Being with him made me feel my own inadequacies and limitations, and I had to give up a lot of myself. But that evening my friend Duke Ellington didn't require that. He wanted more from me, just as he always wanted more from his musicians, and the more he received, the more joy it brought him. He couldn't have given me a better present.

I tried so hard to become my own person and stay out of Sidney's way, but for all my good intentions I couldn't stop thinking about him. Part of me never wanted to hear from him again, yet every time the phone rang another part hoped he was calling to say how terribly he missed me.

Sidney was suffering through the same kind of turmoil. "Oh, if you would just get out of my life!" he raged at me the night we accidentally crossed paths at a cast party, grabbing my face in anger and pulling me toward him, then pushing me away. "If I could only make you disappear . . . not be . . . so I could put an end to this thing!"

We were pathetic. It was like a bad movie. But it was real life, our real life, and we couldn't help it.

By the last week in December we had almost completed shooting. Monte flew over with the baby, Suzanne, and my parents so we could spend Christmas together as a family. But despite the beautiful tree in the living room and my mother's ebullient preparations for the big Christmas dinner, I wasn't able to feel very much of the holiday spirit. Nothing had improved between Monte and me. We remained just as estranged from each other as when we parted at the airport in New York. Both of us were lonely. Both of us were miserable.

The night before Christmas Eve I asked a friend to meet me at a restaurant so I would have an excuse to leave the hotel for a while. As we lingered over our coffee, I turned to her abruptly and announced, "Sidney's going to find me. I know I'm going to see him any second." A few minutes later, almost as if it were in a dream, I saw a shadowy form peering in through the frost-covered window, and there he was. Sidney's family was also in Paris for the holiday, and he also needed to escape for a moment. He had been wandering the streets hoping to find me.

My friend excused herself, and Sidney sat down at the table. Neither of us could believe how we found each other, and we sat there silently, staring and trembling, as we tried to regain our composure. And then, once again, the serious discussions about our future together began. They continued over the next few evenings as we met in secret and took long walks though the freezing Paris winter.

By the end of the week Sidney had reached some conclusions. It was time to stop playing this silly game — he would ask his family to fly home to Pleasantville instead of remaining in Paris until the picture was finished; the two of us would go off to Sweden and make the necessary phone calls; we would return to New York as a couple, then move ahead with our respective divorces. It had been two years since *Porgy and Bess,* two long years standing at the door with my hand on the knob waiting for it to open. Now, finally, that was going to happen. The sense of fulfillment seemed almost too good to be true.

It was.

I felt it coming the moment he began telling me about the telegram. I kept praying I was wrong.

"I received this wire from President Kennedy's inauguration committee," he explained. "I've been invited to take part in the

Gala. I have to fly to Washington. I'm afraid the trip to Sweden is off."

I waited for the next line telling me that when the evening in Washington was over we would go somewhere else — California, Toronto, New Jersey (what difference did it make?) — and resume our plans from there. But the words didn't come. He had done it again. And, as usual, he assumed I understood the importance of his plans.

"You do understand why I have to go back, don't you?" he asked me. And all I could answer was, "I understand, if you think you must go back."

I was too numb to say anything else. Letting myself feel the full pain of the hurt would have made it even more devastating, and I needed every bit of strength I had left to keep from falling apart. But a hundred questions crowded my mind. Who was this human being I had fallen in love with? What did he want from me? It's so simple: either people want to be together or they don't. How could I let myself be fooled like this? Why did I allow it? What do I do now?

Sidney went off to the Kennedy Gala and returned home to Pleasantville. I flew back to New York, alone.

⁂

That was, I told myself, the end of it. And, anyway, what was "it"? It wasn't an affair. It was a torturous, painful, emotionally draining, utterly futile relationship. Sidney's inability to live up to any of his commitments to me was more than I could bear. Somehow I would have to get along without him. Trying to put the disappointment and hurt behind me, I went back to work, singing in hotels and clubs around the country.

And I had my Suzanne. She was wonderful — her smiles filled me with a love and a contentment I had never known. I loved to come home and find her standing in her crib, singing at the top of her lungs. Most of all, I just loved having her with me.

I was booked into the Persian Room for another engagement. As the night of the opening loomed closer, the pressure intensified, and I disappeared completely into my work. And then, the afternoon of my last rehearsal, the phone rang, and there he was again.

I thought I had finally gotten away from Sidney and put all that anguish to rest. Yet the instant I heard his voice I knew I hadn't escaped yet. Paris was many months behind us by now, but Sidney picked up the dialogue as though we had seen each other only yesterday. As always, he knew exactly which emotional buttons to push.

"Hello, Diahann," he said in that incredible voice. "I've talked to my wife, and now I want to talk to your husband. It's the only gentlemanly thing to do. I'd like you to arrange a meeting. It's high time Monte and I met."

Nothing was mentioned about all those broken promises and canceled plans. It was as if they had never happened. Nor did he ask me if I still loved him. Sidney had made up his mind about what had to be done, and there was no need to discuss it further.

I protested weakly that I couldn't possibly do what he asked. It was absurd. We had already been through this twice before. My opening was only a few days off. I desperately needed every second I had left. But both of us knew I didn't mean it. Five minutes later I was on the phone to Monte. I told him everything. I asked him if he would meet with Sidney and me, and he agreed.

"Well, there goes my act," I told myself as I rearranged the rehearsal schedule and tried without much success to focus my concentration on the work. "Here we go again. My life is a mess."

I managed to get through my act. When it was done, the three of us met in a little restaurant on Broadway. Naturally, we were very uncomfortable. I didn't even know where to sit; there was a little table with four chairs, and I wasn't going to sit next to Sidney, and I wasn't going to sit by myself, so I sat down next to Monte.

Sidney was terribly dramatic. "I'm in love with your wife," he announced, almost as though I weren't there. "I've tried, I've really tried to stay away from her. And she's tried too. But this situation has been going on for years now, and we must reach a conclusion."

"I know," Monte answered softly. "She's never lied to me."

"I realize it's been very painful for everyone," Sidney continued. "But perhaps we should try to make this thing come to a head so all of us can get on with rebuilding our lives."

Monte was very quiet. I guess he respected Sidney for being honest, but if the look in his eyes could kill, Sidney would have been a dead man.

"I've already talked with my wife," Sidney kept on going. "We're getting a divorce. I think it would be better for everyone if you and Diahann did the same."

There was a long silence, then Monte answered, "Well, if that's what Diahann wants, I'm not going to stand in her way."

I left the two of them sitting at the restaurant and rambled around the streets trying to sort out my thoughts. If one part of me didn't quite trust Sidney to deliver on his promises, another part believed him more completely than ever. If he didn't really love me, why would he have come looking for me? Why would he be divorcing his wife? Why would he have sat down with my husband? The weight of the evidence seemed overwhelming. The confusion and pain were about to end. Sidney and I were finally going to be together.

Monte and I went to see his family lawyer about starting the divorce proceedings. The lawyer said he couldn't represent both of us and referred me to another attorney on 42nd Street. When I met with the attorney, he only wanted to discuss the financial settlement. I tried to explain that that was not why I was there, but he didn't want to listen. Finally I asked to use his phone and called Monte at the office.

"You'd better come down here," I told him. "This man is acting like a fool. He keeps telling me how wealthy you are and how I should —"

"All right, I'll be right there," Monte answered.

When Monte arrived, the lawyer looked at the two of us and shook his head in confusion.

"Are you kids really sure you want a divorce?" he asked. "Maybe you should give it some second thoughts."

Monte reassured him we knew what we were doing. "You'll get all the details from my attorney," he explained. "I want to support my child, and I want to take care of Diahann for a year. If that's not satisfactory, I'll give her anything she wants."

"Well, what about visitation rights?"

"He can see Suzanne whenever he wishes," I told him. "She's his child too. We both love her, and we both want to raise her."

"Then you really aren't angry with each other?" he asked, not quite believing that was possible. "I understand there's another man involved."

"That's none of your business," Monte snapped at him. "It doesn't have anything to do with how we settle this thing."

"Okay, fine," he said. "I'll draw up the papers exactly the way you want them. And good luck."

Monte and I left the office together. We were so overwhelmed that when we reached the street we sat down on the curb and cried. We were still friends, but the marriage was really over.

∽✤∾

Monte moved out of the apartment, and I began to adjust to being alone. It was the first time in my life I lived alone, and I liked it. I had my baby, and I had the nurse to help me, and I was really fine. I was, in a sense, for the first time since I met Sidney, free. Everything was falling into place. Finally, for me, it became a relationship — a reality — two people really dating. And I didn't have to sneak around or be ashamed.

When Sidney called for a date, I knew this would be the night, so I went to every store in New York City to find the "right" dress. I went to Bergdorf's, I went to Bonwit's, I went to Saks — every place. I must have bought five outfits. Then I went to the beauty parlor. My hair turned out all wrong and I went back. I scrubbed and I bathed. I was immaculate. I remember looking in the mirror and saying to myself, "You look adorable." I was finally pleased and no longer as nervous as I had been in the past.

Sidney picked me up — he looked wonderful, just wonderful. We went to a restaurant and sat in a very dark and private booth. Sidney was very relaxed, and uncharacteristically he ordered a cocktail before dinner, and then wine. So there was something very special in the air. And remember, we had waited for *three years*.

There was nothing forced, nothing unnatural — we had a wonderful dinner. And then we went back to my apartment, and we made love. Finally.

Our relationship grew, and we spent more and more time with each other. In the beginning Sidney returned home to Pleasantville at the end of the night, but that was, he assured me, just to see his children. As soon as he finished hammering out the divorce agreement, he would take a place of his own in the city. Meanwhile, we were together.

The months went by, but nothing changed. The only difference was that Sidney became more and more evasive whenever I asked him what he was doing about his divorce. Eventually, it became apparent that he hadn't done anything. He hadn't filed the papers. He hadn't even seen his lawyer.

To this day, I still can't explain why I didn't put an end to it right there. Was I that hopelessly head over heels in love with him? . . . That pathetically afraid to be alone? . . . That dumb and insecure? By now the pattern could not have been clearer. Each time I pulled away from him and began to show some signs of independence, he stepped up his pursuit and raised the level of his commitment. And each time I agreed to go along with whatever he proposed, he found some excuse to back away. But I didn't put an end to it. Instead, I argued and fought with him, as if forcing him to look at the contradictions in his behavior would somehow make things right between us.

"Why are you spending the night in Pleasantville again?" I would cross-examine him as I watched him put on his clothes. "Why can't you stay in a hotel until you find an apartment?"

"Well, I just can't do that. It would be too upsetting for the children."

"But, Sidney, all that was supposed to have been settled months ago when you sat down with Monte. How can you tell a man you want his wife, then suddenly turn around and announce you haven't figured out how to deal with your children? You can't do that, Sidney."

Sidney was not about to let anyone tell him what he could or could not do, certainly not a woman, certainly not me. As always, his best defense was an attack.

"You're never grateful, Diahann! No matter what I do, it's never enough!"

"But what have you done, Sidney? The only thing you've done is fulfill one-quarter of your promise. The other part of it has to be fulfilled too! Monte could have said, 'Yes, I will divorce my wife,' then tell you the next time you came to him, 'But I didn't say when.' That's the equivalent to what you're doing now. Monte lived up to his word. I lived up to my word . . ."

"Diahann, you just don't understand. I'm doing the best I can. You're such an ingrate!"

"Sidney, we're back at that same old place again."

"Of course we are! Because you keep putting us there! Because you're never satisfied!"

Round and round we went, getting absolutely nowhere, until he would slam the door behind him and storm out in a rage. A night or two later he would return, and once again I would be overjoyed to see him. But then all the anger and disappointment churning inside me would explode, and we would start pounding away at each other again.

There didn't seem to be any way to resolve the conflict. A West Indian man who believes it is his God-given right to dictate the terms of a relationship and an American woman brought up with ideals, ideals such as a man cherished you and didn't humiliate you and lived up to his promises — such contradictory expectations in two people seemed to be irreconcilable.

Thank God *No Strings* came along when it did. It probably saved my life.

Chapter Five

The morning after one of my appearances on the *Tonight Show* with Jack Paar (I had by then become a sort of regular, appearing almost once a week, along with Eydie Gorme and Steve Lawrence — and I loved it!), the phone rang and a voice announced, "Miss Carroll, Richard Rodgers is calling."

"Of course he is," I answered. "And this is Greta Garbo."

I had met Richard Rodgers briefly, but that was four years earlier, in 1957, shortly after I finished *House of Flowers*. He was then casting *Flower Drum Song,* his new musical set in San Francisco's Chinatown, and asked if I would allow Eddie Senz to do a special makeup job for me to see if I might be able to play an oriental. It really didn't work. By the time Eddie Senz was through, the powder and paint were so thick I could barely open my mouth. Rodgers dropped the idea but promised there would be another show some other time. That's something you hear very often in my business, and as the months and years went by I completely forgot about it.

"Who is this really?" I asked, certain it was one of my friends playing a practical joke. But to my astonishment, it actually was Richard Rodgers, and he wanted to talk with me again.

We met for lunch at Gallagher's, the actors' hangout in the theater district. I decided the look would be Givenchy from head to toe — a pale pink wool dress with a matching simple clean-lined pink coat and one of those wonderful little pillbox hats that were popular at the time.

"You look marvelous," he said as I sat down. "That's exactly the way I would like to see you on stage. . . . Have you ever done any modeling?"

I told him I had, that I started modeling for Johnson Publications when I was fifteen and continued until I left college to go to work as a professional singer. That seemed to please him. Obviously he had something in mind.

He asked why I hadn't returned to the Broadway theater, and I explained that I hadn't been offered anything that really interested me. I had been asked to do several plays about ingenues in the West Indies or Haiti who run around in their bare feet, but I felt I had already explored that character in *House of Flowers* and wanted to move on to something a little more sophisticated. I also thought there was a certain danger in being typecast as an eternal ingenue.

Rodgers agreed, and returned to the subject of modeling. Almost thinking out loud, he began to talk about how interesting it would be to do the first musical about a successful black fashion model, someone very much at home in the world of haute couture, who operates at the top of her profession. "Of course it wouldn't be possible for a black model to achieve that kind of success in this country," he went on. (He was perfectly right. This was still 1961.) "But that does happen in Europe. Maybe the story could take place abroad." He seemed very excited about the idea, and asked if I had any thoughts about how it might be developed. It struck me that the main problem would be finding a writer familiar with black people, someone who would be able to write convincingly about the struggles of a young woman who has made her way through the fashion world. When I ventured that opinion, he remained noncommittal.

It was time for the meeting to end. Rodgers assured me he was going to pursue the idea, but since he was on his way to Europe, he would call me as soon as he returned. I told him how very much I looked forward to that, and then put it out of my mind. It was, of course, terribly exciting to meet with a man who was a living legend, then to hear him praise my work and say he would like to write a show for me. But I had been in the business long enough to know that you must never ever let yourself become emotionally involved in the germ of an idea. Not that it couldn't become a reality, but the possibility was equally as great that I would never hear from Mr. Rodgers again.

Less than two weeks later he called from London. Sounding even more enthusiastic than before, he said he was working on the idea with the playwright Sam Taylor and had developed it to the point where he felt certain he had a show. The plot would deal with the romance between an American model living in Paris and an expatriate American writer who is knocking around Europe with the jet set. Sam Taylor had written a number of successful Broadway shows, but what really excited me was that he was also responsible for the screenplay for *The Moon Is Blue,* one of my favorite films. Rodgers went on to say that Taylor was returning to New York to meet me, and they planned to approach Richard Kiley about playing the male lead. Suddenly, the project began to seem deliciously real.

Everything came together very quickly. Rodgers called and asked which arranger and conductor I had worked with and respected. I suggested Peter Matz (arranger, producer, conductor — Peter could do anything!). A month or so later I found myself sitting with Peter in Rodgers's office on Madison Avenue listening to him play his new score for me. I was entranced! The melodies were so beautiful, so appealing. Like practically everything else he wrote, they had a certain something that catches the ear and makes you want to hear them again. When he said, "This is your love song," and played a few bars from "The Sweetest Sounds," it was more than I could bear. Trying to keep both feet on the ground, I kept telling myself, "Come on, concentrate, concentrate. This is the music you're going to have to perform. Pay attention, Diahann." But it was almost impossible. I was floating.

Not until the very end of the afternoon was there any indication that Richard Rodgers was not the epitome of tact and sensitivity. Before *No Strings* Rodgers had always collaborated with a lyricist — first Larry Hart, and then, after Hart died, Oscar Hammerstein. Now for the first time he had composed the words as well as the music, and he was extremely pleased with himself.

"You just can't imagine how wonderful it feels," he told me as we were saying goodbye, "to have written this score and not have to search all over the globe for that drunken little fag."

I was stunned. The unexpected cruelty of the remark shook me to my very being. I hoped I was mistaken, but as he went on there was absolutely no question that he was talking about Larry Hart. All my life Rodgers and Hart epitomized the very best of American popular music. Their partnership produced some of the most glorious songs ever written. I had heard the gossip about Larry Hart's self-destructiveness, and I'm sure he must have caused Rodgers great anguish over the more than twenty years they had worked together. However, it was inconceivable to me that a man the stature of Richard Rodgers could be so lacking in kindness and generosity of spirit. Rodgers had been blessed with an extraordinary gift and been lavishly rewarded for it. Everything in his elegantly appointed office, from the paintings on the walls to the exquisitely beautiful piano, reeked of quiet money and long-time success. If he could be that mean-spirited about Larry Hart, he could be that way about anyone. My respect for his genius was undiminished, but I was so disappointed by the character of the man that, from that moment on, I never quite trusted him.

❧

Soon we were on our way. Richard Kiley accepted the male lead. Joe Layton became the director. Donald Brooks designed the incredible wardrobe. The extraordinarily gifted Ralph Burns wrote the arrangements. Peter Matz was hired to conduct the orchestra. And almost immediately stories started appearing in the press about this new musical Richard Rodgers was writing for a black star. And then the hard work began.

The weeks that followed were, for the most part, like living in a fairy tale. Joe Layton possessed an extraordinary sense of movement and staging and had mastered the art of negotiating egos to get the work done. Richard Kiley was the kindest and most generous co-star an actress could hope for. He knew all the tricks for getting out of trouble when you lose your concentration or your throat starts to close, and went out of his way to share his experience with me.

Donald Brooks's clothes were breathtaking. I still remember the afternoon Rodgers arranged a private showing at Henri Bendel for me to have my first look at them. Sitting there in that lovely room as the models paraded past me in one beautiful dress after another, I couldn't really believe any of this was actually happening to me. Donald Brooks contacted Geraldine Stutz, a woman with a faultless sense of fashion who went on to become president of Bendel's. Gerri took me under her wing — she came to my home, went through every item in my closets, making lists, explaining why this or that was not acceptable, teaching me how to build a wardrobe, helping me shape my style. I never forgot her kindness. Just being in her presence was an education in itself — I was really learning everything about fashion from Gerri.

While I was preparing for the show, Sidney reappeared. Although he had very little respect for musical comedies, he realized it was an important opportunity and tried to be supportive. More than once he came to my apartment and spent the entire evening rehearsing with me. On the other hand, he would have much preferred it if the show had never happened in the first place. As always, he had a great deal of difficulty accepting the fact that I had a career of my own, that I chose to earn my own living and I loved my work.

We were already having enough problems without the added pressure of my taking the lead in a new Broadway show. Sidney was in no great hurry to talk to his wife about a divorce, and therefore our relationship was deteriorating rapidly. I still loved him, but part of me was also starting to hate him. Little by little, I began to pull away. Shortly before I was due to leave New York for the out-of-town tryouts, I found the strength to break it off completely.

"I'll be on the road for at least nine weeks," I told him. "I'll be very busy. This is a gift, Sidney, a perfect opportunity for the two of us to put an end to this madness and stop torturing each other."

Sidney heard me out and agreed it would all be for the best. It was time for us to leave each other.

Overjoyed that I had finally freed myself of him, I went off to Detroit with Suzanne and her nurse to do *No Strings*. One afternoon, as I was standing on the stage rehearsing, I looked out into the audience and there was the gorgeous black panther stalking down the aisle. I suppose I should have screamed at the top of my lungs, "Sidney, please, for God's sake get out of my life!" But I didn't. Unable to think, unable to put a sentence together, I just stood there and sort of beamed. Now it was absolutely clear to everyone to whom I belonged. Sidney remained in Detroit for two days. He was charming and wonderful, and the entire company loved him. Then, having accomplished his mission, he left.

And the show went on. By the time we opened in Detroit (the first stop in our out-of-town tryout), we realized that we had our share of problems. Opening night was a complete fiasco. My fault. Like a lot of people before him, Joe Layton took it for granted that of course I could dance. I kept telling him I could not dance, and most certainly not while I was singing. But he insisted on including me in two of the dance numbers.

"Sure, you can do it," he assured me at the rehearsal. "It's easy. All you have to do is move to the left and go two-three-four, and the kids will do the rest. Then when they cross, move upstage — seven-eight . . . two-three — and you're stage center. . . . All right, let's try it again."

We tried again and again, and by the time I finally did it right, it was five hours later. By then the dancers were so tired and disgusted that the looks on their faces seemed to be asking, "What is this? Can't she count to eight? Does she have two left feet?"

When we opened in Detroit it was our first night before a live audience. Once onstage, I must have blocked out everything except what I thought I needed for the performance, and what I thought I needed was to perform as a singer, not a dancer. In any case, I concentrated so heavily on the singing that I did not take one single dance step the entire night. The dancers were very kind. Some of them grabbed the back of my coat and pulled me out of the way, then the others pushed me off to the side. It was so embarrassing, but I sold those songs!

When the show was over, we all met downstairs in the lower lobby. I was mortified. I thought I'd never be able to live it down.

"What can I tell you, Joe?" I asked him. "Now you have positive proof that we don't all have rhythm."

"All right," he answered, "I'm not going to argue with you anymore. You cannot dance. We'll restage the scenes so you can just walk through them."

"Say it again," I told him. "Say it again: Diahann is right. She cannot dance."

Another problem was communicating with Richard Rodgers. Rodgers wasn't exactly intimidating, but there was never any of that easy give and take and sense of camaraderie between composer and company I had experienced with Harold Arlen. Arlen was a wonderfully warm human being, and everyone in the cast of *House of Flowers* adored him. Rodgers was much more formal. As time passed, I came to the conclusion that he was really incapable of hearing someone else's point of view without regarding that person as a potential adversary, and his frequent insensitivity was appalling.

I will never be able to forget the smile on his face when he informed me that there would be no opening night party for the cast in Detroit because the hostess had refused to invite me. It seems that this local socialite was afraid to have a black person who wasn't a servant around her children, and unless Rodgers could assure her that he had created me himself — trained me to speak and walk and dress properly — she would not allow me to set foot in her home.

Rodgers found the whole episode vastly amusing. He didn't seem terribly bothered by his friend's racism. It only confirmed that he accomplished what he set out to accomplish, which was to present this glamorous, very desirable black woman in a vehicle that would startle the white community. This woman gave a party for Rodgers — and he went. I held my own party for the cast in the restaurant across the street from the theater.

Other problems weren't solved quite so simply. When I first saw the script, I was much too excited even to begin to evaluate it. The author's note stated on the front page that the play never once mentioned the female lead's color, but I didn't allow myself to ask why. I wanted to do it. I wanted to star on Broadway. As we moved into rehearsal, Sam Taylor openly acknowledged that he and Rodgers had quite consciously arrived at that decision and there was nothing more to discuss. "It's a love story," he said, "a beautiful love story with beautiful songs and beautiful clothes, and the fact that she happens to be black and he happens to be white is not going to be discussed. It's just going to be there." But then as time went on, it became increasingly clear that this ridiculous evasion was going to catch up with us, and it finally did. The ending of the show simply didn't work. The plot spent an hour and forty-five minutes getting these two people together. It established that they love each other. Now suddenly, without any explanation, they are made to part. Kiley's character decides to return to the United States so he can resume writing his novel. My character thinks that's a wonderful idea and tells him goodbye. End of story.

"But why can't they go home together?" Kiley and I kept asking.

"If they love each other so much and are so well suited, why do they have to separate?"

Sam Taylor insisted that we were being totally unrealistic, and informed us that the subject was not open for discussion. I guess he felt that it was perfectly feasible for a white man to have a brief affair with a black woman in the fantasy world of Paris, but that was as far as it would go.

"Well, they have to," was the explanation. "You know, they just have to."

The problem of the ending was finally resolved when someone came up with the idea of reproducing the opening scene of the show detail for detail. Kiley and I are on stage together but haven't yet met, aren't even aware of each other's presence. Both of us are singing "The Sweetest Sounds," that beautiful song I had heard that first day, full of yearning about wanting to fall in love. When the song ends, the lights begin to dim and, still not seeing each other, we cross and move off separately into the opposite wings. It was an absolutely brilliant solution, making everything that came in between a fantasy, a love story that may or may not have actually happened.

We opened in New York on March 15, 1962. There were enough rave reviews to make us a solid hit.

Two months later I received my second nomination for a Tony Award — this time for best female performance in a musical. And this time it was a "big to-do" in my life. I was ecstatic that my peers thought so highly of my work. But, in truth, I became a little too full of myself. It was all so much so soon! I had never dreamed that by the age of twenty-five I would have had a Broadway show written especially for me by Richard Rodgers, and then to top it off, a Tony Award nomination. It was a lot for me to handle (and to handle *gracefully*) because I didn't have any experience with this kind of attention.

My friends were wonderful! Everyone called and sent flowers in congratulations. My parents were in heaven, and Sidney was happy for me, too. Almost immediately Donald Brooks and Geraldine Stutz began trying to solve the big question: what *would* I wear? After much discussion we agreed on a white jersey gown that was spectacular because it was so simple. And the day of the awards my old friend and furrier, Abe Rein, sent over a gorgeous fox coat for the occasion. Our friendship had begun when Lou

Walters sent me to Abe's showroom when I was eighteen, and Abe custom-made a black diamond mink coat for a mere fifty-dollar deposit, reassuring his partners that I was to be trusted (and our relationship has lasted thirty years!).

And that evening I sat in the theater in a trance. When they announced the nominees — Anna Maria Alberghetti for *Carnival*, Molly Picon for *Milk and Honey*, Elaine Stritch for *Sail Away*, and Diahann Carroll for *No Strings* — my heart pounded so hard I began to shake. It sounds trite — but it is true. I was so certain I wouldn't win against such competition that I never prepared a proper acceptance speech. When they announced my name, saying I had tied with Anna Maria Alberghetti, it wasn't until I saw the audience turning to smile at me that I knew I had heard correctly and allowed myself to move to the stage.

When I reached the podium, I was overwhelmed! I wanted to thank Richard Rodgers, but instead I was so overcome with emotion I became incoherent and rather theatrical. "Isn't it incredible?" I proclaimed. "*He* knocked on *my* door. *He* called *me*." I'm sure everyone was delighted when I finally finished speaking and returned to my seat.

❧

Receiving that kind of recognition is a glorious feeling, and I was on top of the world for days. But nothing lasts forever, and life is so full of surprises you never can tell what's going to happen next. One day you win the Tony Award and are performing the lead in a Broadway musical Richard Rodgers wrote for you. The next day you pick up the morning paper and read that an actress named Nancy Kwan has just been hired to play your role in the film version.

I was furious. I was hurt. I felt betrayed. And, hearing the news that way was a terrible shock. I assumed that Richard Rodgers would have had, if not at least compassion, then the common courtesy to tell me himself. I understood that he had no legal obligation to do so, but this was not a legal question. There had been rumors about the possibility of a movie sale to Ray Stark at Warners–Seven Arts, and the implication, I thought, was clear that I would be part of the package. But now that the negotiations had been completed, I was suddenly out of the picture, and no one seemed to feel I should be told the bad tidings before the announcement hit the papers.

I would like to believe that when Richard Rodgers stopped by my dressing room that evening of the announcement, he was trying to soften the blow.

"Of course you realize," he told me, "that I had nothing to do with casting the film."

"Well, no, I didn't realize that."

"Not that I have to explain this to you, but I sold the rights to Warners–Seven Arts, and they're free to do as they please."

I found it hard to believe that Richard Rodgers would sell a property outright without retaining some power over the project. But there was nothing more to say. I wished him every success, and he left. It was a very uncomfortable meeting for both of us.

Earl Wilson called the next day to ask if I would come to his office to discuss my feelings. I threw caution to the wind and said that I would. I met him at his office and he immediately got to the point. He wanted to know if I was disappointed by the news. I told him that of course I was. At the risk of sounding presumptuous and naïve, I felt that *No Strings* was my baby. But I made it clear that I was also disappointed about something else. If Warner Brothers didn't think I was right for the part — fine; that was their prerogative. I would have to live with that. But the fact that they didn't select a black actress (Nancy Kwan was Eurasian, a minority, but she was *not* black) told the story. It was explained to me that a black actress was not box office.

I had no idea what a furor Wilson's column would cause when it appeared in the papers the next morning. Almost every show business journalist in the country had something to say. Some of the writers cheered me on. Others accused me of sour grapes. Didn't I realize, they asked, that this sort of thing happens all the time when Broadway shows are made into films? Julie Andrews played *My Fair Lady* on Broadway, but Audrey Hepburn took over her role for the screen version. That was perfectly true, but they seemed to miss my point. Audrey Hepburn and Julie Andrews are both white. And since *No Strings* was written for a black woman, a black woman — if not me, someone else — ought to be given a chance to play the part.

Earlier that month Adam Clayton Powell had held a series of congressional hearings about racial discrimination in the entertainment industry. I had testified about the limited opportunities afforded black performers, and now, two weeks later, here was a perfect example of what I meant. The NAACP sent a petition to Warners–Seven Arts demanding to know how many black people were employed by the company. Several other groups started discussions about boycotting the film. That may or may not have been the deciding factor, but the studio eventually decided to shelve the project.

The experience was more than disappointing. For a long time it marred my work. Whenever I walked onstage I had this terrible feeling that everyone in the audience thought I was good enough to perform in the theater but not good enough for the film. Even though I understood the racism of what happened, and tried to remember my mom's words ("It's their problem, Diahann, not yours"), I felt an overpowering sense of failure that I couldn't shake.

This was hardly the first time I had come up against the reality that parts for black performers were not in abundance. For example, while a Broadway star is in a successful play, he or she often receives many scripts to read for his or her next project. For black performers, this is not the case. Parts have always been few and far between.

I thought I was prepared for the blows, but one never really is. The studio — the entire industry — seemed to be telling me, "We're not doing this movie with a black female lead." And that was something "they" wanted me to accept. But I couldn't. I walk around in this skin all the time. So it wasn't just this one movie that was at stake. It was my very life.

❧

Well, as they say, life goes on. I continued to do the show, and I continued to see Sidney. He still wasn't ready for a divorce, but he did more or less move out of the house, taking a little one-room apartment on West 57th Street. Three evenings a week he went back to Pleasantville to have dinner with his children. The nights I stayed with him I would leave at four or five in the morning, to be home by the time Suzanne awoke and give her breakfast. (One of my joys in life was feeding my sensationally beautiful little monster, who ate by putting one-third of her food in her mouth, a third on her face, and a third on me.)

It was a difficult arrangement for both of us. Sidney was so filled with guilt about being away from his children that he seemed to feel he was somehow betraying them if he were nice to Suzanne or even acknowledged her existence. For my part, I found it increasingly painful to accept the fact that I was now, in effect, his mistress. The more I thought about it, the more it rankled.

Finally, hoping to force some kind of resolution, I set up a meeting at my home between Sidney and my parents. I had the entire scenario mapped out in advance. There would be a moment or two of social chitchat while I served the drinks, then Mom and Dad would gently but firmly confront him with how he was mistreating their precious child. "We don't intend to tell you two how to live your lives," they would say, "but Diahann is terribly unhappy and we would like to see her in a better frame of mind. How are you going to handle this?" Put on the spot by the parents of the woman he loved, seeing their anguish and concern firsthand, Sidney would declare his intentions to do right by their daughter and head straight for the divorce court.

But none of that happened. There was no confrontation. Mom had a great deal to say about our living arrangement beforehand, but when she found herself face to face with the great Sidney Poitier, she was too dazzled to say anything. So was my father. Without even trying, Sidney had them completely charmed. His very presence was enough to reduce them to two adoring, worshipping fans. Sidney still held all the cards, and he knew it. If anything, the meeting only strengthened his hand. One look at the awe on their faces, and he knew as well as I that the pressure was off and he was still free to do whatever he pleased. Mr. and Mrs. Johnson were not about to cause him any problems he couldn't handle with a flash of his famous smile.

Sidney was going through a long dry spell in his career. It made him absolutely crazy. Finally he was offered a film with Richard Widmark called *The Long Ships*. It was a Viking adventure movie that was really about nothing, and he wasn't at all sure he should do it. But he needed the work, so he signed the contract and went off to Yugoslavia, where the film was being shot.

If it weren't for my show, I would have gone with him. We still had our ups and downs, but Sidney's career difficulties had exposed his more tender, vulnerable side and brought us, once again, closer together. While he was away I furnished his apartment, turning the hideaway into more of a real home for us. At first he called and wrote constantly, letters that were heated and passionate and went on for pages filled with the declarations of love he had never been able to make face to face. But then the letters and phone calls stopped. It occurred to me that maybe he had changed his mind about us, was perhaps even having an affair. But rather than confront him I decided to wait it out and see what happened when he returned.

And then one afternoon toward the end of the shooting of his film I received a telegram. All it said was: "Come at once. I need you." He sounded so urgent and I was so relieved to hear from him that I rushed straight to Richard Rodgers's office and asked if I could take my vacation immediately. I realized I was giving him very short notice, I said, but I had never taken a vacation from *No Strings* and desperately needed to get away for a week. (I had had a terrible case of the flu a few weeks before, and had still not recovered.)

Rodgers was, quite rightly, furious with me. "All right, in that case you don't have to come back," he answered. "I have another young lady I'm going to make into a big star." It wasn't until I saw a doctor (who informed me that I was suffering from true exhaustion and could have a relapse of the hepatitis I had suffered years before) and he sent Rodgers a letter explaining it was absolutely imperative I have a little time off that I was able to leave without being fired.

In truth, something was the matter with me. I had never recovered from that flu, and I was working nonstop. But to go to see Sidney in Yugoslavia in the middle of starring in my own Broadway show was not exactly rational behavior. What was I doing flying off to Yugoslavia? I knew I was behaving irrationally. I knew I was jeopardizing my entire career, maybe throwing away everything I had ever worked for. But I couldn't seem to stop myself.

I should have realized I was in serious trouble when we landed in Germany to refuel. When the passengers were asked to disembark, I refused to leave my seat. Looking out the window, I saw the uniformed airline officials riding toward the plane in an old convertible, and I was reminded of the cars the S.S. officers used to drive in many World War Two movies. (My daughter's infant nurse, Ilsa, had been in a concentration camp, and we had spent many hours talking about her experiences. They were so vivid in my mind that this time, in my fatigued state, I saw Nazis everywhere.) I think my mind slipped a gear, and I was certain I was in Nazi Germany and that these were Nazis coming to arrest me.

"I will not leave this plane," I said, and I meant it. "I will not get into that car."

The airline officials explained very kindly that we were just refueling and would take off soon. They escorted me outside and bought me a brandy. When it was time to leave, they deposited me back on the plane.

"Are you sure you're all right?" they asked in perfect English.

"Yes, of course I'm all right," I answered, though everyone could see by now that of course I wasn't.

Sidney was not at the airport when we landed. When I arrived at the resort in Sveti Stevan, Sidney was waiting. He was quiet and distant. It was almost as though he were sorry I had come and wished I would go away. I was astounded. This was not the reception I had expected. As always, trying to understand him, I figured that now I had left a hit show and flown halfway around the world to be with him, there was no question about the totality of my commitment, and Sidney must have been frightened. He was, perhaps, even more frightened by the extent of his own need, for having allowed himself to say, "I have to have her with me."

Things didn't improve. The first night at dinner at this romantic restaurant on the Adriatic Sea, some of the cast gathered around the dining room piano and began singing Broadway show songs. After a while they strolled over to our table and asked if I would care to join them. Immediately, I felt the tension coming from Sidney. They felt it too and retreated to the piano.

"Sidney, do you mind if I join them?" I asked him.

"Diahann, every black person can either sing or dance," he answered, "and I wish you would stop."

He had been trying to tell me that for years, and I still wasn't getting the message.

"But Sidney, I love to sing. . . ."

Glaring in anger, he rose from the table and went off to his room.

When the filming ended a few days later, our taxi broke down on the way to the plane taking us to Paris, and we had to hitch a ride on a little country bus. It was stiflingly hot. There was no place to sit. The dust was flying in our faces. And there we were bouncing along in a bus full of women, children, and chickens with my mountain of luggage. When we finally reached the airport, the plane was about to take off, and the other passengers were good enough to help us unload. The chickens were everywhere, and Sidney looked at me as if he didn't believe any of this was really happening. The whole thing was so ludicrous that, for all his anger, he couldn't keep himself from laughing. (I had to admit that even at this point, I still loved his laughter!)

By the time we reached Paris, he had practically stopped talking to me. He seemed perfectly comfortable and relaxed with other people, but the moment we were alone he lapsed back into the same stony silence. I felt unattractive. I felt like a burden, like something being dragged along that kept him from doing what he really wanted. It was perfectly obvious by now that he couldn't stand being with me. On our second day in town, I went shopping for the afternoon to give him some time to himself. When I returned to the hotel, he was packing.

"I'm going to London tonight," he announced.

"Oh, all right. When are we leaving?"

"No," he answered. "*I'm* going to London. *You're* going back to New York. I'll buy you a return ticket."

There it was once again, that same old sinking feeling in the pit of my stomach. I ran into the bathroom, threw a lot of cold water on my face, and off we went to the ticket office on the Champs Elysées.

Standing there waiting for him to make the arrangements, I felt like a total idiot. When would I ever learn? I had walked out of a hit Broadway show and flown thousands of miles to be with this man, and now he couldn't wait to get rid of me. When Sidney returned from the ticket counter, he threw me a wicked look and asked, "You don't mind going back tourist, do you?" Mind? I immediately purchased my own first-class ticket.

I think if I had just that once taken a swing at him, it would have changed our entire relationship. I would have been clearer to him. I would have had more form, more shape, more reality as a flesh-and-blood human being who had to be reckoned with. Somehow, I could not do it. Each time he emotionally knocked me down, I bounced back almost as if I had no feelings and didn't really mind being hurt. And as soon as I dusted myself off, I was ready to go at it again any way he wanted it. "All right, which way now? Left turn? Okay. Right turn? All right, I'll try a right turn. Down the middle? Fine, I'll try that."

Sidney's flight left an hour before mine. I waited with him silently, keeping my thoughts and feelings to myself. When he disappeared through the turnstile, I became suddenly determined that his last sight of me would be a smiling, whole woman, so I waved goodbye. The moment he was safely out of sight, everything went out of focus, my knees buckled under me, and I collapsed. Some strangers helped me to the first-aid office upstairs. They offered me brandy to keep me from passing out and helped me to the plane.

When Sidney returned to New York a week or so later, I was there at his apartment waiting to greet him with open arms. Neither of us said a word about Yugoslavia and Paris. It was as if the whole insane episode had never happened. Now that we were alone, Sidney didn't have to explain me to anyone, and we stayed up the entire night laughing and talking and making love. I don't know which of us was more out of touch with reality.

❧

Harry Belafonte was one of Sidney's oldest and closest friends. As we came to know each other, he became my friend too, almost like the big brother I never had. He and his wife, Julie, spent enough time in our company to recognize the depth of our difficulties. Shortly after Sidney returned from *The Long Ships*, the Belafontes suggested I talk to Julie's therapist about possibly starting treatment. I didn't really believe I needed help. So I thought the Nazis were coming to force me to get off the plane in Germany and fell flat on my face in the Paris airport. That could happen to anyone. And lots of women have trouble with their boy friends. What's so unusual about that? But they convinced me that I needed help, so I made the phone call and set up the appointment.

It took a while to gain some clarity about my own behavior, to understand why I allowed myself to stay in such a demeaning relationship. But gradually, with my doctor's questioning and probing four and five times a week, the insights began to come.

I saw that even loving, doting parents can create a child with an inadequate sense of self-esteem. As we examined the damage inflicted upon my mother and father by the white community and how, like most black people of their generation, they largely accepted it as their way of life and passed this acquiescence on to their children, I saw how I had been given the message, almost by osmosis, that I was not supposed to be treated like a first-class citizen. And I saw how that fed into my relationship with Sidney. I was willing to take whatever he handed out, as if I didn't deserve his respect.

And I saw how my sexual hangups had only worsened the situation by attracting me to the negative and the unacceptable, even though every part of my conscious mind was screaming for the direct opposite. I surmised from hearing my parents tossing in bed at night while making love, when I was an infant, that sex was a struggle, a fight — a bad thing that nice people do not do. Having made that connection, I carried it with me through all the years I was growing up, to such an extent that every sexual encounter practically had to have the overtones of a rape scene. Obviously I did not like myself too much — no wonder I chose a man who was *totally unavailable* and could only make me unhappy. After all, subconsciously I felt that was what I deserved. If he loved me, there must be something wrong with him. My helpless involvement with a married man like Sidney provided me with a wonderful excuse not to confront my incapability of having a so-called normal relationship. As long as I was in love with Sidney, I would *never* have to *face* all the personal problems that were preventing me from being happy with myself.

It took me years to sort this all out. There was a lifetime of obstacles to overcome. But thanks to my therapy I started on the road and was beginning to see Sidney and myself in a somewhat clearer light, although I wasn't yet able to do very much about it.

స్మ

It was 1963. Sidney and I had been seeing each other for over five years. And, once again, we agreed to part. *No Strings* finished its New York run. Following Belafonte's advice, I decided to take the show out of town. "That's where the real money is," he had said, explaining the financial advantages of the tent circuit. When I looked into it I saw he was absolutely right, so I packed my suitcases, bundled up my baby and her nurse, and left New York for the road.

Harry insisted I bring along my own company manager to run the box office, and recommended a young man named Richard. Richard and I liked each other immediately, and as the months went by we began dating. When the tour ended, he joined me in Reno, where I was working at one of the casinos, then came along with me to my next job in Los Angeles.

I was staying with my mother and my little Suzie at the Chateau Marmont, the same hotel where Sidney and I lived when we first met each other during *Porgy and Bess*. Richard was staying at another hotel. It was six o'clock in the morning when the phone rang.

"You bitch! You whore! You tramp!" the voice on the other end of the line screamed at me. "How dare you!"

If I wasn't too groggy to have a sense of humor, I would have asked, "Who is this, please?" But there really was no need for that. Who else could it be?

"Hello, Sidney. What's wrong?"

As it turned out, Sidney was also in Los Angeles and also staying at the Chateau Marmont. He had gotten up early and on his way to breakfast had met Richard on the street.

"I know he's living with you!" he raged, full of self-righteous indignation. "I know he just left your bed!"

"Richard probably couldn't sleep and left his hotel to get something to eat," I told him, wondering why I was explaining this to him. "But you can interpret that any way you want. Of course he's here to see me. You know we've been dating. You must have known that for months."

"Get up and get dressed! I'm coming down to talk to you!"

"I can't have any scenes here, Sidney, not in front of my mother and the baby."

"Then meet me in my suite."

"No, I'm not going to do that. I've had it with these games. They've been going on forever, and I can't stand it anymore."

"Okay," he answered, softening suddenly, "you're right. It's time to put an end to this foolishness. It's time to work things out for good."

God knows I had heard that line before, but once again my determination wilted. I knocked on the door of his suite. He stretched out his arms and pulled me toward him. I melted. We were so happy to see each other. Fifteen minutes later we were fighting again.

"I won't have you running around with other men!" he shouted. "You belong to me!"

"Who the hell do you think you are? I don't belong to you, Sidney, I really do not! And you don't belong to me. I'm free to live my life, and you're free to live yours."

LEFT: *Graduation picture, Stitt Junior High School in New York.*

BELOW: *This is the photograph I sent to* Ebony *magazine to see if I could become a model.*

Me at age twenty—I couldn't even fill up the gown!

Winning a beauty contest in 1954 at my dad's Masonic Temple.

Carmen Jones—*left to right: Roy Glenn, Pearl Bailey, Dorothy Dandridge, Nick Stewart, and myself.*

The "chanteuse" at the Waldorf, 1956.

Wedding photograph of Monte and me, 1956.

Andre Previn and I, recording the album "Porgy and Bess."

The Garry Moore Show, 1960. *That's Durward Kirby, myself, Garry Moore, Jack Benny, Carol Burnett, and Marion Lorne.* (J. Peter Happel Photography)

Richard Kiley and I in No Strings. (Fred Schnell)

Vacationing at Fire Island during the run of No Strings. (Stewart Associates)

One of my favorite photographs—my baby, Suzanne, and I taken by the incomparable Richard Avedon. I have a series of these hanging in my bedroom, and each time I look at them, they still make me smile. For this, Suzanne's first photo session, I packed a full trunk of dresses that I had bought for her in France and Switzerland. But Avedon chose to shoot her nude when he saw how beautiful she was.
(Richard Avedon)

This publicity shot for Paris Blues, *taken in 1961, is the only photograph I have of Sidney and me.*

From Paris Blues, *Joanne Woodward and I, 1961.*

Marlon Brando and I at the SNCC Dinner at the Hilton in New York, 1962.
(Mike Zwerling)

President John F. Kennedy and I at Arthur Krim's home in 1962.
(Cecil Stoughton/White House)

Here I am accepting my Tony Award for No Strings. *(That's Jason Robards, Jr., in the background.) I am making my rambling speech.*

With the Tony Award for No Strings, *1962. Left to right: me, Robert Morse, Margaret Leighton, and Paul Scofield.*

Jane Fonda was one of my co-stars in the movie Hurry Sundown. Poor Jane just couldn't seem to bring herself to slap me. I kept saying, "Slap me!" but she just kept tapping me on the cheek.

In my New York apartment that I had just finished decorating, in 1967.

Dinner at Arthur Krim's house with President Lyndon Johnson and Camille and Bill Cosby. (Cecil Stoughton/White House)

Lloyd Nolan and I in our first publicity photo for Julia, *1968.*

That's I and "Corey," played by Marc Copage, in Julia.

John and Mabel Johnson—my father and mother—on the set of Julia.

Hal Kanter holding my Golden Globe Award.

Fred Astaire, Barbra Streisand, and I when we won the Golden Globe Awards in 1968. Mine was for "Best Newcomer in Television." (Peter C. Borsari)

Harry Belafonte and I on my television special, Diahann Carroll, *1970*.

David Frost and I at our engagement party in November 1972. (Bert Glinn)

My wedding to Freddie Glusman in Las Vegas.

Closing shot in Claudine.

Claudine.

With Robert DeLeon at our wedding in New York.

My first job after Robert's death — co-hosting the Mike Douglas Show, *September 1977.*

Entertaining with Bob Hope, May 1979.

The one and only Roy Gerber, my manager and friend, who has been at my side for thirty years, and has promised to stay for another thirty. (Harry Langdon)

At Caesars Palace in Las Vegas, 1985: that's Harold Melvin, Sammy Davis, Jr., myself, and Julie and Harry Belafonte.

Portrait, (Victor Skrebneski)

"The Girls"—top are I and my sister, Lydia, and at bottom, Mom and Suzanne. My sister is laughing because I pinched her—she was so intent on being demure and elegant that I decided the only thing to do was to make her laugh.
(Harry Langdon)

My beautiful daughter, Suzanne, at age twenty-four, in 1984. (Tony Mallone)

With my friends Candy and Aaron Spelling. (Las Vegas News Bureau)

Power in White—Joan Collins and I in our Dynasty *best* (ABC/Bob D'Amico)

My first photo session in Dynasty, *here with Billy Dee Williams.* (Harry Langdon)

With Damone, 1985. (Jim McHugh/People Weekly)

At age forty-nine, and still going strong. (Harry Langdon)

"What is it, then? What do you want? Why can't you be content with our relationship?"

"Oh, for God's sake, Sidney, we don't have a relationship. We haven't had one for ages."

"What do you want of me?" he reiterated, throwing up his hands in exasperation. "What is it you want me to do?"

"I've said the same thing so many times I can't bear to say it again. It sounds so stupid. Why don't you tell me what *you* want, Sidney, what *you* want to do?"

"I'll tell you what I *don't* want. I don't want any more Richards in your life."

"Fine," I answered. "Now how do you intend to accomplish that?"

He took a deep breath and plunged ahead.

"All right, suppose I put a ring on your finger."

"What?" I asked. I couldn't believe what I was hearing.

He looked at his watch. It was almost ten o'clock. We had been going at each other for hours.

"Come on," he said. "We'll drive over to Beverly Hills, and I'll buy it now."

If I had heard him correctly, he seemed to be proposing.

"Sidney, I don't want to seem tedious about little details, but I can't be engaged to a man who is married."

"Well, I'll get the divorce in Mexico. We'll fly down together. And as soon as the papers go through we'll get married."

I don't know if I believed him. I'm not sure I wanted to. Part of me was finally beginning to suspect that perhaps this wasn't really the right thing for me. But I couldn't admit that yet, not even to myself. I still loved him.

I ran upstairs and told my mother I was going with Sidney to buy a ring. We were about to become engaged. Mom didn't believe it either. She was so upset she burst into tears.

"Oh, no, not again. Where will it lead this time?"

"I don't know. I'm not sure."

"I've never seen anything like the two of you. It's like an illness."

"You're right, Mom," I told her. "It is an illness."

We drove to a jewelry store on Beverly Drive. I waited outside while Sidney bought a diamond engagement ring. That afternoon he called his wife, then arranged with his attorney to serve her with papers. I, in my turn, apologized to Richard and said goodbye.

Sidney informed the press about our engagement, and two days later we flew to Tijuana. Sidney met with the Mexican lawyer and signed the documents. We had dinner and a marguerita, then returned to Los Angeles. We were now, so it would seem, free to move on with our lives together.

❧

Sidney left California for Kanab, Utah, to begin shooting a western with James Garner. I joined him for a few days, then flew back to New York. Shortly before he came out to Los Angeles he had purchased a large nine-room apartment on Riverside Drive and hired a decorator. Now that we were back together, he asked me to work with her to make it a real home for the two of us and our children.

I had just returned from looking at some fabric for the sofa when Sidney called from Utah with a piece of very bad news. His wife was having second thoughts about the divorce agreement. Our wedding plans would have to be postponed until he finished his movie and met with the lawyers.

Much to my amazement, the news wasn't really that upsetting. I suppose I had progressed far enough in my therapy to question some of the values with which I was raised, and that had freed me from the shame and guilt I always felt about our illicit relationship. I wasn't in as much of a hurry to be married. I was quite prepared to go on with our plans and move in with him even if *he* was still married, and I didn't think that made me such a terrible person. If anything, it seemed to me that living together openly for a while was probably a very good idea. What better way to find out whether or not we really ought to be husband and wife?

I continued decorating the apartment — meeting with the plasterers and electricians, looking at bunk beds for the children, having my old furniture recovered to fit into the new decor. And, although Sidney and I were sharing the expenses, the place was costing me a great deal of money.

Sitting there in Utah watching this whole thing become more of a reality with every passing day, Sidney must have panicked. I don't know how else to explain what happened next.

My secretary, her husband, and small son had already agreed to take over my old apartment. Everything was packed for the movers. The day before they were to arrive, Sidney called and announced, "I don't want your daughter moving in with us. And I don't want you to ship any of her belongings to my apartment."

I couldn't understand what he was talking about. We had agreed that Suzanne would stay with my parents for five or six weeks to give us the needed time to adjust to each other, but there was never any question about her living with us. She was always part of our plans. Her new room was ready and waiting for her.

I begged him to explain why he was suddenly telling me this, but he had no explanation. His only answer was "Do as I say." The longer we argued, the more adamant he became. Nothing I said seemed to make any difference. Not knowing where else to turn, I told him I had better discuss all this with my analyst. "Fine," he answered. "You can discuss it with anyone you want. But this is the way it's going to be."

There was never any question that I would not leave Suzanne. But I knew that Sidney had to hear this from a higher authority.

I immediately contacted my doctor and asked him to explain again to me how this trauma could do Suzanne irreparable harm. When I called Sidney to repeat the conversation, he replied, "To hell with you and your doctor," and slammed down the phone.

Our engagement ended as abruptly as it began. As I thought about what had just happened, I realized that Sidney knew I would never leave my child. He just needed an excuse to get out of his commitment.

Early the next morning Sidney's business manager appeared at my home.

"I don't know how to tell you this," he apologized, "but don't go over to the new apartment."

"Why not?"

"Because you won't be able to get in. Sidney called in the middle of the night and insisted I change the locks."

"Really? . . . Well, what am I supposed to do?"

"He says that if you give me a check for forty-seven thousand dollars, you can take over the lease. Those are his expenses to date."

I withdrew every dime I had in the bank and borrowed the rest. When I handed Sidney's business manager the money, he gave me the keys, and Suzanne and I moved in.

Taking over the apartment had left me financially strapped, and I had to go back to work immediately. It was probably the best thing that could have happened. Knowing how Sidney felt about being married to someone in the business, I had pretty much stopped working during the months of our engagement. I hadn't been sure that I would be able to lay aside as much of my career as Sidney expected, but I knew that if the marriage were to have any chance of succeeding I had better start thinking about myself more as a wife and helpmate than as a performer. If the decision left part of me feeling at loose ends, I chose to ignore it.

Suzanne and I were together and happy!

Now I was a full-time working woman again, and I went back to doing what I knew best. I found a new manager, Martin Bregman, and his enthusiasm rekindled the vital interest I had lost. I started working every day — rehearsing new arrangements, hiring writers to help me overcome my inability to talk on stage, exploring new songs like "Going Out of My Head" that were a complete departure from the Cole Porter and Harold Arlen standards I had usually performed. When I went on the road, my manager traveled with me. In between shows we had long sessions together criticizing my performance and analyzing how to improve it. I was back in familiar territory, and I began to come alive again.

But neither Sidney nor I was quite ready to let go. One day, some months later, he telephoned me in California as I was finishing a long nightclub engagement at the Cloisters. He said he had chartered a boat down in the Bahamas and would be sailing around the islands for several days. Would I care to join him? It would be just the two of us and the crew. We would relax. We would talk. Maybe we could finally make some sense out of all the confusion and pain of the past nine years. That sounded like a very good idea (don't ask me why), and I arranged to meet him in Nassau.

It was glorious being out in the middle of the ocean, away from all the normal pressures and cares. I had been working two shows a night, seven nights a week, and some time in the sun was just what I needed. Lolling around the deck in my bikini, I assumed Sidney and I would get around to the promised conversation as soon as we both had a chance to unwind a little. But that's not quite how it worked out.

As we pulled into the dock at our first stop, Sidney casually mentioned that we would be picking up some of our guests. A high-ranking politician from the West Indies and his bodyguard were waiting for us. Then we sailed on to the next island and picked up the politician's friend. Suddenly the small boat was crowded with people, and the only conversation was social chit-chat.

Sidney had done it again. Instead of dealing honestly and aboveboard, he had promised whatever had to be promised to get what he wanted, then promptly forgot all about it once that was accomplished. But this time it didn't take the same toll. I suppose all those many months of therapy had been quietly doing their work. "Okay, so he wanted to make sure you came on this trip," I found myself thinking. "Why don't you just accept it as that and relax? As long as you're here, enjoy yourself."

Following my own advice, I shifted gears and adjusted. The politician was charming. His bodyguard was very bright, and we spent a lovely afternoon discussing some of the books we had both read. "I don't think Sidney likes me talking to you," he told me as the black panther skulked past us with a scowl on his face. "Well, we'll just have to let him work that out for himself," I answered. I wasn't angry with Sidney, but neither did I care very much whether I pleased him or not. I had taken another step forward and was no longer quite the same woman I had been.

Sidney was not at all happy about this new show of independence but managed to maintain his composure until we came ashore for the night a few days later. After we all dined together in the romantic courtyard dining room of the beautiful little hotel, I explained to our guests that I wanted to sleep late the next morning and wouldn't be joining them for breakfast. "I understand," the politician answered. "I know you've been working very hard, and of course you're tired. Please take care of yourself. We're very proud of you." I said good night and went off to my room. Sidney followed me upstairs. He was furious.

"How dare you tell him you won't be down to breakfast?" he raged. "How can you be so rude? Don't you realize who he is?"

"But, Sidney, why is that rude?" I asked. "This isn't an official visit. He's on vacation, too. I'm exhausted. I need a bit of time to myself. I have some things to take care of in the morning."

"What things?"

"I have to find a telephone and call my daughter. I have to speak to my manager. I have to send off some telegrams."

Sidney slammed the door behind him. I was just falling asleep when he returned. I suppose sex had become the final battleground in the war between us. But those nights were over.

"No, Sidney," I told him. "I prefer to sleep with a man who likes me, who is nice to me and makes me feel good about myself. I don't want to feel like a naughty child who is being punished."

I moved over to the other bed and closed my eyes. I was at peace. I had finally discovered that I was becoming an adult. I was not allowing myself to be subjected to something I didn't want. When I woke up the next morning, he was gone.

I spent a leisurely few hours making my calls and sending off my wires, then hired a cab to take me back to the dock. After lunch on the boat, we had planned to return to Nassau, and our little holiday excursion would come to an end.

Halfway to the pier we passed another cab racing full speed in the opposite direction. "That's Sidney Poitier!" the driver exclaimed. Like everyone else on the island, he was tremendously excited by Sidney's presence. Not only was Sidney a famous movie star, he was also a fellow West Indian. I asked the driver to stop. The other cab screeched to a halt. Sidney jumped out and came running toward me. Flinging open the door like a Nazi storm trooper about to place me under arrest, he ordered me to come with him. I knew he expected me to be devastated by his displeasure, but I wasn't at all intimidated. Quite matter-of-factly, I paid my fare and climbed in next to him. There was no need to make a scene.

We arrived at the dock and stepped into the little dinghy that would take us back to the yacht. Sidney had a great deal of trouble starting the outboard motor. The young men on the pier, who absolutely adored him, wanted to help, and when he waved them away they began teasing him a bit. "Ah, come on, Sidney," they laughed. "Why don't you let us help? You're an *actor*, Sidney. You know you don't know anything about boats." It was all quite loose and good natured and filled with affection, and I laughed along with them. But Sidney was much too angry to see the humor in the situation. As we pulled away from the dock, he glared over at me and stabbed out the words with his finger: "Don't you ever — ever, *ever,* as long as you live — laugh at me again."

It had been coming for days, and now it finally snapped into focus. Sitting there in the dinghy watching Sidney nurse his imagined humiliation, the veil dropped from my eyes and I saw him for the first time. I saw the incompleteness. I saw the insecurity and fear. I saw the lack of humility and the need to be regarded as some sort of god. I suppose the evidence had always been there, but I had never been able to look at it. Even in our darkest moments, Sidney *was* almost like a god to me — all-powerful and all-knowing and all-wise. Both in his life and his work he was able to touch people and make them care about him in a way I never thought I could. I suppose that was how I needed him to be. Everything I wanted in myself and couldn't find I had projected onto him, never really allowing him any room for falsity or weakness. Now that I was able to see his imperfection, I understood that I was actually growing up. But I also knew that the dream was over.

There was some sadness in the recognition, yet there was also a fantastic feeling of relief. For the first time in nine years I was breathing clean air. I felt eleven feet tall. I finally had a handle on the two of us. I could finally look at the relationship and understand it, rather than be manipulated and pushed around by it while I waited for the next turn of events to catapult me into something else that I didn't understand.

When we left the boat in Nassau, Sidney and I shook hands and said goodbye. We never had the promised conversation, but we really didn't need to. Both of us knew it was over — really over. Walking away from the pier with my suitcase in my hand, I felt as if I were in the closing shot of a movie. I could almost visualize "The End" coming up on the screen as the music swelled and we faded to black. The image was so absurdly theatrical I had to smile. I wasn't playing a role here, I reminded myself. This was all quite real. One part of my life really was coming to an end, and another part — who knew what? — was about to begin.

A few minutes after I arrived home, the telephone rang. "Well, did the two of you come back married?" a mutual friend asked. "No," I told her, "I think we did something better than that. We finished it. Nine years," I said with quiet amazement. "It's hard to believe. Nine years, and we have finally put it to rest."

Chapter Six

Another chapter in my life began the day Dave Tebbett, an NBC executive, called me from Los Angeles.

"Let me ask you something, Diahann," he said mysteriously, "and I don't want you to give it a great deal of thought. I just want to know whether you might consider moving to California."

My immediate reaction was to say, unequivocally, "No." Although I hadn't made any movies in Hollywood after *Carmen Jones* and *Porgy and Bess*, I did fly to Los Angeles every now and then to perform on TV (and I do mean *fly* — because Hollywood made me so uncomfortable, I would ask the director to film my segment first so I could take the midnight flight back to New York). I did *The Danny Kaye Show, The Carol Burnett Show, Hollywood Palace,* and specials with Dean Martin and Frank Sinatra. I loved these appearances because I loved to work. And some of the shows hold special memories for me. I still remember my first *Dean Martin Show.* I flew to the Coast with Suzanne and my mother. Suzie was now nearly five, and to make sure she was busy while I was rehearsing, I had given her a large pad of paper and a pencil. As I was singing, accompanied by a huge orchestra, Suzie went wandering around looking for a table so she could put her paper down and draw. Her search was fruitless until she discovered Frank Sinatra sitting on a chair with his legs crossed. She then quite forthrightly asked Frank to uncross his legs, which he did, and then proceeded to put her pad on his lap, and began to draw. I looked at Frank while I was singing, and motioned him to remove Suzie. He refused, and sat still for nearly fifteen minutes while she finished her drawings, then presented them to Sinatra for his approval. I couldn't believe how much fun this legend was having with my curly-haired, slightly pushy little doll. I had often witnessed such vulnerability and kindness from this man. Once, at the Copa in New York after a very crowded opening-night performance by Sammy Davis, Jr., I was caught in the crush of the departing crowd. Sinatra spotted me, stood up at his table, and demanded at the top of his lungs that I be given protection. Immediately three huge men lifted me off the floor and never left my side until I was safely delivered to my limo. Through the years, Frank has shown concern and affection — when he cares, he never hesitates to let that be known.

Warm personal memories abounded, but I was still uncomfortable working in Hollywood. By now it was 1966, and I was enjoying a very nice career singing the music of all my favorite composers — Cole Porter, Harold Arlen, and Duke Ellington. Twice a year I played the Persian Room at the Plaza Hotel, then I'd fly off to the Fairmont in San Francisco, the Sheraton in Washington, or the Sands in Las Vegas. I worked hard at jobs I could handle and had a marvelous time being a mother to Suzanne. It wasn't easy combining the two — often I had to devote so much time to my work that my private hours became even more precious and important. Since I could never give up my work — this "sickness" I have which makes me want to perform as much and as often as possible — I had to be flexible in my choices. Once, when I was appearing at the Persian Room the week of a big blizzard, I didn't want to be separated from Suzie, so I moved her and her nurse into the Plaza and she learned to play baseball in the elegant halls (I used to call her the "Black Eloise"). My work and my life were complicated, difficult, rewarding, and very clear. Why would I want to change all that by moving to Los Angeles?

So I finally answered, "I don't think so, Dave. Like the song says, 'Hate California, it's cold and damp. That's why the lady . . .' "

"Well, would there be any circumstances that might change your mind?"

"For how long, Dave?" I asked him, weakening ever so slightly.

"I'm not sure. Suppose it was for three, four, five years?"

"Dave, are you serious? What *are* you talking about?"

"I don't really know yet. I just want to find out if you'd consider it."

"Well, it would have to be something I'd love," I answered, still not knowing what he had in mind.

"Okay, well, let's see what happens. I'll talk to you soon."

As time went by, and he didn't call, I forgot the conversation had even taken place. Every now and then I heard a rumor that NBC was toying with the idea of a TV series starring a black actress, but it didn't really matter to me. I was doing what I loved. I was perfectly content.

Then, about a year later, I was in Los Angeles once again to tape a show with Danny Kaye, a very complex, yet sometimes charming man. As I was getting ready to pack, my agent called.

"There is a man named Hal Kanter," he told me, "a very successful television writer-producer, who is putting together a project for NBC and Twentieth Century–Fox. It's a TV series, a sitcom about a black woman, and I'd like you to meet with him for five minutes."

I heard a certain reticence in his voice that piqued my curiosity.

"Oh," I answered. "Tell me more."

"Well, the truth of the matter is, Hal Kanter doesn't really want to see you. But he's talking to every black actress he can find. I think I can set up a quick meeting with you."

That's all I had to hear. Tell me I'm not right for a part, tell me you *don't* want me, and I'm yours. I'll do pratfalls, I'll do handstands, I'll do anything — but please tell me you love me. Suddenly I was very interested in Mr. Kanter and his project. It wasn't so much that I wanted the part; I wanted to be wanted for it.

"Why isn't he anxious for me to have the role?" I asked.

"He thinks you're too sophisticated, Diahann. You represent glamour and elegant nightclubs and couture clothes, and that's not the image he wants to project. He's going for a different audience."

"But I am an actress," I answered. "I hope my range is a little broader than that. Can you send me the script? I'll read it immediately."

The script was about a young, very middle-class Vietnam war widow named Julia who goes to work as a nurse in the aerospace industry. The one really special aspect of the plot was that Julia and her five-year-old son were black.

Everyone and everything in the script were warm and genteel and "nice" — even the racial jokes I knew would be there. For example, when Julia telephones her boss-to-be, the crotchety-but-lovable Dr. Chegley, she tells him, just to make certain he understands, "I'm colored." "What color are you?" he asks. "I'm a Negro," she says, setting up the punch line that follows: "Have you always been a Negro, or are you just trying to be fashionable?"

"Well, I suppose this is a kind of progress," I thought. "First television pretended there wasn't any prejudice. Then it pretended there weren't any racial differences. Now it has reached the point where it can not only acknowledge there *are* differences, but a white man can write jokes for a black woman to say about them."

The use of the word "colored" in 1968 seemed a bit stretchy and out of step, but I understood that the joke was trying to make a very mild racial statement. The attitude toward every other meaningful issue the script touched on — a woman alone, a woman on a job, a woman who's a widow raising a child — was equally mild. Julia was a terribly mild statement about everything — period.

What captured my attention was Julia herself. From the very first scene I understood her completely. She was a situation comedy version of many ladies I had known my entire life, most certainly part of the product Mrs. Mabel Johnson had brought up to be Carol Diann Johnson a.k.a. Diahann Carroll. Behind the stylized cuteness of the dialogue, Julia's conversations with her son reflected many of the same middle-class attitudes toward parenting I experienced in my own childhood. I could relate to that very easily, just as I could relate to Julia's desire to make a place for herself in the world. She wanted a good job. She wanted a nice apartment. She wanted to give her child a decent education.

By the time I finished the script, I had gone beyond understanding Julia's character — I saw her actual physical presence. I knew exactly how she should look.

I asked my agent to set up a meeting with Hal Kanter the next day, changed my plane reservation to later that night, and began forming myself into this lady. My hair stylist brought his scissors and hair dryer to my suite at the Beverly Hills Hotel; a bob blunt haircut was our final decision. I hunted though my closet and found exactly the right dress: black wool with a short skirt, simple and understated. (The script had made a point about Julia's great legs. If mine aren't spectacular, they ain't half bad, and I figured that was bound to help.) And I wore subtle makeup and no jewelry.

By the time I entered the Polo Lounge, I was positive I was just what Hal Kanter wanted to bring into the homes of America.

I spotted him sitting with my agent the second I stepped through the doorway. To make sure he had a good look at me before we got down to business, I pretended I didn't see him and stopped to ask the maître d' for his table. When Hal swiveled around in his chair to watch me walk across the room, I knew I had his attention and headed for his table like a nice middle-class housewife meeting her husband for dinner. From the smile on his face, he seemed to like what he saw. I hoped what he saw was Julia.

There is a special Polo Lounge noise in the late afternoon — a low, steady hum of agents and movie stars and producers talking business deals. To be a part of it, not just an onlooker having a drink before taking a limo back to the airport, was, I have to admit, exciting. I felt light-headed sitting there discussing the possibility of starring in a television show of my own. All those years of lessons about how to walk, how to talk, how to sing, how to act, how to conduct myself in meetings led up to this present moment. And I was ready.

Hal Kanter, a tall, pleasant-faced man with a black mustache, seemed a bit cold and aloof at first as he explained why he hadn't wanted to see me. (I later learned that, like me, Hal is a bit shy!)

"This is a very simple middle-class woman. I want her attractive but not glamorous. The television audience has to be able to relate to her."

I assured him I understood. Over the years, the long fingernails and coiffed hair and designer clothes had become something of a personal trademark. But clearly such attire and attitude were not appropriate for Julia.

Once we realized we had no disagreement, we both relaxed, and Hal began telling me about how he got the inspiration for the show. He had heard Roy Wilkins, then head of the NAACP, speak at a luncheon and was so moved that he wanted to do something to forward the cause of mutual understanding and goodwill. *Julia* was to be his contribution, using the most powerful communications medium of our time to help counteract the hateful effects of racial bigotry.

"You must remember some indignities that happened to you in the past?" he asked.

I had heard that one before. It is often assumed that once a black person achieves a little success, all the problems that come with the color of your skin automatically disappear.

"What do you mean, in the past?" I answered. "The day before I left New York I waited on Fifth Avenue for an hour before a cab would stop for me."

"Oh, well, that's just New York for you. It happens to me all the time," he smiled.

"Really, Hal? Do they slow down for you, stick their heads out of the window and shout, 'I ain't goin' uptown, baby!'?"

We both laughed — out of discomfort — but the point was made.

Hal went on to say he thought a series starring a black woman was timely and could attract a large audience. A number of black actors were already appearing regularly on popular TV series. There was Bill Cosby on *I Spy* (I adored that show), Greg Morris on *Mission Impossible,* and supporting performers on *Ironside* and *Star Trek.* We were ready for the next step forward, for a show that had a black actor as the lead, not just the sidekick to the star or part of the supporting cast.

Despite a few bumpy spots, the meeting went well. As it came to an end, I noticed Hal was no longer talking quite so much, but I knew his silences did not mean a rejection. Believe me, I recognize rejection when I see it! He smiled as he stood up to shake hands and said, "Well, Julia, it's nice to have met you."

"My pleasure," I answered, thrilled that the part was mine.

Can you imagine how I felt riding back to the airport in the limo? Me, star of my own television show? Not to be believed!

༚

Two months later I returned to L.A. to shoot the pilot Hal needed to sell the show to the network. Because he had insisted that Julia should not be too glamorous, I was a little surprised by her opulent wardrobe and very attractive apartment. They were certainly beyond what could be afforded on a nurse's salary. But I reminded myself that even with the racial angle, *Julia* was still a fantasy like every other situation comedy on the air.

The gifted Lloyd Nolan played Dr. Chegley. After seeing two hundred children for the part of my son, Hal decided on the first one he interviewed — a little five-year-old named Marc Copage, who was so irresistibly delicious he must have been made in the adorable child factory. We all worked hard and well together, and shortly after the pilot was finished NBC bought the series.

While packing for the move to California, I decided to take just enough clothes for a thirteen-week visit, which should indicate how skeptical I was about *Julia*'s future. I assumed it was just a fluke that NBC had bought the show in the first place, and though it would probably create a mild stir when it aired, once the thirteen-week commitment was over, the network was sure to cancel. If I had done my homework and spent more time monitoring other situation comedies instead of watching only old movies or the news and documentaries, I might have appreciated that *Julia* was a cut above the pap we were being fed on television — better written and a lot more charming.

I also believed that in the larger scheme of things *Julia* was not terribly consequential. The entire country was undergoing one of the most traumatic upheavals in its history. There was rioting in the ghettos. Students were marching against the war in Vietnam. Civil rights workers were being murdered. And then, in April of 1968, Dr. Martin Luther King, Jr. was shot to death in Memphis. Two months later Robert Kennedy was gunned down in Los Angeles.

In the face of this kind of national tragedy, could anyone really care about Julia and her humorous little racial and personal difficulties?

But life — and show business — go on.

Hal Kanter most definitely had his finger on the moment. By the time we aired in September 1968, more black actors were working on television than ever before. Along with half-a-dozen holdovers from the previous season, Gail Fisher had been added to *Mannix,* Clarence Williams III was on *Mod Squad,* Otis Young was playing a black cowboy on *The Outcasts.* There was even a black actor on *Peyton Place.* I'm sure this was partly a response to the pressure brought about by the murder of Dr. King and the Kerner Report's urgent recommendation that blacks be given greater visibility in the media. CBS issued a directive "to intensify immediately the portrayal and use and actual number of Negroes," and the other networks came out with similar statements. I'm sure it also had something to do with the fact that after a long dry spell Sidney Poitier finally emerged as the first black superstar. In 1967 he had three smash hits — *In the Heat of the Night, To Sir With Love,* and *Guess Who's Coming to Dinner?* — and now the race was on to find the next black moneymaker. There was even some talk in the press that it might be me.

❧

Julia turned out to be exactly what Hal envisioned. It was slightly controversial, but not enough to interfere with the ratings. The scripts were charming and in their way really quite involving. NBC had scheduled us against some tough competition. *The Red Skelton Hour* on CBS and *It Takes a Thief* on ABC were both established programs with loyal followings. But not only did we capture our time slot, when the first national Nielsen ratings came out in October we were ranked the number-one show on the air. We were a solid hit, the hottest new TV series in the country.

The success of *Julia* was remarkable. It was such a wonderful feeling to know that I was being accepted into millions of homes every Tuesday night. It was thrilling to read all the reviews praising the show. It was even more gratifying to read the letters from mothers who wanted me to know they liked the hardworking, disciplinary aspects of Julia's character. Some of them went on to say that for the very first time their children could go off to school bragging about this terrific new television show both white and black children were exposed to on a weekly basis. (There were other letters, of course — hate mail from bigots — but that was to be expected. I'd long ago learned to protect myself from that kind of insanity by having my mail screened.)

There were, however, some unexpected problems for me.

The time pressures had begun to put a strain on my relationship with Suzanne, the single most important person in my life.

Suzanne, who was then eight years old, was a bright, beautiful, talkative child with large, expressive eyes and curly black-brown hair that was in constant disarray. Oh, how I adored her! She was a warm, sensitive little girl, wise beyond her years. My assistant, Louise Adamo, often joined us for dinner, and I still remember my astonishment the night Suzie turned to her and said, "We're all part of a pie — a pie of life — and if you were not here we'd be missing a slice." I not only felt blessed to be the mother of this special child — I felt honored.

In the early days of *Julia* we lived in a little cottage, just off Benedict Canyon, that reminded me of the cottage in *Mrs. Miniver*. There was a small pool in the back, and it was wonderful watching Suzanne swim and thrash about in the water. Saturdays and Sundays we always played together. We loved to watch Frankenstein films. We'd pull the bed covers over our heads and take turns peeking out to make sure the scary part was over and it was safe to come out. But then, as the season progressed and the pressure mounted, I began seeing less of her.

I was required to be in the makeup room between 5:30 and 6:30 each morning, and by the time Suzanne awakened I had usually left for the studio. We still ate dinner together almost every evening, but now I would immediately disappear into the bedroom to prepare for the next day's shooting. Instead of playing with her on the weekends, I memorized the next week's script so I could concentrate on rehearsing and blocking when we started in again on Monday. I felt so guilty about my hours that when we moved to a new, much larger home, I spent a small fortune turning the parklike yard into an elaborate playground. And I tried (unfortunately, only when I had the time) to arrange for my mother or friends or other children to spend time with Suzie. But that wasn't the same thing as having a mother around. We both longed for more of each other.

Another major problem was my closeness with the little boy who played my son. Marc's real mother had disappeared when he was just an infant, and he needed maternal affection badly. As the weeks went by he began to attach himself to me almost as if I *were* his real mother. He always stayed close to me while we were working on the set, and during the breaks followed me into the dressing room so he wouldn't lose contact. When Marc misbehaved, the way any five-year-old will do, I was the one the assistant director came looking for to quiet him. When the cast and crew dispersed at the end of the day to return to their families, Marc was overwhelmed by the feeling of abandonment and often asked me to take him home. I was exhausted by then, but Marc was so damned cute, with his little fat cheeks and little lisp, and so hungry for mothering that I couldn't turn him down. "All right, Marc,"

I would answer. "You're the best offer I've had all day. Let's go."

It took a while for me to realize how badly this affected Suzanne, though it should have been obvious. "You're not his mommy," she would pout. "You're *my* mommy." When the kids at school questioned her about her brother, she screamed at them, "That's not my brother! I don't have a brother!" Soon it reached the point that when *Julia* was aired Tuesday night, she refused to watch. "I don't want to see that dumb show!" she would announce and storm off to her room.

Eventually I had to confront the reason for Suzanne's anger and begin to remove myself from Marc. "Suzie's my real daughter," I explained. "And you're my television son. That doesn't mean I don't love you very much. I do. But when the day is over, you must return to your home and I want to do the same." It was such a painful moment. Marc couldn't understand what was wrong and was terribly hurt.

I don't think Suzie really understood, and I can't blame her. Her mother was deeply involved in her career, and she must have felt somewhat abandoned, too.

❦

There is no way in the world you can prepare yourself for all the unnatural attention national television exposure brings in its wake. Such strange things happen.

One day the mailman delivered a package of shaving gear, magazines, and men's clothing that had been sent from a California penitentiary. The accompanying letter said they belonged to an inmate who died. He had informed the warden I was his only living relative and he wanted me to have his effects. I just stood there staring down at the tattered odds and ends that were all that was left of the man's life, overcome by a dreadful feeling of disconnection. I couldn't begin to figure out what he was thinking while he watched this lady, Julia — me — on television each week.

Then there was the series of phone calls from a young thirteen- or fourteen-year-old boy in Cleveland. His parents told him I was his long-lost sister. They had been forced to give me away because they were so poor. He said that if he was only allowed to speak to me, perhaps I would forgive them. This child wanted to come live with me. Half-a-dozen times he called crying and begging. "Please forgive them. They're sorry for what they did. They really are. We love you so much. We're so proud of you." I could always hear his father in the background telling him what to say. I tried to be patient, to explain I was certain of my family background and his parents were mistaken. But when he announced they were bringing him to Los Angeles for Christmas to meet me, I panicked and went to the studio security office. The next time he called, the guard picked up the extension phone and said, "Young man, I have recorded this conversation, and if you don't stop harassing Miss Carroll, I'll have to notify the Cleveland police department." It was heart-wrenching. One moment the boy was happily proclaiming, "We're coming to see you at Christmas!" The next moment he was screaming in terror, "Daddy, it's the police! Why are the police on the phone?"

❧

Not everyone loved Julia and wanted to be part of her family. Along with all the praise for the show there was also criticism attacking its distorted, unrealistic portrayal of the lives of black Americans. The criticism started before the actual air date. Looking back now, I can understand that we were probably asking for it, because there was a great deal of advance publicity hyping *Julia*'s significance as a racial breakthrough. It was the first situation comedy about a black family. I was the first black actor or actress to have the lead in a weekly dramatic series. In a humorous, gentle sort of way, it would be the first show to mirror the realities of racial discrimination in this country. "We're going to tell the truth," Hal promised the interviewer from *Daily Variety*. "We're going to show it like it is."

When I read Hal's words, I couldn't decide whether he really believed them or whether, as a good businessman, he knew they were trigger statements that were bound to cause controversy. I suppose they were a little of both. I thought controversy would be good for the show. I thought it would create interest and give us visibility. I certainly didn't think *Julia* offered the viewing public some deep truth. When a reporter from *Time* magazine asked me to comment on Hal's statement, I tried to make that clear. *"Julia* is a comedy," I told him, "a half-hour sitcom, and there isn't a half-hour sitcom on television that gives us any real information about anything or anyone!"

But when the publicity releases described the characters and situations and quoted some of the dialogue, it became fairly obvious that *Julia* was just too fragile to carry the weight of all that

[143]

promised significance. In April 1968 — months before we went into full production — Robert Lewis Shayon, the television writer for the *Saturday Review,* devoted his entire column to an attack on the show. Its plush, suburban setting was, he wrote, "a far, far cry from the bitter realities of Negro life in the urban ghetto, the pit of America's explosion potential." Even worse, there was "no adult Negro male as an effective role model" for the character of Corey, the young son.

Five weeks later Shayon wrote another attack on the show, then two months after that a third one. By now there was an entire chorus of critics complaining about *Julia*'s harmful inadequacies. I thought the criticism was wildly overstated, but it troubled me deeply, especially the accusation that the series failed to offer a proper role model to black children. When I met with Hal Kanter to discuss this charge, he pointed out the reason there was no man in the family had nothing to do with race — it had to do with the fact that single parents were then a proven television format. The coming September when we premiered, several other new shows with widowed mothers would also be introduced. There was one with Hope Lange, another with Doris Day, a third with Lucille Ball. The format worked, and there was no arguing with success.

Television, during those years, consistently skimmed the surface of something more profound, and women were finally beginning to discuss their rights, to express their dissatisfactions with their assigned roles as wives and homemakers, and to look around for some new possibilities of freedom in their lives. None of this was terribly well defined at that time. But the image of a youngish widowed mother on her own, exploring the workplace, experimenting with new male relationships, seemed to provide a powerful fantasy that touched a large part of the viewing audience.

But many critics thought that *Julia* was a cop-out. Blacks didn't really live like Julia, they said. Why wasn't there a black father figure? (I don't remember any criticism of white single women on television for not having white father figures around.) Harry Belafonte seemed to agree with this criticism the night he came to see me.

Belafonte was a good friend. He had always been extremely supportive of my work and had molded my understanding of the business — or "money" — end by generously sharing his knowledge. When he called a month or so before I was due to leave for

California to complete the first thirteen episodes and said he wanted to meet me, I assumed he was going to advise me how to capitalize on the financial concerns that come with a weekly television series. I was surprised when he walked into my dressing room and launched a full-scale assault on *Julia,* then asked me not to do it.

I forced myself to focus in on his criticism and weigh each of his charges. Even though I understood, I really could not refuse to do the show. True, the format did not deal with the absence of the black male — that was a perfectly valid complaint. But I felt very strongly that any one piece of work should not be held responsible for answering all of society's problems. After all, *Julia* was not conceived as a documentary. It was a situation comedy, and calling upon my own experience as a child, I didn't find it such a poor representation. I thought its middle-class aspect was a positive. There *is* a black middle class, with middle-class values and aspirations, and I had never seen it shown on TV before. I thought the humor of the show was also a positive, as was the relationship between the mother and son. As Belafonte and I discussed this problem back and forth, I really could not convince myself that this was a harmful way for children to be exposed to black people on television.

Maybe I wasn't trying to be convinced. To be completely honest about it, I had also begun to understand that there are certain opportunities one does not take lightly. I wanted to test myself in a broader setting and find out what I might accomplish in the area of television. More people would see my work in one evening than if I worked in nightclubs the rest of my life. It's called running a career.

The argument continued over dinner. By the end of the evening, the two of us had reached an agreement: We would pool our resources and raise enough money to shoot our own pilot that embodied all the principles we felt necessary. We would hire the writers, finance the filming, then sell the show to a network ourselves. Within the next month he would get back to me. But the month came and went without another word; and when it was time for me to begin to film *Julia,* I left for California.

∽≫

I was thrilled when we went on the air and became a hit. Yet success only made the complaints louder. And as the star of the show, I was the one who was expected to deal with the criticism.

The fact that I had no decision-making power at all didn't seem to matter. I was still held responsible.

The studio hired two full-time assistants just to answer my mail. I had endless meetings in my dressing room with psychologists, journalists, and heads of organizations who were so concerned about the show's impact they felt compelled to discuss it with me personally. Some of them had flown to Hollywood solely for that purpose.

"Don't you realize you're letting the white community get away with murder by not insisting it address itself to the black male?" they asked me. "How do you reconcile Julia's lavish life-style with her nurse's salary? Do you know how many black nurses there actually are in America? . . . Is there any truth to the rumor that Julia's going to have a white boy friend? . . . Don't you feel guilty about doing this show?"

The white journalists asked about *Julia,* then quickly moved on, expecting me to give them my philosophy about the overall state of black people in this country. Some performers are equipped to be spokesmen. I was not. The fact that I made my living as an actress in front of millions of people certainly did not mean I was qualified to speak politically for anyone. But *Julia* was so popular that everything I said was practically front-page news, and I became carried away with myself. I fell into the trap.

It took a while, but eventually I realized that not every person who came to see me representing a newspaper or magazine was really as well informed as I wanted to believe. Many were racially ignorant and didn't have the vaguest understanding of what I was saying. And of course that came through in the way I was quoted. The misrepresentations were so upsetting that I insisted that all quotations dealing with race be read back to me for my approval.

But the damage had already been done. One reporter had encouraged me to dismiss the black nationalist groups as detrimental, and seemed positively shocked when I refused. "In spite of our many differences, one of their primary purposes is to give dignity, education, and economic opportunity to young blacks," I told him. "And *that* I support."

The fact was so obvious, but coming from Julia's mouth the words appeared to surprise many people. They seemed even more surprised when I decided to sponsor the only fund-raising dinner in Southern California for Shirley Chisholm, a black woman, and the first woman to seek the office of President of the United States. Who knows what they made of me when I agreed to extend an invitation to Huey Newton, founder of the Black Panther Party? I certainly did not agree with everything Huey Newton stood for, but I thought he was brilliant. However, as is so often the case, his brilliance walked hand in hand with a kind of madness. The heavy macho rhetoric about guns and fighting in the streets was bound to entice a lot of innocent people into suicidal confrontations that could not possibly be won. But the Panthers' community work was positive. I especially admired their sense of purpose and the camaraderie they shared, which did so much to relieve that terrible feeling of separateness that is a fact of life for so many young blacks.

There was no question in my mind that *Julia* had the responsibility to set a positive example in the way it presented the black family. And it didn't take long to realize that it was largely up to me to try to make that happen. For all Hal's good intentions, it became increasingly difficult for him to write meaningfully about black people. How could he? He had never really been exposed to blacks. It was inevitable that as the season progressed the writing would become more and more problematic.

I began scrutinizing the scripts for blatant examples of racism or just plain ignorance. When I found them, I usually went straight to Hal to discuss them. He always tried his best to hear me, but sometimes we ran into serious problems. We had an especially rough time with the script about Julia's first encounter with bigotry. The episode began with my son's coming home from school terribly upset because someone called him "nigger." After trying to ease his pain, I go downstairs to my white neighbor's apartment to tell her what happened. "When did bigotry come into your life, Julia?" she asks, and off we go with the story:

All the kids in high school were going to the prom. My mother made a beautiful yellow organdy dress for me with a big bow and ruffles at the bottom. But then when I arrived at the gym, no one asked me to dance — and I learned for the very first time that there was such a thing as racial prejudice.

The scene was written to be extremely moving. I was to be filmed in a tight closeup with tears streaming out of my eyes so all America could see this horrible hurt on my face as I related what happened. But the whole story was so naïve, so completely unreal, that I couldn't take it seriously.

At first I tried. Rather than complain to Hal, I learned my lines, then began rehearsing the scene with my assistant, Louise. Louise is an Italian-American. However, she immediately saw the absurdity of the situation. When we came to the big moment, she stopped reading the neighbor's dialogue, put down her script, and looked at me straight in the eye.

"That was the first time?" she asked. "The first time Julia experienced prejudice?"

"Yes, that's what the script says."

"Well, let me ask you something, Julia." She laughed. "Did you ever think maybe it was the yellow organdy dress?"

That did it. I was still laughing when I went off to shoot the scene the next morning. Then I had the nerve to repeat Louise's line to Betty Beaird, the actress who played my neighbor, and she began to laugh, too. By the time Hal appeared on the set, the cameraman and the gaffer and the rest of the crew were also in on it, and no one could keep a straight face.

"You're just so terribly sophisticated," Hal grumbled. "You've forgotten what a terrible shocker this kind of moment can be. You're not being honest about it."

"Okay, Hal," I answered. "*But where has Julia been?* Until this high school dance she never knew anything at all about racial prejudice? She never experienced it even once? Nobody *ever told her* — not her mother, her father, her sister, her uncle? *Nobody?* There was no television set or newspaper in Julia's young life?"

We tried desperately to pull ourselves together. But either I broke up or Betty broke up or someone on the crew started giggling. I don't blame Hal for becoming furious. He had written these beautiful words and, goddammit, we were going to do them and do them right. The fluid that's used to make your eyes tear was squirted into my face so often that my eyes turned the color of stoplights.

༄

The laughs were actually rather few and far between. The harsher the criticism became, the more obsessively I scrutinized each and every detail in the scripts and the more fiercely Hal and I argued. The whole routine was so depressing I could hardly think about anything else.

One day it all came to a head. The next week's script showed Julia's son running around the apartment playing cowboys and Indians with his friend, then telling him, "I'm John Wayne and you're an Indian, and bang-bang, I just shot you dead." By now I was so sensitized to anything that might have the slightest wrong racial connotation that the line sent me immediately to the telephone.

"Hal, Corey cannot say that!" I insisted, maybe more upset than was necessary.

"Why not?"

"Because John Wayne is not the idol of black children. Because black parents don't think of him as a role model."

"Diahann, John Wayne is the most famous cowboy in the history of motion pictures."

"That may be true. That may be absolutely true. But I have to take the responsibility for those words. No one ever reprimands you, Hal. No one ever keeps you up till four in the morning wanting to know how-could-you? I don't know why, but everyone behaves as though I write this show. So I'm taking a stronger position here. And I'm telling you, I can't be a part of this script."

There was a long silence before he answered, "Well, look, we can't use Roy Rogers's name. Roy Rogers retired years ago."

He doesn't get it, I thought to myself. He just doesn't understand. "You're the writer, Hal. I'm sorry I can't be more helpful. But Corey cannot say this."

"Diahann, you are doing a half-hour sitcom, remember?"

"I realize that, Hal. But I'm beginning to feel overwhelmed by the pressure. I don't know how much more of it I can take."

The morning we were scheduled to do the scene, the script still hadn't been changed. When I telephoned Hal to find out what was happening, he had left the lot. His secretary kept telling me, "He'll be back soon," but he didn't show and he didn't return my calls. The director did what he could to shoot around the cowboys-and-Indians, but by early afternoon we had taped the rest of that day's shooting schedule. I didn't know what to do. Finally, out of anger and frustration, I said, "All right, if that's how Hal is going to handle it, I'm going to leave the lot too."

And that's what I did. I went home.

The phone was ringing off the hook when I walked through the door.

"Mr. Kanter calling. Please hold on."

Hal was in a rage. "What do you think you're doing?" he demanded.

"I don't know, Hal. What are *you* doing? I left a dozen messages this morning that I needed you, but I didn't see you all day."

"Jesus Christ, you can't just take off like that!"

"Let me tell you something, Hal. *You* can't do it either. *We* can't do it. It's called out of order. You can't walk out on a problem."

To solve some of the problems, we discussed getting someone else to evaluate the racial content of the scripts. "It has to be done, but I just can't handle it anymore," I explained to him. "I cannot spend every weekend studying each word, writing an analysis of everything I think may possibly be insulting, then presenting it to you in the hope that we might come to an understanding. You can see it — I'm falling apart."

He agreed. I recommended a black psychologist who had been one of my earliest, most articulate critics. Dr. Maris had come to see me soon after we went on the air to inform me of our special responsibility to black children. He had shown the proper concern. He had the right credentials and the right attitudes. So Hal put him on the payroll.

I assumed Dr. Maris was doing his job and began to relax. Then one Saturday afternoon about a month later I picked up the next week's script and found it full of the most awful insults about black children. I immediately telephoned Hal to ask him for Dr. Maris's comments.

"Well, I haven't heard from him," he answered. "As a matter of fact, I haven't heard *anything* from him yet. . . . Yes, the scripts have been sent to him as regularly as clockwork. And yes, he's been collecting his check just as regularly."

When I called Dr. Maris at home, he finally admitted he had never read a single word of any of the material that had been sent him over the past month. He hadn't done a damn thing for his money. Nothing. And this great protector of black children wasn't even embarrassed about it. "What can I tell you?" he laughed. "You caught me."

Because I had recommended the man, I went to Hal and apologized. "It's my fault. I feel as though I've been had," I told him.

He was perfectly understanding. "I feel like I've been had, too," he said. But there we were, back to square one again.

By the end of that second season, my 5-foot, 6-inch frame carried only ninety-nine pounds. I had cystitis so many times I could hardly stand. I was seeing a shrink again. I had become a total wreck.

⌘

I don't suppose any of this pressure was apparent. To the outside world I was a huge success, a woman who had everything. I was the star of a hit TV series. I was on the international best-dressed list along with the likes of Jacqueline Onassis and the Begum Aga Khan. I was invited everywhere — premieres and parties and openings — and everywhere I went was news. The paparazzi photographed my every move. I was constantly in the newspapers and magazines — the glamorous Diahann Carroll caught in the act of living her marvelous life. I was smiled at, congratulated, pinched on the cheek and told I was wonderful, and all I had to do was go along with the program.

A lot of the "glamour" was strictly business, of course, a way for the studio and network to promote the show by giving me visibility, and they took care of all the details. Very often at the end of the day racks of clothes were rolled onto the soundstage, so I could select my getup for the next evening's premiere or the big party for the out-of-town affiliates. There was the same kind of pampering when I played Las Vegas during the hiatus from *Julia.* After I finished work for the evening, I went back to the biggest suite in the hotel where my every whim was catered to. Do you want your nails done? Do you want your teeth polished? Do you want a B_{12} shot? Do you want, do you want, do you want?

Fame and success are a very seductive high. They weren't entirely new to me. I'd had a modest taste of them when I starred on Broadway and performed at the Persian Room. But I had never before experienced fame on this grand a scale. And I found it very confusing. After a while my head was so full of cotton candy it became increasingly hard to separate the real from the make-believe. Without realizing what was happening, I floated off into the clouds and started playing a part, behaving as if I were living a movie in real life. It was so much easier than constantly fending off all the criticism.

I began to lead the life that was fed to me in the news media, giving myself over to the glamour and luxury.

When I felt like taking a peek at the latest designer collections, I reached for the telephone and they were rushed to my home so I could try them on in private.

I bought a hugely expensive house in Benedict Canyon from Lance Reventlow, Barbara Hutton's son. The place was truly breathtaking. The downstairs had two living rooms, a den, a sauna, a beautiful kitchen done in barn siding and old pegged wood floors, fireplaces in almost every room, a dining room with a gigantic round table, a bar, a floor-to-ceiling wine cellar. An elevator transported you up to the second floor, where there was a billiard room done in burgundy and loden green.

The grounds included a waterfall that cascaded down forty feet from the side of a mountain. The swimming pool looked like a black lagoon. The entire pool area was covered in slate, with underground heating to take away the chill. A projection booth with two theater-sized projectors stood next to the cabanas. Push a button, and the outdoor barbecue in the conversation pit automatically ignited. Beyond the pool area was a small park where Suzanne ran around the mulberry bushes and played on the trampoline.

The place cost a fortune to buy, a fortune to furnish and decorate, another fortune to run. One morning I counted nine workmen going about their business. I don't know what I was thinking. I must have assumed *Julia* and the high-paying Las Vegas engagements would last forever.

I was going a little crazy. I was so caught up in the fantasy that no one was able to get through to me. Not even my own parents. They were as bedazzled by my success as I was. Before *Julia* they would have had no difficulty telling me, "Diahann, perhaps you're not seeing things too clearly." Now, they weren't so sure. If I had been able to accomplish all this by the age of thirty-four, maybe I had discovered some sort of secret. Mom was so overpowered by my new celebrity status that she often introduced herself to people as Diahann Carroll's mother rather than Mrs. Johnson. My father is a very proud man and must have resented that terribly, but not being quite sure what to do about it he suffered the indignity in silence.

My girl friend Judith did try to talk to me. "You're moving too fast," she warned. "You're always getting sick. Why don't you take off on your next break? Go to the ocean, someplace where nobody knows you, and wander around in old shorts and a T-shirt for a few weeks. Relax. Try to clear your head." I knew it was good advice, so, perversely, I ignored it. I lost track of my other good friends for a while. Unless they were willing to pursue me one thousand percent, I was not really there for the feedback. There wasn't much give and take with me during those years. It was always I, I, I, me, me, me. The truly important things like friendship all seemed to be forgotten. I was busy with unimportant things — I was busy being glamorous. I was busy being seen. I was busy getting more. When Suzanne complained about her nurse, I refused to believe her because it was easier not to.

"Mom, she doesn't really like me," she tried to tell me while I was getting ready to go out one evening. "You think she took me bike riding this afternoon, but she didn't. She left me alone in the Thrifty for an hour, and I didn't know where she was."

Suzanne was not a complaining child, so I made a halfhearted effort to ask the nurse what happened. When she answered, "Oh, no, I was on the other side of the store the whole time," I accepted her explanation without any further questions. It wasn't until much later that I discovered Suzanne had been telling the truth. As it turned out, the nurse was a highly disturbed young woman. She had been stealing all along — major things like furs and cases of brandy. Yvette had done it before with other employers and was so well organized she had a fake psychiatrist ready to back her alibi that she was a helpless kleptomaniac. And I had left my daughter in her care. I still shudder when I think of it now.

I was just as irresponsible when my father left my mother after thirty-seven years of marriage. I was shocked to hear the news, but I was also preoccupied with my own life. My parents had been having problems for many years, but my mother is a very strong, private woman, and put up a good front whenever I called her in New York to find out how things were going. But when my father actually left, she was totally devastated.

"My God, Diahann," my aunt told me on the the telephone, "she just sits in the house all day with the tears streaming down her face. She won't eat. She won't change her clothes. She won't even turn on the lights at night. You're going to have to do something."

I flew Mom out to Las Vegas, where I was working at the Hilton, bought her some pretty clothes, and sent her to all the best shows to take her mind off her troubles. But at the end of my engagement, she broke down again. When we returned to L.A. she stayed with me for a few weeks, and that's when I finally realized she was seriously out of control. I set her up in her own little apartment. As far as I was concerned, I had done my duty and now she was fine. But she wasn't fine. She was still in terrible pain, still crying day and night, still unable to get back on her feet after this terrible trauma.

Selfishly, I didn't want to have to deal with their divorce. I wanted it over. Her problems only got in the way of my own little fairy-tale life. I became increasingly impatient with her unhappiness, so irritable that sometimes I called her on the carpet about all the things she had done wrong to cause my father to end the marriage. Too often I left her alone, and she was forced to turn to Monte, Louise, and my childhood friend Sylvia. It is sad for me to think that my friends were more helpful to my mother than I was during that awful time.

❧

Every fairy-tale princess needs a fairy-tale prince to complete the picture, so of course I had to find mine. First there was an actor named Don and then another strikingly handsome young actor named Alan.

When I began to date Alan I thought I had discovered the Holy Grail: a beautiful, successful black man. Someone whose aspirations were equal to my own. Who was not content with the mundane but wanted to accomplish something extraordinary.

That was precisely what he wanted me to think. Alan knew the dialogue I needed to hear, and that's what he gave me. It was not difficult to recognize I was involved with my child and my parents, so he regaled me with stories about his own family — that made me comfortable. He was serious about his work — that made me respect him. Most important, he expressed a lot of righteous discontent with the circumstances put upon minorities in Hollywood. Once he found out about my own dissatisfactions, he began telling me tales about all the things he was doing to improve the situation. He was developing scripts that would present black people honestly. He was trying to organize black actors into a unified body so we would have more power in the business.

I couldn't put my finger on it, but I sensed from the start there was something about him that didn't quite add up, that wasn't entirely trustworthy. But I was so desperate to fall in love that I pushed aside my apprehensions. For a woman who was raised in my generation, being without a man was like having a huge gaping hole in the middle of my body. I tried to keep it hidden, but I knew it was obvious to everyone, that I would never be complete until the hole was filled, until I found a man and fell in love. So that's what I did.

A woman that needy is perfect victim material, just waiting to be captured and used. I'm sure I carried my vulnerability like a banner, and Alan was very clever, very good at manipulating. Once the hook was in, he backed off a little. He canceled dates. He no longer seemed quite so interested. And I found it more than I could bear. I had to have his total attention, and I pursued him until I finally won it.

But he still knew how to keep the upper hand. Everyone else in my life may have been awed by my success, but not Alan, not for a second. From the picture he painted, he was on the verge of his own breakthrough. The money and celebrity I already had were waiting for him right around the corner. He was as thrilled as I was by the Hollywood glamour and luxury that had my head spinning, but was clever enough to appear unimpressed. He came along when I went to see Lance Reventlow's house for the first time and reacted as though it was nothing out of the ordinary. "Well, I think that's a pretty nice place," he said on the way back, as if we had just looked at a two-bedroom cottage. "You and Suzanne ought to be comfortable. There's plenty of closet space." Plenty of closet space? My God, the closets were the size of anyone else's living room. I was so out of my mind it didn't even occur to me this was coming from a man who lived in a tiny one-bedroom apartment. "Yes, I think you're right," I answered, echoing his nonchalance. "It is a pretty nice place."

When I beheld Alan and myself in the mirror, I thought we were the two most beautiful Barbie Dolls I had ever seen. We were obviously meant to be together. That's how deeply I examined the relationship. Being connected to a man was so much more important than the man himself that I never once stopped to ask, "What is the substance of this human being? What is this mind? What is this person?" I wanted him to be the fairy-tale prince I needed, so that's what I pretended he was — even after it became perfectly clear he was nothing of the sort.

I found out there were other women. I was supposed to find out — he gave them my telephone number, and they called looking for him. He dated salesgirls in the stores where I shopped, and of course they had to tell me all about it the next time I came by.

"Oh, I went out with Alan the other night," one cute little eighteen-year-old announced as she wrapped my packages.

"Really?"

"Yes, we went to the Candy Store, and then he drove me up Benedict Canyon past the house you're buying for him."

(Buying for *him?* I kept my astonishment to myself.)

"Oh?"

"Yes. It's so-o-o beautiful."

I overheard dialogue that revealed a completely different face from the one I thought I knew. At the end of a dinner party he was seeing a friend to the door when he suddenly became so angry his voice carried into the living room where I was saying good night to the friend's date.

"But you know I didn't pay for it! You know she paid for everything!"

"Well, yes," his friend answered, trying to calm him down. "We figured that. But I want to thank you for the evening just the same."

"No, don't thank me!" he snapped back, almost shouting. "That bitch does everything by herself! She doesn't need anybody!"

Stupidly, I let that pass too, as if it never happened.

I was the same way with the physical abuse. Never would I have then accepted the information that I was a battered woman. I thought that my therapy had helped me to like myself more. But I guess the lesson had not yet been learned. The abuse started as early as our third or fourth date. We were at a discothèque, and I had excused myself to go to the ladies room. As I was taking out my makeup case, he stormed in behind me in a terrible rage. "You were flirting with that guy!" he growled. "Don't tell me you weren't!" I didn't know what he was talking about, but there was no time for questions or explanations. Spinning me around, he shoved me hard against the tile wall. Then he shoved me a second time, and a third, and kept on doing it over and over again until his anger subsided.

The next day my dresser asked me, "What happened to your back? It's black and blue." I couldn't believe what I saw, but in my determination to make myself believe that all was okay, I dismissed it immediately. I felt I had made my selection, and if I examined Alan's behavior, I would also have to examine my own. I would have to admit, "This isn't working, so I'd better call it off." But the prospect of being alone again was too unbearable to face. That was the lesson I had not yet learned — one must learn to be alone; I could be alone; I did not need a man to make me whole.

A few weeks later it happened a second time. Once again we were in a discothèque when I spotted an old friend, Mary Wilson of the Supremes, sitting at another table and went over to say hello. When I returned five minutes later, Alan was seething. There were more accusations, more shoving and hurting.

"I cannot have this!" he pronounced. "I thought I made that clear!"

"What are you talking about?"

"You were flirting with that woman! I saw you with her!"

That was so preposterous I didn't know what to say, so I said nothing. I was terrified about what might happen once we were alone, but when he was ready to leave I meekly followed him to the car. I was unable to say, "I'm not about to go with you. You're insane. I'm taking a taxi." I didn't say, "You can't treat me like that. I won't allow it." I could not say anything that showed I had the least amount of self-respect. And it was clear to both of us that my silence gave him the license to do whatever he wanted.

In this kind of abusive relationship, the moment that the woman allows such abuse to take place, a pact has been made, a pact that can be broken only if her behavior changes. When she doesn't complain, he knows that she thinks of herself as "nothing" and that gives him the license to continue his behavior.

There is a kind of dialogue that goes on between couples who travel down that dark and twisted path, a pattern of behavior that becomes so predictable that after a while one could chart it on a graph. Something — almost anything — triggers the tension. It starts to build. The two of us would ride it like a wave. Finally it would crest:

He begins to berate me: "You did such-and-such to embarrass me. Don't you understand you're not supposed to do that? I'll have to teach you a lesson."

I do not become indignant — indignation would put an end to the danger, and the danger is part of the pattern — we both recognize the deal — what happens is by unspoken mutual consent.

I try to defend myself from his accusations. "I didn't do that! You know I didn't!" But the defense only lends credence to the charges and engages him in battle. When he finally hits me I don't just take it. I struggle to hit him back. But that's impossible — he's much too strong for me and my blows only stoke his rage, provoking him to a higher level of violence.

Anyone in her right mind would walk away. But an abused woman doesn't always have that strength.

After it's over, we break up. But we're not done with each other, not yet. He is remorseful: "Please forgive me. My God, I'll never do it again." Somehow he denies it ever happened: "Oh, come on. It was nothing like that at all. Sure, I got angry, but you've blown it completely out of proportion." Then he puts on his best behavior: "I called my mother last night. Talked to her for an hour. I really want you to meet her." He says anything he must to get me to relent. And I do. And then it starts all over again.

It was such an insecure, guilt-ridden time that I thought maybe I deserved to be treated badly, to be punished. I was guilty about my success, about creating a career for myself and having a good, comfortable life. I was guilty about being acclaimed for work I didn't completely respect. Most of all, I felt guilty about the unending criticism that *Julia* was a disgrace, a sell-out. Alan was the personification of all the voices that kept hammering away, examining and reexamining the show, giving me hell for being part of it. He knew what buttons to push, and he pushed them with expertise.

I thought that I loved him. I don't know if that was true. I know that I needed someone. He was necessary to complete the picture that I carried around in my mind. Remember, I grew up with the teachings that a woman marries and has babies and lives in a house on Long Island. The main purpose of her life is to support her husband in all his endeavors. Anything else she might do is strictly subservient to that holy obligation. That's the way I was raised, and I still believed it. I was too confused to understand that those values don't have much relevance to someone pursuing her own all-consuming career. I was too guilty to think honestly, too busy pretending it wasn't true or didn't matter, and too sick to realize what a disaster this had become. I wanted to believe we were something we weren't — happy and intelligent and working our lives out just fine. And as long as that need was there, I would always be his victim because I would put up with anything to hold on to the relationship. It lasted for two long years.

And then one day I couldn't deny the insanity any longer.

It was a Saturday morning, and Alan and I were getting ready to meet some friends at a country club to play tennis. By now he was spending more nights at my home than he was at his own. (I told my daughter we were engaged.) When the doorbell rang, he went to answer it. The man at the front door said he was the new gardener and asked to speak to Miss Carroll about some work. I talked to him for a minute, then went back to the bedroom. When I looked over at Alan, his face was contorted with rage. He was furious that the gardener had asked for me instead of him and that I had dealt with the man myself rather than let him do it.

Once again I had castrated him, taken away his manhood. And once again it was how-dare-you? and I'll-have-to-teach-you-a-lesson. The shouting brought Suzanne running into the room. It was the first time she actually saw him hit me, and she began crying hysterically. The shock of her tears finally brought me to my senses.

"Come on, Suzanne, we're leaving," I told her.

"Where do you think you're going?" he demanded. "We've got a tennis date."

"We're going shopping. I'll see you later."

I drove to my girl friend's place and arranged to have Suzanne stay with her for the night. Then I returned home. Alan was waiting for me, still seething from the imagined humiliation of the morning.

I told him, "Look, I want you to leave." He knocked me to the floor and then, with his shoes on, kicked me in the face.

The pain was excruciating. I wanted to pass out, but all I could hear was Alan screaming in fury, "You will belong to me, and only me!" I think he believed that once he destroyed my face, that would be it for me. When I think about it now, I can't believe it happened to me. It is totally inconceivable that I let someone treat me like that. I was on top of the world, and a man I thought I loved was literally trying to destroy me.

It was the worst beating he ever gave me. It was also the last.

The doctor wasn't positive he'd be able to save my eye. "But

I'll tell you one thing for sure," he said. "This is the last time I'll treat you without calling the police. This isn't just a case of slapping someone around. This is assault and battery. You have got to stop this madness and get help."

The thought of reading the story in the gossip columns snapped me back to reality. To make certain Alan stayed away, I hired private detectives to guard my house twenty-four hours a day.

The doctor had given me some shots to reduce the swelling quickly. But I was still much too battered to go in front of the camera. By the end of the week one side of my face was almost back to normal, and I reported to work on *Julia*. When I walked on the set, the director and cameraman were appalled. Putting their heads together, they decided the only way they could do my scenes was by shooting just my good side and changing all the closeups to long shots. The crew was just as angry and upset when they saw how I looked. They were a tough bunch of guys who weren't fazed by much, but I couldn't help noticing the tears in their eyes.

❧

I was alone again. There is no question that it was better than living that incredibly horrible nightmare. But my life was not happy. And to make matters worse, the pressures of *Julia* were mounting. In September 1969, my contract came up for renewal, and I didn't know what to do. I was torn between being happy with the success of the show and being tormented by the criticism.

My friend James Garner tried to warn me about other considerations.

"You should get whatever you ask for," he said, "because you're going to be stuck with that character for years. Believe me. I know — you can't get away from it. It will hamper you in the film industry; it will hamper you in television; it will hamper you in clubs. The dollars you're earning now will have to sustain you for a long time to come, because no one will know what to do with you. So don't think you're being paid just for the labor of the moment. You also have to be paid for that long, dry period while you regroup and regather."

I realized he was talking from his own experience, after *Maverick* went off the air, but the words didn't register. I was still too caught up in my own success to hear his advice.

But the warning signals couldn't have been clearer. When I opened at the Sands Hotel in Las Vegas during one of my hiatus periods (at the time, it was one of the most prestigious places to play), my friend and press agent, David Horowitz, came back to the dressing room, almost in tears, to prepare me for the shock.

"I don't want you to have any surprises," he said, "so I'd better tell you now. There are maybe a hundred people out there."

"That's impossible. You've got to be kidding," I answered in disbelief. I'd been working Las Vegas for years and never — ever — played to less than a full house, which was about seven hundred people. But that night I was almost snowblind from the sight of all those bare tablecloths.

When the show finally ended, Jack Entratter, who ran the Sands, called me for a meeting.

"We're going to have to do something, Diahann. You're going to have to let me put 'Diahann Carroll — TV's Julia' on the marquee."

"What are you talking about, Jack? Everybody knows me. I've worked here forever."

"Well, they know you as 'Julia' now, not 'the chanteuse in the beaded gowns,'" he answered. "Those who knew you then are gone — they're not interested in who they think you have become — that nice mother on television. So now we have to go after your new audience, and they recognize 'Julia' before they remember Diahann Carroll."

It was unbelievable to me. I'd been singing in clubs for fifteen years, almost always to packed houses. How soon they can forget. But he was perfectly right. The public association with *Julia* was so overpowering that I'd lost my original audience and had to try to find my way to a new one. I'd had a gambling audience, a money audience, an audience that wanted to see a certain kind of mystery and sophistication and glamour that mingled well with late nights and luxurious dining. Now that one could turn on the tube and see me every week as a middle-class mother moving through the same familiar family routine, the whole mystique was destroyed. The identification was entirely different now, and the Vegas gambling crowd didn't find it appealing.

It's always risky for a performer to become too diversified. It's especially risky for a black performer, because we have so few opportunities to present ourselves to the public. In the long run it's probably better to present the same persona at all times. Lena Horne, for example, has never tampered with her sensuality. For years Sidney Poitier was always that same refined, totally respectable gentleman. Cicely Tyson has moved in a straight line her entire career — just say her name, and you think of black ladies who are purpose-oriented. It's clear to the public; it's clear to the creators and producers who she is. But Jack-of-All-Trades, here — I confused everyone, including myself.

The nightclub business was also beginning to change. The headliners were now the record stars who sold millions — they attracted huge audiences and spent enormous amounts of money on production. I'd never had a record that was in the top ten, but to attempt to compete I started making my shows more elaborate. Joe Layton, who had become, if anything, even more brilliant, designed a gigantic Lucite staircase with huge crystal chandeliers, and when I made my entrance I swept down the stairs à la Loretta Young. I never believed I would have to resort to superficial, overproduced pizazz, which was totally foreign to me. I was a chanteuse, and a chanteuse stands there and delivers a song, creating the scenes and weaving the spells without anything but her skill. I considered my work an art form. I didn't really respect the act that required a small fortune to produce. It was not my style. But my style had apparently gone out of fashion.

The pressures really began to take their toll. A few nights later, for the first time in my life I lost contact with my audience. I was singing "The Man I Love" when, suddenly, there was a thick invisible wall between us, and I couldn't penetrate it, couldn't connect with the people out there no matter how hard I tried. Sometimes that will happen to a performer who has spent a great deal of time in front of the camera and has forgotten the art of seducing a live audience. Because of this, many performers don't ever want to return to the stage when they've been away from a live audience for a while. It's too demanding, too immediate, too on the line. Remember, once your name is announced, you can't stop the cameras and ask for another take. So that night, I continued going through the motions, but inside I panicked. We all panicked, everyone out front and everyone backstage. I could see it in their faces. They were all pulling for me to break through that barrier, but I just couldn't seem to do it. It was terrifying.

The entire engagement was a disaster. I was frightened to death that I would never again be able to make contact with my audience. (As a matter of fact, it took me years before I did.) Whenever I would return to the singing, I needed time to find my way to some kind of rapport. Then *Julia* began filming again; when I returned to the clubs, once more "it" was gone. Not until the series ended and I began working consistently did the problem finally disappear.

By the third year of *Julia* I was sleepwalking my way through the show. I was exhausted from the daily grind of the work. The unending criticism and the renewed hassles with Hal Kanter had also worn me to a frazzle. It seemed to me that the show's format had become very dated and needed some serious revamping before time passed us by. I thought we needed new writers — especially black writers — to inject fresh life into the scripts. I thought it might be a good idea to introduce a new character with a completely different point of view, who would make fun of Julia and her nice, warm, gentle middle-class values.

Hal wasn't at all happy with my suggestions. I can't say I blame him. After all, *Julia* was his creation. He had created the show, developed it, turned it into a huge success. I was being presumptuous — who was I to tell him what was wrong with his baby and what ought to be done to set things right? We were both stubborn, both highly emotional, so we locked horns many times.

However, Hal was intrigued by my one suggestion to introduce a new character. I was certain my childhood pal Diana Sands would be ideal for the part. She was so feisty and full of life — I felt she would be absolutely perfect as someone who questions Julia's values with humor. At first Hal didn't want to use her — his feeling was that she was a stage actress and would overproject in front of the camera. But I begged, pleaded, and then insisted until he finally relented. I wanted to work with Diana so badly because I knew she would knock me off my pins and stimulate me and let me know I was still alive. Once Hal met her he fell in love with her — everyone always did — and he wrote her into the script. Diana did thirteen shows and was sensational. Not only did she add an immeasurable amount of talent to the show; she also made my work better.

That helped, but when, in 1970, the time came to renew my contract again, I decided to ask for my release. I was exhausted. I had had, to put it simply, enough.

Financially, it was a very foolish decision. My business manager, Martin Bregman, tried to make me see that. "Don't you realize," he argued, "that if you hang on for another two seasons you'll have piled up enough episodes to go into syndication and your whole financial picture will change? You'll have enough money to be comfortable the rest of your life. Sure, the ratings have dropped, but if you and Hal could pull it out, could push yourselves back up there long enough to last out the five years, you'll have it made forever."

I knew Martin was making sense, but I was too stubborn and tired to listen to him. I think Hal had also had enough by now. He was not a martyr or masochist — he had been creating successful television shows long before he met me and must have felt ready to move on. We were both exhausted.

And so the show went off the air. I remember feeling so relieved, so free. I was emotionally drained — the hours and the conflicts had taken their toll. But I was also sad. I had had fun, I had done good work, and I hoped that I had made some inroads in television for other black actors. But enough was enough.

❧

What now?

After all this time, where should I go? Should I return to singing, try to recapture that audience I had lost? Should I return to films — what films? The last one I had made was *Paris Blues,* ten years earlier. I didn't know what to do next — and I didn't have a manager around to help me make that decision.

It is important to understand that this was my time. I was still riding high, and the philosophy is — grab hold of this moment, this success, before it begins to fade (as it's bound to do), and take full advantage of it. Especially if you're a woman, you must face up to the fact that the young, vibrant years will not last forever and not everyone will be quite so interested in you once the little wrinkles start to show. I understood all that — but I was alone. I had had various agents come in and out of my life, particularly Freddie Fields and David Begelman during my *Julia* years, but I didn't have a Chuck Wood anymore. Elvis Presley had his Colonel Parker; Diana Ross had her Berry Gordy. But, unfortunately, I was without a knowledgeable personal manager to advise me, to make me realize that I should capitalize on *Julia*'s success. Such help and advice and loyalty are very hard to find. Thinking of my future should have been my primary concern, but it wasn't. I must have assumed the career would take care of itself, the way it had in the past. I had always gone from one project to the next, constantly moving up without very much planning or effort, and that had spoiled me. I suppose it crossed my mind it wouldn't always be this way, but I didn't actually believe it — I didn't want to believe it.

When *Julia* went off the air, I was offered another series immediately, but it was practically the same role, doing the same kind of thing, so I thought I'd better not take it. I was also offered a few film roles — small, token parts meant to capitalize on my recent television exposure. I turned them down, too. Because of *Julia*'s success, I was certain the larger, more significant roles were bound to come my way eventually. But as the months went by, they never materialized.

I began trying to put together my own film and television projects. As a child, I loved the interplay between William Powell and Myrna Loy, and I wanted to create a show like that — a Mr. and Mrs. South. And the other series I always wanted to do was a fantasy show about a superwoman. (There is never a truly original idea — in fact, years later, both concepts would indeed end up on television, but for white actors.) I wanted to keep the image of a black woman who has to be dealt with, a woman who could fall in love and have a romance, a woman who could travel the world and not find it necessary to remain solely inside the black community.

I didn't want to appear in either show — but I loved the new experience of putting the deals together. It wasn't difficult to get an appointment with almost any producer in Hollywood. I had just come off a successful series. People returned my calls. We had meetings. Lots of meetings. And then I waited and waited, but nothing ever happened. It took me a while to stop kidding myself, but I finally faced up to the fact that I was just wasting my time. None of those projects was ever going to see the light of day.

That came as a bitter, bitter shock. It shouldn't have. I had known for years that any success a black actor finds in Hollywood is only momentary. But I had allowed myself to be sucked in by the fantasy. I fell head over heels in love with it and fooled myself into thinking that now, in 1971, I had made it and would go on from series to series and film to film like many other successful actors pursuing a career. I had forgotten the lesson I thought I had learned.

❦

And so, once again, I returned to basics. I returned to singing.

A long time before, when I was eighteen and singing at the Waldorf Astoria, Phil Moore was listening to me rehearse a rendition of "Over the Rainbow." I had just finished that last line, "Why, oh why, can't I?" The room was dark and quiet, except for the sound of waiters scurrying about, preparing for the night ahead. When I was done, Phil sat beside me. And I still remember his words.

"You can sing," he said.

I guess I was anxious, but mostly I remember being excited, and eager. Very eager. I just wanted to sing.

And Phil said, "You *can* sing, Diahann. And that's important. Because in good times and bad, people will always come to hear a singer. So you'll always be able to make, say, three hundred to seven hundred dollars a week. Making money at what you love to do — that's the dream, Diahann."

I think of these words today. And I thought of those words then. And so I sang.

Chapter Seven

I don't want to paint David Frost as the perfect man. But he really was one of the best things that ever happened to me.

David and I met for the first time in the spring of 1970. Sidney was two years behind me at that point. My TV series *Julia* had come into my life and we were moving into our third season. I was on hiatus at the moment and had taken a job singing at the Ambassador Hotel. David was doing his own very successful television talk show in New York and had come to Los Angeles to film some interviews with celebrities like Jack Benny and Carol Burnett. One night just before I went on stage, my manager, Roy Gerber, mentioned that David was in the audience. As a professional courtesy, I sent him a note inviting him to my dressing room after the performance. We hit it off immediately. Neither of us was ready to say goodbye when he finished his drink, and we ended up going out for dinner along with our dates.

The four of us went to Bumbles, a popular disco club, where we danced and talked and shot pool until three in the morning. Despite the large antique pool table sitting in my house in Benedict Canyon, I didn't know anything about playing and was the joke of the evening. It was all light and happy and up. David struck me as a warm, worldly, unusually intelligent man who wore his success with a kind of easy grace, and I was definitely attracted to him. The attraction was mutual, though we tried our best to be discreet. At the end of the evening he said that he would love to interview me on his show when I came to New York. The subtext of the invitation was perfectly clear to both of us.

I telephoned Roy at three A.M., waking him from a deep sleep, and told him I had decided on the spur of the moment to fly into New York for a few days when I finished the Ambassador engagement. Could he try to schedule an interview with David Frost? Roy sounded very surprised, since we had agreed that I ought to avoid talk shows for the time being (we both felt I had been overexposed — and that many of the interviews were rather superficial).

Now, Roy is no fool. He has known me since I was nineteen, and has been in and out of my life (it's been "in" for the last twenty-seven years, thank God!) ever since. Roy makes my life better, easier, fuller — he makes me believe that anything is possible. Anyway, that night, Roy saw trouble immediately. He had seen me on the prowl before. He knew things were not what they seemed. But, despite his suspicions of my motives, he made the arrangements.

As I sat in the dressing room of the Little Theater waiting to go on, I began to feel some of my old apprehensions about television interviews. That's the sort of thing one usually keeps to oneself, but when David swept through with his producer to say hello, I just blurted it out.

"I hope you won't find me too boring," I told him. "I don't know what I have to say that would really interest anyone."

David dismissed my concern with a wave of his hand. "That's up to us," he answered, breaking into a wonderful smile filled with reassurance. "You've created a life and you've led the life, and now you can just let us do the rest. There's nothing to worry about. And by the way, you look absolutely smashing."

The hour we spent on the air seemed to fly by in seconds. David put me at ease immediately and knew exactly what questions to ask to draw me out of my shell. Before I realized it was happening, I had dropped my usual meet-the-press façade and found myself telling him about my childhood in Harlem, my experiences as a black performer, and my relationships with my parents and daughter. We were so comfortable together and had so much fun talking that it felt more like a couple getting to know each other on their first date than a network television interview. We kept wanting to touch each other; the only thing that held us back was the realization that millions of people were watching. None of this was lost on the audience. The next day the papers were filled with comments about how personal the interview had seemed. Several columnists felt that the viewing public was having a sneak preview of a romance in the making.

The photographers waiting outside on the sidewalk took our picture as we left the theater together. I saw the photos later, and we looked like two little kids about to sneak a cookie out of the cookie jar.

The laughing and talking continued for the rest of the evening. As we walked along Park Avenue at five o'clock in the morning, we were still engrossed in conversation and enjoying ourselves immensely. The moment we stepped inside my suite at the Waldorf, we began attacking each other. I wanted to make love as much as he, but something compelled me to stop. David didn't understand that at all, and I can't say I blamed him. We were both adults; we were both single; the desire was mutual.

"My head's swimming," I apologized. "I'm not used to moving so fast. I think we need to take a little more time."

"Well, how much time?" he asked, looking amused as he reluctantly left.

We saw each other again two nights later. In the interim David flew to London for a business meeting, but he promised to return to New York the next day, and he did.

The months that followed reminded me of those stories in movie magazines I read as a girl — days and nights filled with champagne and flowers and limousines that whisked us to one airport and restaurant and nightspot after another. Both of us were extremely busy with our careers. I was finishing *Julia*, and it was a difficult adjustment for me. David understood perfectly, and spent a lot of time helping me, even though he was riding the crest of enormous success on both sides of the Atlantic — hosting talk shows in New York and London, overseeing the production of *London Weekend Television*, trying his hand at all sorts of other entertainment and business ventures. Yet somehow we managed to juggle our schedules so we could be with each other as often as possible.

"I have to fly into Los Angeles for a meeting Thursday morning," he would telephone from New York. "Isn't that marvelous? We can have the entire evening together. And set aside some time — I want to take you away for four or five days."

There were constant, unbelievable trips to Bermuda, yachting in the Grenadines, a glorious weekend in Hawaii, quick excursions to London and Greece. Best of all were the quiet afternoons in Manhattan buying posters and records in Greenwich Village and wandering around Central Park. It sounds trite, but it was so wonderful! Wherever we went and whatever we were doing, David always made me feel wanted and cared for and adored in a way I had never known, and I responded to his attention with an enormous hunger. We enjoyed every moment we had together.

It was such a change from being with Sidney. David was proud of me and never ceased telling me so. He loved the fact that I had a career. He reveled in my talent and achievements. He had no qualms at all about sharing his business with me and asking for my opinions. When I told him something helpful, he praised me. When I was off the mark, he gently explained why without making me feel ignorant or foolish.

David liked and respected women, and he enjoyed the differences between us.

"I'm calling you now, darling," he would tell me, "because we have to be there at eight, and I want you to look beautiful. It's already four o'clock, so why don't you start doing all those things you have to do to get yourself ready?"

I had a great tendency to overexamine everything and focus on the negative, and David was forever pulling me out of my momentary depressions.

"You Americans take yourselves so seriously," he would laugh. "Something didn't go right on the set? Oh, darling, how awful. Now what time will you be ready for dinner? Wear something lovely and forget the problems of the day. Did you receive the champagne? All right, then, have a nice, cold glass and I'm sure you'll feel better. I may be running a little late tonight. Would you like the car to pick you up, or would you rather wait?"

David was such a caring, considerate man, and everything about me was important to him. When the curtain rang down on *Julia*, he flew out to California to help me through the trauma of the closing. It was a terribly difficult time for me — one part of my life was ending, the next was yet to begin — and he put everything aside to be with me.

I'm forever grateful for the way he took charge the afternoon of the wrap party. The cast and crew and production staff were waiting for me on the set to exchange our last goodbyes, but I was still in my trailer with my lawyer and business manager, being pressured to make important decisions about money and contracts and career moves. I knew I belonged outside with the cast and crew and that's where I wanted to be, but they hammered away so relentlessly I was too dazed to pry myself away.

Seeing the strain on my face, David stepped in and very tactfully put an end to the meeting. "I think maybe she's had enough of this for the moment," he suggested. "She has to attend the closing party. Why don't we get the social part of the afternoon under way? She can deal with these other matters tomorrow." As we left the trailer he turned to me and said, "Let's forget about business for now. Just smile and laugh and try to enjoy yourself. You deserve it." It was so reassuring to be able to lean on his arm and know that someone was there to take care of me.

❧

For all the differences in our personalities and backgrounds, so many things about us were similar. When I met his relatives in England, it was as though I had known them for years. Like most of my family, they were uncomplicated people of simple tastes and down-to-earth attitudes. Our mothers were practically black and white versions of each other. When they visited us in New York and we sent them off to the theater together, they were wearing almost identical little mink jackets and tailored suits.

Both David and I were driven by the same need to step out into the larger world, to accomplish and contribute and become visible. I understood how far he had to travel from his beginnings as a minister's son in the provinces who went on to Cambridge as a scholarship student. He understood how far I had come. Our journeys down the road had been similar: I had wined and dined on mulligan stew and gone on to caviar with great ease, and so had he. The difference in color wasn't very important to either of us. Every now and then we would run into someone with a racial problem, but both of us understood from past experience that the problem was his, not ours, and was not to be taken to heart.

That's what happened when we went island hopping in the Caribbean and stopped off for the day at Moustique. The only hotel on the island was still under construction, but the manager insisted we stay for dinner along with his other guests, an English airline executive and his family. We all dined together out on the patio at a long table lit by candlelight, and everything was green and lush and terribly romantic. The manager was extremely solicitous, and tried very hard to make us all happy.

The airline executive had consumed rather too much wine, and during the main course he turned to me and exclaimed, "What an extraordinary feast! Isn't our host a wonder? He's worked all day like a black!"

The man's wife and daughters shrank down in their seats. Not quite believing his ears, David looked across the table and asked, "*What?*"

"You heard him," I answered. "He said the manager worked like a black."

"Oh, I wasn't sure I heard right."

"Well, he'll say it again for you in a moment. Just wait."

Sure enough, he did. "Like a black he's worked. Just like a black."

By this point David and I had to bury our faces in our napkins to keep from laughing. There was no need to confront the man on his racism. What would it accomplish? He was obviously drunk. His prejudices were so old and boring. It had been such a beautiful evening, why spoil it? I poured him another glass of wine, hoping he would fall asleep, and David and I began playing footsie under the table. The line became one of our favorite running jokes.

Nor were we overly concerned about how the relationship might affect our careers. It seemed to me that the days of the weekly television show *The Bell Telephone Hour* calling my agent to announce, "We're not going to use Diahann Carroll because she's married to a white man" were very much in the past. We were a bit uneasy at first about a possible drop in David's ratings, but they remained high. Westinghouse, the broadcasting company responsible for the syndication of his show, was extremely enthusiastic about the relationship and wanted us to know that it had not affected David's relationship with them in any way. David's mail was overwhelmingly positive — if there ever were any hate letters, we never saw them.

There was hardly a newspaper or magazine in the country that didn't want to write about us. Within weeks after we met, some of them were already speculating about whether or not we would marry. I wasn't at all prepared for this kind of intrusion into my personal life. Sometimes, the questions and requests surprised me. For example, very early in our relationship *This Is Your Life* was planning a show about David, and the production staff became quite insistent that I take part in it. I thought the idea was in very bad taste and would make us look ridiculous.

"We're just beginning to know each other," I explained to David. "I'm not an old friend or a member of your family. I'd be so out of place." Even though David loved showing me off, he finally agreed.

He was a good bit more adamant when he was invited to the White House to entertain President and Mrs. Nixon and wanted me to accompany him. "I may not be the most political person in the world," I explained, "but I feel this would be a very grave mistake. It could be misread as a political endorsement." My refusal mystified him.

"Darling," he answered, "it will be such a wonderful evening. What's the difference between going to the White House to meet the President and going to Buckingham Palace to meet the Queen?" It was our first serious political argument, and it didn't get resolved until his close friend Clay Felker, at the time the editor and publisher of *New York* magazine, convinced him that my concerns were warranted. (Thank you, Clay — you knew it was out of the question for me to have gone!)

ॐ

We continued seeing each other all through the summer and into the fall. Neither of us questioned where the relationship was heading, but clearly it was headed somewhere. As we neared the end of 1970, David asked me to come to England to spend Christmas with his family. When I told him I couldn't leave my mother and daughter for the holidays, he thought for a moment, then in typical David fashion found a way to turn the negative into a positive.

"All right, here's how we'll handle it. I'll have to be in London for a few days to tend to some business, but I'll return as quickly as possible. We'll have Christmas with Suzanne and your mother in California, and then we'll all fly to England for a second Christmas. That way your family can meet my family, and everyone will get to know each other."

David was always terribly busy in London. When we stopped over for a few days before running off to the country, his schedule was so hectic I spent an afternoon in Harrods with his secretary helping her buy Christmas presents for the last twenty people on his enormous gift list. But once we drove away from the busy city to his little cottage in Kent and began visiting with his mother and sisters and the other relatives who lived in the nearby villages, he was able to put his work aside and relax. Undistracted by the demands of his career, David was at his very best, warm and loving and full of fun. The night he took us to dinner at a wonderful old inn, the Fox and Hound, was sheer perfection. David played darts and shot pool with Suzanne in the game room and made sure my mother tried out the various local specialties on the menu.

"This is really English, and you've never tasted it before," he teased. "Don't tell me what they make in North Carolina. This is different." Mom was in heaven from all the attention he lavished on her, and so was I.

Shortly after we returned to New York, David moved out of his hotel and took a large suite at the Plaza. I still maintained my own home on the Upper West Side, but whenever we were both in town we essentially lived together. (David immediately set aside one bedroom in his suite for Suzanne.) I worked with the Plaza staff to plan the redecorating. I selected a soft pale green silk moire for the walls, then ordered lovely Irish linen sheets with his initials from Saks Fifth Avenue. Next on the list were Baccarat goblets and beautiful Waterford china for the dining table, even though the tiny kitchen was seldom stocked with anything more than tuna fish, caviar, Dom Perignon, and a few bottles of club soda.

When David saw my handiwork, he was delighted. He was forever buying paintings, records, and books, but decor and furnishings and the other accoutrements of success were an enigma to him. His house in London was furnished with only the barest essentials, and despite his passion for music his sound equipment was antiquated. As always, David showered me with praise whenever someone stopped by to visit.

"Isn't she marvelous?" he would say. "She's attended to every small detail. Isn't this place beautiful?"

David loved creating extravagant evenings filled with good food, good conversation, and fascinating people. It was part of his madness, part of his craving attention, part of his zest for life. When he called from New York to say he was throwing a dinner party in honor of Rose Kennedy, he indicated that he was very pressed for time and would appreciate my assistance, so I hopped on a plane from Los Angeles (where I was filming a television special) to help him with the arrangements. Together, we selected more appropriate china, silver, linen, and flowers (his menu and wine list were already quite perfect). The evening was especially a lot of fun for me because I sat next to Henry Kissinger, who was charming, and to my surprise and delight very, very funny. And the next morning I flew back to California.

I always felt extremely comfortable talking to David about my career problems. "Tell me, David," I would ask him, "where does one go after a television series? What's my next step? I think I may have mishandled this whole thing rather badly." I had such confidence in his understanding that I was even able to discuss some painful things in my personal life without feeling embarrassed and ashamed. That's what happened the night we went to see *Klute,* the film about a call girl pursued by a homicidal sadist. One of the scenes involved a brutal beating, and I was terribly upset because of my own experience with that kind of illness. Instead of hiding my feelings, I told David exactly what had happened to me when we returned to the hotel. He couldn't have been more supportive. "There are certain things we must put behind us, my darling," he answered, taking me in his arms as I began crying uncontrollably. "That time of your life is over now, and you have to move on."

David was always there for me, always finding ways to share his boundless enthusiasm and energy. "You must join me for dinner tonight," he'd announce on the telephone after I dragged myself home from a grueling day on the set. "I know you're exhausted, but I'm dining with Bob Evans and I want him to meet you — you should be a movie star. Besides, I promise we'll make it an early evening."

David's own career was so successful by now, and yet he was forever encouraging *me* to stretch out and try new things. Once, when he had to leave New York unexpectedly for the day, he insisted that I take over his talk show.

"Of course you can do it. You have the gift of gab. You know how to make people comfortable and reveal a little more than they planned. You've watched me put the show together. You know how it works."

"But, David, I don't want to embarrass you. What if I panic?"

"Oh, don't be silly. That's not going to happen. Besides," he smiled, "I need you. You know how you'll be good for my ratings."

⁂

Our relationship became closer and closer. But a little voice inside began nagging at me. The more David was there for me, the more he showed how much he really cared, the less secure and trusting I became. That tiny baby girl who had been left alone by the two most important people in her life, who trusted them so little when they finally brought her home, was still lurking somewhere inside me, and she began to make her presence known.

"It's too good to be true," she whispered. "It can't possibly last. You know you don't deserve this man, so don't be a fool. If you open your heart to him, you're sure to have it broken. That's what always happens. It happened with Sidney. It's bound to happen again if you still haven't learned not to give yourself completely."

The whisperings started early, during one of our first weekends together in New York. We spent a lovely afternoon in the Village wandering in and out of the little art shops, and we had so much fun we lost track of the time. Suddenly it was evening, and the world began to close in on us. David was running late for a meeting. I was due at the airport to catch my flight back to California. As he dashed out into the street to hail a cab, I looked over at him and found myself thinking, "Oh, no, don't fall in love with this man. Please don't fall in love with him." That was, of course, exactly what was happening. I should have been ecstatic, and in some ways I was. Yet the anxiety and fear triggered by this realization kept me company all the way to Los Angeles. The moment I landed I called him just so I might find some reassurance in the sound of his voice.

Neither of us had started out thinking we were becoming involved in anything very serious, and the fact that the relationship had taken a turn in that direction was a surprise to us both. Obviously, we needed time to find out who and what we were before plunging ahead with the "I love you"s and running off to buy the ring. We were two adults moving step by careful step through the inevitable twists and turns of a mature relationship, not a couple of children caught in the agonies of teenage passion. When we were together, we were together; when we were apart, both of us were free to do whatever we wished.

David was perfectly candid about the other women passing through his life. "Oh, I had dinner with so-and-so while I was in London," he would say. "She's very pretty, and we had a lovely time. Now tell me, darling, what have you been doing?"

Sometimes I feigned a bit of jealousy, but there was really no need for it. Everything in David's behavior showed me there wasn't. Whether or not he declared himself in so many words, the seriousness of his feelings was obvious. He was always searching for ways for us to be together and would make plans months in advance.

"This summer, would you prefer a house in the Hamptons, or do you think you'd rather go off to the coast of Spain?" he would ask. "What shall we do during Suzanne's Easter vacation? I've found a wonderful spot in Greece, and we could do that, but I don't know if that's quite the right thing for her."

"Well, if he doesn't really love me," I reasoned with my infant self, "then why is he acting like this? Why is he always thinking about us as a couple? Why is a man as busy and pressured as he is always considering not only what's best for me but also what's best for my daughter? Why is he pursuing this relationship in the first place?"

I wish I could tell you that my arguments stilled the childish insecurities and put the fears to rest. How beautiful it would have been to trust my heart and take the chance, to make the commitment on my own without worrying about the consequences. How beautiful to say, "I know he loves me, but that's not the point. The point is that I love him. I don't care what he wants to give. I want to give. I like what I see, and I'm going to make a run for it. And if I get hurt in the process, so be it. Twenty years from now I'll be able to look back and say, 'Well, it was worth it. At least I didn't cheat myself. At least I had the courage of my emotions.'"

But the child inside was not stilled. The sense of security I felt when David and I were together was not enough to sustain me when we were apart, and then the child took over. Still scarred by the memories of abandonment and betrayal, I needed to arm myself against the strength of the feelings he evoked in me. I needed to find protection against the horror of the inevitable moment when I would be forced to hear once again, "I don't love you as much as you love me . . . I don't need you as much . . . I don't want you as much . . . I'm going to leave you." The infant needed to find an "out clause," and she found one.

Slowly, almost imperceptibly, I began to turn all my fears and uncertainties into criticism. To keep myself from loving him too much, I began to discredit everything that was wonderful in David and to concentrate on his shortcomings. Well, seek and ye shall find. What human being is perfect enough to withstand such scrutiny?

I started complaining that David's high-pressure, fast-moving life-style was taking too heavy a toll on me. Jetting back and forth from Calforina to New York to London, popping sleeping pills on the plane to catch a few hours sleep before we arrived at our next destination, left me feeling like a zombie for weeks. I was losing weight. I was exhausted and bedraggled. And, of course, it was all his fault. He was the one making the plans and orchestrating the moves, wasn't he? Look what he was doing to me.

I began accumulating evidence of just how selfish and self-involved he could be. A few days before I was due to open in Las Vegas he called from Long Island and insisted I come to him immediately. He was breaking in a new act as a standup comedian on his first U.S. tour, and it wasn't going well.

"I think I may have gotten in over my head," he explained. "Practically all my writers are English, and they don't seem to understand American humor. I need you to help me pinpoint the flaws. I need your advice. I'm afraid all of us are beginning to feel very confused, and I don't have to remind you that the opening is tomorrow."

Forgetting all the times he had answered my own cries for help, I argued that he was being unreasonable, that my Vegas opening was only a week away and I needed to plan and rehearse. Eventually I relented, and boarded the private jet he sent for me. It wasn't until I saw the nervousness on his face when he picked me up at the airport that I finally snapped to my senses. "My God, how could you be so insensitive?" I berated myself. "The man you love is in trouble, and he needs your help."

I concocted problems everywhere. I knew David's reputation as a ladies' man and began convincing myself that he was sleeping with other women. When he went off to Northern Ireland to cover the mounting conflict between the Protestants and Catholics, I almost drove myself insane. David had been asked to moderate a televised town hall meeting between the opposing factions, and the journalist in him jumped at the opportunity, even though it was terribly dangerous.

"You do understand why I have to go?" he asked when he saw my apprehension. "If you were in my place, wouldn't you do the same?"

I knew he was right, and part of me loved him for his courage. I stayed in his flat in London, watching the escalating violence on television, waiting for the phone to ring, trying to tell myself that it was just a job and he was going to be fine. But as the days went by without a call and the political situation worsened, I started thinking that surely he had taken up with someone and was having an affair. The longer he remained away, the more certain I became that I was right. By the time he finally returned home, I was so happy to see him that I fell all over him. Later, I accused him of being unfaithful. David was very patient with me.

"How can you say that?" he reasoned. "What have I done?" The unassailable logic of his response only heightened my rage.

"All right, you don't have to tell me about it!" I screamed at him. "I know what really happened!" That insecure two-year-old inside me just wouldn't let go of her martyrdom. She needed to believe that once again she was being pulled down and betrayed, that David and I weren't really as wonderful and honestly committed as we seemed, that he really didn't love me.

All my doubts and ambivalences came to a head a few months later when we returned to England to spend our second Christmas together. I knew I wasn't well. I was exhausted from the constant running around, and the fatigue had triggered off the old cystitis I had contracted during the long hours I spent standing on the cement floor of the sound stage while I was shooting *Julia*. But, foolishly, I chose to ignore it. I didn't want to tell David I was feeling ill. It was clear by now that he didn't have time for me to be sick. I didn't have much time for it either, and I wanted us to have our Christmas. Trying to put it out of my mind, I decided to wait until I flew home to California before seeing a doctor.

It turned out to be a bad mistake. We were attending a large dinner party in London, and toward the middle of the evening I began to shake uncontrollably. My hands were so cold I couldn't pick up my knife and fork, and I thought I might be starting to hemorrhage.

"David," I told him, "I'm not feeling very well. I think we'd better go. I need my fur jacket."

"Just a moment, darling," he answered, then blithely went on laughing and talking with the other guests. David was so involved establishing relationships and making business conquests he didn't realize how ill I really was. He reached for my hand but continued ignoring me until the gentleman on my left said, "I'll get your jacket for you." When he rose from his seat, David looked over and told me, "Oh, I would have done that."

"That's all right," I snapped at him. "It's no longer necessary."

I was absolutely furious. I felt he was taking me much too much for granted. I felt that he thought the wheelings and dealings of the moment were far more important than any problems I might have. I felt, in a word, rejected. It was an absurd overreaction, but I had an enormous amount of anger in me.

"I'm leaving!" I announced. "I can't stay here another moment. I'm afraid I'm ill."

"But, darling," he whispered, "you can't leave. How will we explain it? Try to wait a bit. Let's see if anyone else is leaving."

"I don't give a damn about anyone else!" I answered. "You stay if you want to, but I'm going. I'll send the car back for you."

"No, no, no. You cannot go without me. It isn't appropriate."

That did it. The insistence on social protocol pushed me over the edge. Like a spoiled, self-indulgent child, I barked a curt "Good night!" to the astonished onlookers and stormed out of the ballroom. David was utterly baffled by my behavior.

"That really was unnecessary," he told me on the drive back. "You know that, darling. If you have problems, you keep them at home." Of course he was right, but at the moment I didn't want to admit it.

By the time we were ready to leave for the country to spend Christmas with his family, tempers had cooled and I felt sufficiently recovered to go on with our plans. But then while we were sipping eggnog and exchanging presents at his sister's home, my hands and feet became icy cold once again, and to my dismay I found that I was bleeding. Trying to play down my concern, I said I would like to rest for a while, but on the way upstairs my legs buckled under me and I fell against the wall. The next thing I knew I was being helped into bed.

David is the kind of human being who will deny a migraine headache until the pain is so excruciating it has him writhing on the ground, yet this time he could not have been more caring and attentive. He whisked me back to London, put me in the hospital, and made sure I had the very best doctor he could find. The doctor was quite cross with me.

"You knew you weren't well," he admonished. "Now you must have surgery. . . . Don't be absurd. Returning to California in this condition is absolutely out of the question. Of course you can't fly home. You'll have to have surgery here in London."

A few days after the operation, David had to return to the United States to tend to some business. I was still in the hospital recuperating when the phone calls began.

"Darling, you sound ever so much better. I know you'll be fine. I'm sure you're doing beautifully. I have a marvelous idea. Why don't you check out of that dreary place and join me in Florida?"

David was his incurably optimistic self again. I can't blame him entirely for what happened next. I knew how weak and fragile I was feeling. I heard the doctor's adamant disapproval when I asked about leaving. All I had to say was, "No, David, I'm not well enough to travel." But I didn't.

I flew to New York, took another plane to Miami, then met the private sea plane David had waiting. The plane was a few feet from the beach, and everyone else walked through the water to get to it. Like an idiot, ignoring the fact that I was sick, refusing to ask anyone to carry me, I, too, stepped into the water. By the time I climbed on board, my feet were soaking wet. We flew on to the little island where we had arranged to meet. To make matters worse, the air conditioning in the hotel wasn't working properly, and I was so cold I had to sleep in my fur coat. Not surprisingly, I woke up the next morning with a relapse. I returned to Los Angeles, and my doctor immediately insisted I go back into the hospital, where I remained for another ten days.

"What do you think you're doing?" he asked angrily, chastising me like an irate father. "This isn't to be taken lightly. If you don't allow yourself to heal properly, you can have this condition the rest of your life. It's time you and David had a serious talk."

I tried, but David didn't like me to be sick. He wanted me to be with him.

"Yes, of course, darling, you must do exactly what your doctor says. But wouldn't you like to come to New York next week, and then we could scoot off to Bermuda to rest for a few days? I have to return to London tonight, but I'll call you as soon as I arrive. And don't forget Bermuda. Or perhaps we should go to Hawaii."

My hospital room overflowed with flowers and gifts. David telephoned every day. But that wasn't enough for me. Lying there in bed, mulling over the events of the past few weeks, I began to construct a solid case against him:

David hadn't taken care of me. When I was sick in London, he should have said, "Stay there, stay there until you are well." Now I was back in the hospital again, and it was all his fault. Because of his selfishness I might not recover. Because of his selfishness he had abandoned me and left me alone in London and then again in California. And he still couldn't address himself to the fact that I was seriously ill. Yes, of course, the two-year-old inside me had been right all along. Once again I had made the mistake of trusting someone.

When David called to say he was flying to California to see me, I asked him not to come.

When I finally left the hospital, I was confined to bed for a while, but a month or so later I felt strong enough to visit David again in London. The doctor wasn't happy with my decision but thought I might be all right as long as I didn't push myself too hard and spent most of the time resting. "That sounds perfectly fine," David assured me. "We'll stay at home. You'll have your meals in bed. I promise to take good care of you."

Several nights after I arrived he invited a few friends over to dinner. About eleven o'clock he came up to the bedroom and asked me to join them for a brandy. I was so furious I began to cry. I thought we had agreed to curtail the socializing, but there he was, back to his old ways again.

"Oh, for God's sake, David," I sobbed. "Why can't you take this illness seriously?"

"Oh, must we be so dramatic?" he answered. "I don't think it will hurt you to come downstairs for a few minutes and have a brandy with us. I told them you're not well, but they're your friends, too, and they'd like to say hello before they leave."

I felt like the worst bitch in the world. What was he doing that was really so terrible? He loved me. He was proud of me. He wanted me to be a part of the evening. Maybe he was right, and I *was* carrying on too much about not feeling well. Maybe I *was* making more of it than I should.

The following morning David brought me breakfast in bed, then announced, "I've planned a little surprise for you. I didn't expect you to be ill again, and if you're not quite up for it I'll arrange a postponement. But I think you're well enough."

"What is it?"

"I have a plane waiting for us, and I'd like to take you to see a house I've found in the country. I think it's exactly what you've been looking for, exactly what you wanted."

Some months before, David and I had visited Fleur Cowles at her country home. It was a wonderful house about an hour outside of London, and I had fallen in love with it. On the drive back to town I casually mentioned that this was just the sort of place I would like to have for myself some day. David had remembered my words and, without telling me, had scoured the countryside for a comparable home for us. Now that he had found one, he wanted me to see it before I returned to California. It was such a kind, loving gesture, and it left me feeling just awful.

"You're the most lovable, wonderful human being I've ever known," I told him, "and I could kill you. Maybe you should have changed the appointment without telling me. Maybe I am well enough to go. But I can't deal with it right now. I can't even think about it."

David was crestfallen but tried to pretend it wasn't important. I knew that it was, because David wasn't simply talking about a house. He was indirectly saying that he loved me and wanted us to live together on a more permanent basis. But I couldn't allow myself to hear it.

In the week that followed I continued finding fault. I can imagine his relief when he finally deposited me at the airport and I boarded the plane home. It was not one of our happiest visits.

∾§∾

David and I continued seeing each other, but we also started to back off a bit. We had reached the point where we needed to move on to a firmer sort of commitment, yet neither of us was quite ready. I didn't make any demands. Neither did he. Both of us allowed the relationship to float, and little by little, while we waited to see what happened next, the deterioration began.

I think David felt I was much more secure about us than I really was and that I was handling the situation very well. But I wasn't handling it well at all. I thought maybe I was finally ready for a new kind of maturity, another way of life that wasn't so hopelessly old-fashioned and naïve. I began to rethink my beliefs that marriage is the only answer. "There are all kinds of relationships in the world," I found myself thinking. "They don't all have to be love and marriage."

It happened sooner than I thought. In February 1972, when I went off to Las Vegas to work at the Hilton, I met another man. Freddie Glusman owned a number of women's shops in the various hotels. In his style and manner, he was as different from David as two people could possibly be. He had a deep, raspy voice and a jagged, unfinished, dangerous-looking face. He wore loud sports jackets, expensive alligator shoes in garish colors, enormous diamond wristwatches, lots of gold rings, and more chains around his neck than could be found in many jewelry counters I had seen. Yet, quite frankly, there was also a gruff, animal sexuality to this man that was different from anything I had known and I found myself attracted to it.

Freddie and I met for the first time the night of my opening when he invited himself back to my dressing room. I had just finished performing and the room was crowded with visitors. Freddie took charge immediately, pouring the drinks and attending to everyone's comfort. He was obviously trying to attract my attention, but I didn't think very much about it.

The presents began to arrive the next morning — large bouquets of flowers, beautiful negligees from one of his shops, and a dozen bathing suits for my approval. When Dave Victorson (who was in charge of buying the entertainment for the Vegas Hilton) invited me to dinner with his wife a few days later, he asked if I would mind if Freddie joined us, and I agreed. The four of us had a marvelous time dining and dancing and laughing until four in the morning. It was the kind of fun I'd never had in Vegas before. In the past I had always just worked and slept — performing twice a night, doing whatever publicity had to be done, then spending the rest of the hours in my room with my arsenal of humidifiers, trying to ward off another attack of "Vegas Throat" (better known as laryngitis).

At the end of the evening, I invited everyone to my suite for a nightcap. After finishing their drinks, the Victorsons left. Over the course of the evening Freddie had made me very aware of his interest — there was nothing subtle about him. Now that we were alone, he made no secret of the fact that he was attracted to me, and I couldn't deny my own response. And that made me very uncomfortable, because, whatever our problems, I was still involved with David. Even though I was trying to be sophisticated (in my mind meaning being able to have casual relationships without the license), I found it troubling that I could be attracted to someone else.

The following day I received a telephone call from Mrs. Victorson.

"What are you going to do about this?" she asked. I didn't know what she was talking about. "Well, he's mad about you," she explained.

I told her not to be ridiculous, but in actuality, more flowers and presents were already scattered about the room. In all fairness to the man I ought to have put an end to it then and there. But I was still trying to play this sophisticated game. So, when Freddie telephoned a few minutes later and invited me to lunch, I accepted. We had a casual, fun time, and the next night we went out to dinner again.

What I hadn't yet completely learned was that there is a certain kind of person who wants to be involved with people in show business. Such a person always will seek out performers and become so good at knowing their needs that he or she becomes indispensable.

At that time, Freddie had many of those characteristics. And as the days passed and we saw more of each other, he began devoting himself to taking care of me. I was vulnerable, and Freddie smelled it. As he began homing in on me, I responded. (For all his garishness and flamboyance, Freddie was appealing — he was always *there*.)

"I think you should go to bed early tonight," he would tell me, "because we're spending tomorrow at Lake Meade on my boat. We'll return early so you can rest. . . . Suzanne's coming to visit? My daughter's about the same age, and she'll also be in town. I'll take the two of them waterskiing. . . . Would you like to play tennis this afternoon? Oh, you don't know how? I'll set up some lessons — my country club isn't five minutes from here — I'll arrange it with the pro."

Freddie loved people and loved to socialize, and he introduced me to a world I hadn't even realized existed in Las Vegas, a world of yachts and tennis courts and afternoon barbecues. It was great fun, a welcome respite from my old dreary, two-shows-a-night routine.

I assumed the relationship would come to its own natural conclusion when I finished the engagement and left town. But Freddie had other plans.

"I'm not ready for this thing to end," he told me over our final dinner together. "I want to keep seeing you." He was perfectly aware of my involvement with David and interjected a few underhanded jabs into the conversation to make his feelings clear. "Are you sure you really belong with that guy?" he asked.

In my mind, the answer was yes. David was still the one important man in my life, and as far as I was concerned whatever went on between us had nothing to do with Freddie. When I returned to Los Angeles Freddie called to say he had some business in L.A. and would like me to keep my evenings free. We continued this way for several months, seeing each other in L.A. and Las Vegas.

I'm not entirely sure why I encouraged his attention. I am sure that the strong sexual bond between us dictated much of our behavior. But I'm just as certain that there were other, far more neurotic reasons at work. I think perhaps my enormous fatigue and insecurities allowed me to be drawn to Freddie's roughness and lack of sophistication at the same time as they repelled me. I knew that life with David would have to be a constant process of learning and improvement — he would expect me to grow, expect me to be the very best I could be. It was easier with Freddie — he made no demands other than the pleasure of my company.

To be honest, it was nice to be in control for a change.

Freddie was aware that his garishness put a distance between us, and he was determined to correct it. He accepted my criticisms with enormous good humor and patience. He really was the perfect foil.

And I kept at it.

"Do you have to wear forty-two gold chains around your neck?" I would tease him. "Please, at least button your shirt so we can get through this dinner without looking as though you're up for sale. Why do you always wear shirts that make you look like the lead singer in a rhumba band?"

"What's wrong with my shirts? They wouldn't dress this way in New York, is that it? Everybody has to walk around in navy blue blazers and shirts from Brooks Brothers."

"Surely you're not going to wear those green alligator shoes to dinner this evening?"

"Well, they match my green Piaget watch."

I suppose I was really attacking myself. I still wasn't strong enough to say, "Diahann, you don't have to be here."

❧

It was now the summer of 1972, and I returned to my apartment in New York. Shortly before I flew to Paris to shoot a television special (a show about Paris with Charles Aznavour, Twiggy, Louis Jourdan, and Perry Como), David and I had a dreadful falling out over dinner at the Plaza. He was in great high spirits, but I was feeling rather sullen and moody. I really needed to talk to him about us, but he was enjoying himself too much to listen to anything serious. Each time I tried to broach the subject, he interrupted by raising his glass and proposing another toast.

"Here's to your show. May it be a wonderful success. . . . Here's to our next vacation in Hawaii. . . . Here's to this. . . . Here's to that. . . ."

On and on he went, until out of frustration and anger I smashed my glass against his, spilling the champagne all over the table. Everyone in the restaurant turned to look at us. David was stunned, and stared at me in disbelief. I was almost as stunned as he, but, by God, I was furious!

"I'm not hungry," I informed him. "And I'd like to leave."

We went back to his apartment and talked about what had happened, but got nowhere. By the end of the evening we decided to let the relationship cool for a while.

Somehow Freddie found out about my trip to Paris. A few days before I left New York he called to say that he and one of his pals were flying to Paris, too. He suggested that we take the same flight and spend our evenings together, and I didn't put up a fight. But by the time Roy Gerber and I arrived at the airport, I had forgotten about Freddie and was surprised to see him. It was too late to say anything, but I promised myself to be discreet. Despite what had happened between David and myself, the press was still treating us very much as a couple, and I didn't want any publicity (nor did I want David to find out).

Allowing myself to travel with Freddie was a mistake, to say the least. Not that we didn't have any fun, but it was too much, too soon — and it just wasn't right. In fact, the day we returned to New York we had a terrible argument, and he left for Las Vegas full of anger.

To prevent David from finding me, I had bypassed my apartment and checked into the Regency on Park Avenue. But somehow he managed to track me down. A day or two after Freddie left town the telephone rang, and there he was.

"Welcome back, darling," he said. "Did you have fun? I read about your new companion."

There was a long, uncomfortable pause in the conversation. Then David went on.

"I need to see you. Are you free for dinner this evening? There's something important I want to discuss with you."

We dined at the Regency. I realized immediately that something about David had changed. He wasn't his normal light, breezy self. There was an undercurrent of seriousness in his manner — maybe he was annoyed that I had gone off with Freddie and was getting ready to tell me so; maybe he was priming himself to say that he realized he was more emotionally involved than he thought and was ready to take our relationship to the next phase. I was prepared for all sorts of possibilities, but not for what happened when we returned to my hotel and he settled down to the business of the evening.

David can be extremely theatrical, and he was never more so than at that moment. Staging the scene as though we were in a play, he sat me down on the sofa, turned me toward him, cleared his throat, and began.

"Darling, I have something to say to you. I know there are differences between us, but I don't want to discuss them — they're not really that substantial. Nor do I want to pressure or frighten you. But in my jacket I have two boxes. The box in my left pocket contains a brooch. The box in my right pocket contains a ring you once admired in Asprey's in London. I would like you to accept one of them. If you accept the brooch, we will continue to be friends. If you accept the ring — which is what I hope you will do — then that means we're engaged and you've agreed to become my wife. I'm going to put both of them here on the table, and I want you to make your choice. Which one shall it be?"

I was too stunned to answer. I thought we understood we were playing this sophisticated game I was so busy learning. At one point nothing would have made me happier than to become his wife, but now I wasn't so sure. I was too flustered and bewildered to be certain about anything. So we sat there and stared at each other. Both of us were terribly nervous. I had never seen David this way before, flushed and apprehensive, with his heart in his hand.

After a while he began to press me for an answer, but I couldn't give him one. I told him, yes, I probably did want to marry him, but I needed his understanding and patience. He asked me to take the ring and give him my decision whenever I was ready.

I returned home to California, taking my new ring with me. But I didn't wear it very often — I felt it was unfair and improper to wear it until I made my decision. Over the next few weeks I almost drove myself mad trying to figure out what to do. I knew that I loved him, but that little frightened child inside me was overwhelmed by the magnitude of the commitment to David. Caught up in her panic, I began to look at all the reasons why we really should not marry.

I felt that David's life-style was wrong for me. I was afraid that I would never be able to keep up at his pace. Inevitably, there would be long periods when we scarcely saw each other — David most certainly had another fifteen or twenty years of working at that same frantic tempo. He loved it more than anything. And the things that I needed were too demanding. If the marriage were to succeed, I would have to make the necessary adjustments in my own career. Could I do that? Did I really want to exchange my life as a performer for the role of hostess and helpmate and homemaker? Perhaps David wasn't aware of it yet, but I was sure that eventually he would come to expect that of me. Sooner or later there would have to be compromises. Would I be unselfish enough not to resent them?

And what about children? I knew how David felt about babies. He would want to have them immediately. True, I wasn't a young girl anymore, and the sooner I became pregnant, the easier it would be for me. Yet I wasn't so sure I wanted to rush into it. I knew from my own experience how much time and effort it takes to raise a child, and I was working a minimum of forty weeks a year. Yes, David would probably be a wonderful father, but the brunt of the burden would fall on my shoulders. That's what David would expect, and, once again, the adjustment would be very difficult.

On the other hand, David and I did love each other, and that wasn't to be taken lightly. Neither was the fact that when all was said and done, we were very well matched. For all our differences, so many of our needs and desires were exactly the same. I loved David — and perhaps if I acted like an adult and made adult demands about how the marriage would have to operate, we could make it work.

I still hadn't thoroughly analyzed what to do when I returned to perform in Las Vegas a few weeks later. Freddie was there waiting for me. I told him that David had proposed and had given me a ring. Freddie was unimpressed.

"So he gave you a ring," he scoffed. "Big deal. You want a ring? I'll give you a ring."

The next day he did. It was the largest, gaudiest ring I had ever seen — there must have been fifty diamonds in it. It looked like one of those shiny revolving balls on the ceiling of a dance hall.

"Wear it for a while," he said as he slipped it on my finger. "I got it on approval from a friend of mine in the jewelry business. If you like it, I'll buy it for you."

I don't know what I could have been thinking. Obviously, Freddie was putting himself in direct competition with David, but I was so confused I barely noticed. For two or three days I did wear it, and then I returned it to him.

By the time I left Vegas for my next job, in New Orleans, I had made up my mind. It seemed to me that the positives outweighed the negatives and that David and I should be able to have a good life together if we both worked at it. I reached for the telephone and called him. He sounded ecstatic and I was happy too. It was, I assured myself, the sensible, the right decision. Yet part of me was still terrified.

We began compiling the guest list for the engagement party Clay Felker was throwing for us at his lovely home. Then things began to move fast. Our press agents called the newspapers. Our mothers flew into New York. I telephoned Freddie, and he was furious.

"Don't ever call me again," he seethed. "I'm not going to be played with. You made your choice, and that's that."

I heard him, but, frankly, I was too busy with my plans to give his reaction much thought. What I was not prepared for was the mad amount of public attention brought on by the engagement. I suppose I should have been. David and I were extremely popular at the time, and the fact that this heavily publicized interracial romance was finally heading for the altar was deemed newsworthy enough to put us on the front page of the *Daily News*.

The morning the story hit the street, David and I were leaving the apartment at the Plaza for lunch in the country. The moment the elevator door opened the cameras started flashing, the microphones were thrust in our faces, and the crowd of well-wishers surged toward us. There must have been three or four hundred people waiting for us in the Plaza lobby. I couldn't believe it!

"Yeah, David! Yeah, Diahann!" they screamed. "Congratulations! We love you!"

There was the same kind of excited response a few weeks later when I went off to play Australia for the first time. Scores of young people surrounded my hotel and shouted their blessings. Everyone was so happy for us.

Everything was much too dreamlike and unreal. I felt as though I were sleepwalking my way through the excitement, putting one foot in front of the other as if I were on automatic pilot. I knew that marriage was what we both wanted, and I hoped all the questions that still troubled me would eventually be answered.

A few days after I returned to New York from Australia, David flew off to London. There was certainly nothing unusual about that. Yet this time it left me feeling terribly isolated and alone. "Well, here we go," I told myself. "You better start getting used to it." I was ashamed of myself for being so childish, but I was also angry at David, even though I knew there was no valid reason for my anger. I had, after all, just been away attending to *my* own business.

Lying around David's Plaza apartment while I waited for him to return, I kept thinking I didn't really belong there. It felt so different from all those times when I worked at the Plaza. Then I had been surrounded by my manager and my assistant and my musicians, and I was there for a reason — I had a job to do. Now when I walked through the lobby I was David Frost's fiancée. I didn't pay my own bills. I didn't feel as though I had a real purpose. I felt that I had relinquished all my authority. It was a whole new role for me, and I wasn't sure that I liked it.

We announced our engagement in November of 1972 and planned the wedding for the following spring. As far as David was concerned, we were doing just fine. Whenever one of my uncertainties raised its ugly little head, he would wait for it to go away or say whatever had to be said to make me comfortable for the moment. He was perfectly happy. Most of the time so was I. But as the weeks passed and I began to confront all the arrangements that had to be made, I became more and more unsure.

Arnold Scaasi was designing my wedding suit and a travel wardrobe for the honeymoon. Scaasi makes the most beautiful (and expensive) clothes in the world, and I was delighted with his designs for my trousseau. We selected a pale pink suit for the marriage ceremony, three or four satin and silk blouses and a marvelous gray wool coat lined in sable that had matching pants for excursions to the country, a long skirt for evening and a short skirt for the afternoon. They were all absolutely gorgeous except for one — nothing about the wedding outfit seemed to please me.

"I don't want to get married in pink," I complained. "Pink is not a serious color. I know I chose it, but maybe we should try something else. . . . And the collar on the blouse is all wrong. We have to do it over." After a time, I think Scaasi understood it wasn't the suit that was the problem — it was the wedding.

Things were better when David and I flew to California to spend the Christmas holidays at my home. The comfortable familiarity of my surroundings made me much less anxious. We had breakfast together on the patio surrounded by the trees and flowers. We swam. David shot pool with Suzanne and, to her squeals of delight, allowed her to win. He was his usual busy self during the day but always found a moment to call.

"Shall we go out to dinner tonight," he would ask, "or would you rather stay at home?"

Most of the time we dined out, and if that troubled me a bit, I thought we would settle down eventually. Yet the day after Christmas I was sitting across from my analyst, regaling him with the list of my misgivings.

When the holidays ended, David picked up his pace and once again began jetting off to London and New York and wherever else on the planet his business took him. I didn't want to return to New York, so I remained in California. Now that I was alone again, all my anxieties resurfaced and started playing havoc with me. And as the weeks went by, the feeling of desperation became more and more overwhelming, and I couldn't seem to shake it.

"Why don't you just take off and go somewhere?" I kept asking myself. "You don't have to be here. At least call someone." But I couldn't seem to do that. Instead, I wandered around the house on automatic pilot, becoming angrier and more frightened with every passing day.

Toward the middle of February, a little over three months after we announced our engagement, I picked up the telephone and told David, "I think we should call this thing off." He was astonished. I felt both miserable and relieved.

David said I was being unfair to us. He knew we had some problems, but given half a chance, they were bound to resolve themselves. He said I was being too impatient and much too impetuous and felt that I needed to give the decision some further thought.

"Let's talk about it tomorrow," he concluded. "Sleep on it tonight, and see how you feel in the morning."

But by the next day nothing had changed. I asked if he wanted me to return the ring. He said, no, I should keep it. When I hung up the phone, I wanted to dial him back immediately. The finality was more than I could bear. But I didn't. That was that. The engagement was over.

❧

I was still in a daze a week or so later when Freddie invited me to Las Vegas to visit for the weekend. "Let's not talk about anything," he said. "Let's just take it easy and try to relax." I didn't know if I really wanted to be with him, but I needed the rest, so I accepted the invitation.

I slept on his boat. I sat in the sun. I drifted from the health club to the beauty parlor back to the health club. I was a total zombie. But that was fine with Freddie. He accepted me that way.

We were lounging around the country club, having a drink with some of his friends, when one of them casually said, "I don't know what the two of you call this, but from where I sit, it looks like you're both in love."

I didn't say anything.

"Well, I know I'm in love," Freddie laughed. "She doesn't know what she is."

"Yes, I do," I answered. "I know what I'm doing."

"Then why don't you guys stop playing with each other? Why don't you get married?"

"I would marry her this second," Freddie told him. "That's how much I love her. But she won't marry me."

"I'm not so sure about that." The words just fell out of my mouth.

"Well, what about it then? I could call downtown right now and make the arrangements. We could get married today."

"Is that a proposal?"

"That's what it is. So what do you say? Do you want to marry me?"

"Well, I guess so. Why not?"

Freddie ran to the telephone. I sat there watching his excitement as he called city hall and arranged to have the waiting period waived.

"I really am doing the best thing," I told myself. Being with Freddie was so easy, so safe, so free of pressure. He would take care of me forever — I would never have to worry about being alone, and I wouldn't have to change. I wouldn't have to grow. Nothing would be required of me.

The silly little child inside me was delighted. She had won again.

By the time we returned fom city hall with the marriage license, Freddie's house was overflowing with people. In the midst of the pushing and shoving, someone led us in front of a microphone and performed the wedding ceremony. The next thing I knew I was being whisked off to some hotel, where a wedding dinner had been arranged. And so, on February 21, 1973, I again became a wife.

Toward the end of that evening David called from New York.

"I just heard the news on the radio. Are you all right?"

"Yes, I'm fine."

"You haven't had too much champagne, have you?"

"No."

"Are you sure you know what you're doing?"

"Yes."

"Then let me wish you every happiness."

Freddie and I remained in Las Vegas for a while. If I felt any vague apprehensions that perhaps I really *didn't* know what I was doing, I chose to ignore them. When Freddie suggested we have another, more elaborate wedding in Los Angeles, I said that would be fine. We booked the Bel-Air Hotel for the reception. We mailed the invitations. I selected the colors and swatches for the wedding wardrobe. This time around, Bob Mackie and Ray Agayan designed the wardrobe for the wedding, and I went along with their recommendations.

The wedding lunch was big and lavish — and that's all I remember.

I floated through the next few months like a sleepwalker. Freddie seemed as happy as a little kid with a new toy. He took me to beautiful restaurants, was a wonderful host when we entertained, showered me with gifts and surprises. Knowing how I felt about my mother and daughter, he always included them in our plans and was unstintingly kind and attentive. Knowing how I felt about his garishness, he began to dress more conservatively and take on a new sophistication. "This is the lady who brought Lalique crystal and Limoges china into my life," he would joke with his friends. "Isn't she something?"

Freddie seemed so pleased with the marriage that I didn't take it very seriously when he began to exhibit a bit of jealousy toward some of the men who worked with me. First there were a few insinuations about my friendship with my manager, Roy Gerber, who was like a combination of big brother and father confessor to me. Then there were more heated accusations about the relationship with my new record producer. The producer was a large, blond, sullen man who was extremely ill at ease with people, and Freddie interpreted this discomfort as evidence of some kind of involvement with me.

I knew Freddie took enormous pride in his sexuality but had no idea he could feel so insecure when he thought it was being threatened. Then, about three months into the marriage, his insecurities got the better of him, and he exploded like a bomb.

It happened the night of my opening at a hotel in Lake Tahoe. It had been a long and difficult day. I had rehearsed for five hours, performed two shows, and in between performances joined Freddie and his daughter and some friends for dinner. Now it was almost three o'clock in the morning, and I was exhausted. All I wanted to do was take a bath and go to sleep. Freddie, though, was feeling amorous. When I explained that I was very tired, there was a quick exchange of words, and then without any warning he suddenly began cursing and hitting me. Before my very eyes, the nice guy, the fun guy had turned into an angry, raging stranger.

Lying there on the floor I caught a glimpse of myself in the mirror. The sight was all too familiar. I had experienced this degradation before. But this time was going to be different. I was not about to stay here. Not for one minute more.

I ran into the bathroom and locked the door behind me. While Freddie tried to break it down, I telephoned my secretary, Louise, and blurted out what had happened. A few minutes later the local police and hotel security guards rushed into the suite and asked Freddie to leave. He packed his bags and left. It was the last time I ever saw him.

The next morning I received a phone call from a lawyer in Reno. He told me that Freddie had filed papers for a divorce. By afternoon the whole ugly story was in all the press.

Freddie called me a few weeks later. He said he had wanted to spare himself the embarrassment of having me file the papers first, but now that he had a chance to think about it he would like to stop the proceedings. Would I consider meeting him to talk about a reconciliation? He said he was sorry about what happened in Tahoe and promised it would never happen again.

I'm sure he had no idea how familiar that dialogue sounded to me. I knew by now that this wasn't the first time he had become physical with a woman and it wouldn't be the last. I explained to him that anyone who allows herself to put up with that kind of abuse is even crazier than the person who administers the beating. And I wasn't about to let it happen to me. I told him that the marriage hadn't made any sense in the first place, and it was just as well for both of us that we were out of it.

In a way, the beating was exactly what I needed to bring me to my senses. Now that I was finally awake and back in the real world, I could see what a botch I had made of everything by not taking responsibility for my own actions. Operating out of weakness and fear and desperation, I had hurt David, I had hurt Freddie, I had hurt myself.

Well, you live and you try to learn. The mistakes had been made. The damage had been done. The moment for David and me had passed. It was over between us. There was no place to go but onward. But the consolation was — and it gave me great comfort, as it does even today — that David and I would always be friends.

Chapter Eight

About three months after the divorce I received an excited phone call from my manager. "I'm sending over a movie script," Roy told me. "I want you to stop whatever you're doing and read it immediately. If you like it, I'll come by and fill you in on the details."

I more than liked it. I *loved* it. With humanity and humor, *Claudine* told the story of a mother's determination to bring her six children safely through the perils and poverty of the Harlem ghetto. The cards are stacked against her: her fifteen-year-old daughter is pregnant; one of her sons has dropped out of school and become a street-corner gambler; another is so traumatized he refuses to speak. Out on her own without a husband, she has to resort to welfare to supplement her meager income as a domestic and is forced to endure all the attendant humiliations — hiding her toaster from the social worker, concealing her relationship with the new man in her life, a fiercely independent garbage collector with some money and family problems of his own. Claudine is harried and exhausted by the pressures that beset her on every side, yet she is so strong-willed and persevering, so committed to the well-being of her family, that somehow she manages to survive these adversities with her dignity intact.

I have known this woman all my life. We grew up together in the same neighborhood. She was one of those girls who married too young and had babies too fast, and now that her middle years were upon her has to live with the consequences of her mistakes. Who can say for certain — if I had had different parents and hadn't been blessed with some talent, I could easily have become Claudine. And we *were* similar — we were both the same sort of verbal, highly protective mothers, and I understood all too well how her sensuality kept getting her into trouble, how more than once she had placed her trust in a man without really evaluating what she was doing.

There was so much of Claudine in me that I couldn't see anyone else in the world playing her. I felt I could give life to her humanity. I felt I could make people care about her. And I knew it was an incredible opportunity to test my skill as an actress — the opportunities had been so few and far between, and none of them ever required me to create a character of this dimension. I couldn't wait to put aside the couture gowns and to work without glamorous makeup. I looked forward to the challenge: I wanted to let my talent out, to expose it, to test it. I had always believed I had the ability to be a good film actress. If I landed this part, I would finally discover whether that was actually true or not.

My hands were shaking as I returned Roy's call. "I want to play this part so badly I'll do it for nothing," I told him.

"Okay, I'll be right over," he answered. "There are some things you have to know."

Twenty minutes later, Roy was sitting in my living room. He took a deep breath, then lowered the boom. The film was already in production — Diana Sands had been set to play Claudine. The film was her baby, the major project of her career. She had fought long and hard for it, and then the first day of shooting she collapsed on the set and was rushed to the hospital. She had terminal cancer. She was dying.

It took a minute for the news to sink in. I just sat there, but Roy kept talking. He explained that it was Diana who wanted me to take over her role. Everybody involved in the production felt I was wrong for it, for the same reasons I had heard before *Julia* — I was too chic, too much of a jet-setter, too far removed from the gritty reality of Claudine's world. But Diana was adamant and insisted I read the script.

At first all I could think about was Diana. The news tore my heart out. She was so bright, so feisty, so bursting with life — my

God! How could she be dying? It didn't seem possible. In a special way, I loved Diana — she was part of my childhood; we had attended elementary school together. We were always very different. Diana was the smart one, the funny one, the talkative, outgoing tomboy who ran everything and sailed through school with straight A's. I was understated and quiet — I remember that my desk was as neat as a pin, and Diana, the gregarious one, always had the messiest desk of all.

We became friends. Diana helped me with my history and math and came to my defense when someone threatened me. I helped her a little with her hair and clothes. After graduation our lives went their separate ways, but we always liked each other and respected each other's work. Years later I badgered Hal Kanter into signing her for *Julia*. Now she was reciprocating with *Claudine*.

I flew to New York to meet the director, John Berry. I liked him immediately. He seemed completely up front — honest and kind. He was interested in *me* as a person, and I felt comfortable talking to him, especially since he had a definite and positive view about my work. We began by talking about Diana. He told me she realized she was dying and kept asking everyone, "When is Diahann coming? Have you sent for her yet? What are you waiting for?" I found out later that Diana had known she had cancer for quite some time. Somehow, through sheer guts, she kept working until she collapsed.

We then talked about the character of Claudine, and because I felt that John thought I *could* play her, I found it easy to express what I felt about her. And then, miracle of miracles, we agreed that I would do the film. I would have to start shooting immediately. *Claudine* was a low-budget independent production well out of the Hollywood mainstream, and there was no time or money to waste.

I was leaving for the hospital to see Diana and thank her when the telephone rang. Harold Melvin, a very dear mutual friend, was on the line.

"I don't want you going over there to visit her," Harold insisted. "There's nothing you can do for her. She won't even recognize you. Her condition will only upset you."

Less than two weeks later she was gone. We were shooting on the set the day she died. Ironically, we were shooting the same scene she had been filming when she collapsed. All of us held hands and prayed for her and thanked her for bringing us together. Without Diana's perseverance, I'm certain the film would never have happened.

When I went to the wake I was shocked by how the cancer had ravaged her. She had lost so much weight, and the morticians had done such dreadful things to her.

"Oh, Diana," I said to her, "if you could see what they've done to you, you'd be furious! For once in your life you had to turn the controls over to someone else, and look what happened." I was angry, and started to shake. She was too young to have left us — it was as simple as that. As I said goodbye, I told her how much I would miss her and promised to be the best damn Claudine possible — the best ever!

❧

Playing Claudine became everything — there was nothing else in my life. Suzanne, who was by now fourteen, was away at school in Lausanne, Switzerland, and this let me devote all my time to my work. And work was *it* — that was all that I did, all that I was. And I loved it all. Every incident, every scene was a joy — it was wonderful to work again.

The first day of shooting, John Berry decided to have me begin with a nude scene with James Earl Jones, Claudine's boy friend. I think John was trying to throw me off my well-focused, serious approach to the work — that defined refinement that I always carried with me. So he scheduled the scene between James and me in bed. As they called us to the set, James walked in — totally naked. Not a stitch of clothing was on that body! I was absolutely stunned! My first instinct was to look the other way. But then I said to myself, "Don't be a child. You're not Diahann — you're Claudine, a mother of six (each of the kids fathered by a different man), and this is not the first time you have been to bed with this man. So relax and get into it."

When it was over, James paid me a compliment — I think.

"You're really into this part, aren't you?" he asked, smiling.

"Why do you say that?" I asked.

"I was really looking forward to doing this scene with you. But not once did I get a hard-on for Diahann Carroll — you were always Claudine."

John Berry must have been right — it worked, as did everything else with *Claudine* from then on. But other scenes were more difficult, both on the soul and on the body. There was one very traumatic scene — with my teenage daughter — that I will never forget. Let me back up for a minute. To understand the power and pain of this scene, you have to remember that Claudine is a very moral person in her own way. She has worked very hard to bring up all these kids, and to keep them on the straight and narrow. They are all living examples of how difficult it is to be fatherless, so when Claudine finds out that her daughter is pregnant, she goes berserk.

When we prepared to shoot the scene, we set it up, laid it out, carefully blocked out what we were to do. The following day, John Berry and I rehearsed it with the adviser (it is required that there be a physical adviser on the set when there is going to be a lot of action). And then I said to John, "I want to think about this scene, so I'm going upstairs, and when I come down, I'll be ready to shoot." When I returned, John saw that I was ready to go for it, so instead of shooting piece by piece, he decided to shoot the entire scene in one take.

I find out from my son that my daughter (played by Tamu) is pregnant. I turn around and go right upstairs, march into her room, and start beating her unmercifully. Something inside Diahann cracked, and Claudine's emotions matched Diahann's perfectly — whether it was that Suzanne was far away from me and this could have happened to her; whether it was for all the young girls I had known who had been in this position; whether it was for this woman, Claudine, who was trying so hard to hold everything together and finally realized that she really didn't have that kind of control — I don't know. All I do know for sure is that when it was over, John yelled, "It's a take," and all of us — the actors and the crew — fell into each other's arms, crying. The next day both Tamu and I were swollen and black and blue from head to toe.

Other moments were much less painful. I enjoyed working with the children. Often, we ate our meals together. They were constantly in my dressing room, as they would have been with their real mothers. This kind of chaos was terrific for me, both because I missed the interaction with my Suzanne, and because it allowed me to experience firsthand the harassment and fatigue of having to cope with a brood of six lively, demanding youngsters. Often I actually *was* that exhausted woman on the screen.

And I looked it, with a little help from my friends the makeup artists. At first the brass upstairs insisted that they didn't want me to wear makeup at all. So I did the first test with a bare face. The next day the same brass arrived on the set and informed me that since I looked about fifteen years old without makeup, they had decided that I needed makeup after all to make me look older and more fatigued.

That little bit of makeup, and a $40 wardrobe (the average cost of one of my dresses was $7.98), was all I had to cover me, and I loved it. No false eyelashes! No beaded gowns! No fancy hairdos! It was me and the camera, and I was in heaven.

Every day after the shooting, I returned to my home and worked with Alice Spivak, a wonderful drama coach Belafonte had recommended. I understood Claudine so well I didn't have to make any of the usual mental adjustments, but Alice was insistent that I bring out the fine details of her character. We would sit on my living room floor with cartons of Chinese food and spend hours going over the next day's scenes — dissecting Claudine's behavior, examining what worked for me and what didn't, talking about ourselves as we related to her personality and situation. Alice and I were both single women trying to raise children on our own, and sharing our common experiences gave us a closeness that exists to this day. Very often I was too weary to crawl into bed by the time we finished and would wake up on the living room floor the next morning. But the work was so rich that I wanted to bring to this part everything I had in me, and the exhaustion didn't matter.

Neither did the fact that I didn't make a cent on the film. Every penny of my salary, which was not very large (this *was* an independent production), went to pay for my coaching. And it was worth every penny. I really would have done this film for nothing; it gave me the chance to work as a serious actress, and it also gave me the opportunity to work with James Earl Jones. He was simply brilliant. I realize that I received a lot of attention and publicity for *Claudine* because no one expected it of me and everyone already knew that James was incredible. But I have always felt that he did not get his due — that his performance was extraordinary and he should have received many more accolades for his work in this film.

As luck would have it, much of the film was shot around 145th

Street and Convent Avenue, the very same neighborhood where I was raised. I hadn't been there for years, but every building, every doorway, every little storefront still held its own special memory. There was the corner where my first boy friend and I would meet each other. Right across the street was the swimming pool where I went swimming as a child. There was the church where I attended Sunday school . . . the beauty shop where I first had my hair pressed and rolled into the big puffy curls popular at the time . . . Cushman's bakery that made the delicious chocolate cake Mom brought home every weekend.

Many of the people I had grown up with were still there. Some had been destroyed by drugs, but others seemed to have weathered the years without any visible scars. "Is that Carol Diann Johnson?" they would ask, tapping on the window of my limousine or stopping me on the street. "Remember how we sang in church together? . . . Remember how you and Sylvia used to come by my father's store every Friday for a knockwurst and sauerkraut? . . . Remember how we went bike riding in the park?"

My instincts told me that I was right for this part, and now that I was back in the neighborhood again I knew it for sure. Claudine and I were sisters, alternate versions of the same little girl who made her way so long ago through these same Harlem streets.

༄

And then it was April 1975 and *Claudine* was over. The reviews were wonderful — and some of them quite funny. Headlines like "Can you imagine Jackie Onassis as Claudine — Well, it works!" and "Songstress Diahann Carroll Pulls It Off" made me laugh out loud, and stories about the wonder of Diahann Carroll, best-dressed-list member and jet-setter, playing a welfare mother and playing it well made me extremely proud.

It was gratifying to receive good reviews, but as a low-budget independent production without major distribution I felt we had no chance to make any real impact on the industry. But then the following February, while I was vacationing in Mexico, I received an unexpected phone call from my press agent, David Horowitz.

"Are you sitting down?" he asked. "I have some fantastic news for you. You've just been nominated for an Academy Award!"

I was dumbfounded — and speechless. It hadn't occurred to me that anyone in the academy had even screened the film for possible consideration, and I was ecstatic — no, shocked — that they nominated me. After a giddy afternoon of Mai Tais and manic calls to friends and family, I returned home to start the round of interviews David had begun to schedule. I certainly didn't expect to win Best Actress, and as it turned out I didn't (the award went to Ellen Burstyn for her work in *Alice Doesn't Live Here Anymore*). But the honor of the nomination was, and remains to this day, thrilling.

⤙❦⤚

Among the journalists who came to interview me about the film and the nomination was the managing editor of *Jet* magazine, a young man named Robert DeLeon. Standing there at the bar of the restaurant where we arranged to meet, he cut a strikingly handsome figure. He was tall and slender, with skin the color of caramel, and impeccably dressed in a dark blue suit, white shirt, and neatly patterned tie. For all his studied nonchalance, he was too young to disguise the fact that he knew he was attractive, and I found that quite charming. When we finished lunch, he snapped open his Gucci briefcase, took out his tape recorder, and went to work. He was very good at his job, warm and relaxed, with a nice sense of humor that put me at ease, yet never drifting too far away from the business at hand.

When the interview ended, he didn't seem quite ready to say goodbye. "I'll be in town a few days before I return to Chicago . . . ," he told me as David and I began to leave, letting the sentence trail off without further explanation but looking at me straight in the eyes to make his meaning clear. I thought it a bit forward of him and pretended not to notice. Over the course of the afternoon he had mentioned more than once that he had a wife and baby. "Oh, why are the nice men always married?" I found myself asking on the ride to David's office. David stared out the window, ignoring my little joke. Clearly he had some reservations about this young man, but he kept them to himself.

About a month later I saw him again. I had come to Chicago to work at the lovely Palmer House Hotel, and he showed up at the press conference the afternoon of my opening. I didn't know how to react, but the way he conducted himself made me extremely uneasy. All the other reporters were busy taking notes and asking questions, yet he just sat there in the back of the room with his arms folded, silently watching my every move almost like a hunter stalking his prey. When the conference ended he waited until everyone left, then came over to say hello. *Jet* magazine had decided to do another story on me, he said. So few black actresses had ever been nominated for an Academy Award that his editor thought it would be a good idea to follow my steps through the day of the actual ceremony. He had been given the assignment and would meet me in Los Angeles later that week. Louise admitted to feeling a strangeness about this man — that he made her immediately uneasy.

The day of the awards was so hectic I found it impossible to think about anything else. Yet Robert seemed determined to capture my attention. Shortly before we were due to leave for the theater, he interjected himself into the middle of the turmoil and, with a grand flourish that brought everything to a stop, presented me with a gift, a gold bracelet with the twin masks of Comedy and Tragedy. It felt a bit off, a bit too personal. He was, after all, a journalist covering a story, not an old friend (who in any case would have known better than to break my concentration at such a tension-packed moment). He was also a married man with a child, and the way he presented the bracelet was rather too much like a suitor bestowing a present on a loved one. As we left my house for the ceremonies, Robert climbed into the limousine and took the seat next to me. My mother was to be my date for the evening. Now we unexpectedly had an escort.

The following morning I received a very disturbing piece of news from my press agent. It seemed that Robert had spoken to Joe, the man I was dating then, and had been told that the two of us were living together. Before he put it in his story, Robert wanted to know whether or not it was actually true. David had assured him it most certainly was not, but thought I ought to be aware of what was going on. I called Joe immediately and he denied he had ever said anything of the sort. But then when I spoke to Robert, he insisted that Joe was lying. Robert was so filled with righteous indignation — "What a despicable thing to do! I can't understand how someone like that can even be allowed in your presence!" — that I never thought *he* was lying. I called Joe back and said we better stop seeing each other. When I arrived at the airport later that afternoon to return to my engagement in Chicago, Robert was waiting in the passenger lounge. He was booked on the same flight and had reserved the adjoining seat.

Robert called from his office the next day and invited me to have dinner with him. He had mentioned on the plane that he had separated from his wife a few weeks before and was now sharing an apartment with a friend, so I agreed to see him. True, Robert was younger than I — he seemed rather vague about it, but from what I could piece together he was either twenty-seven or twenty-six or twenty-eight. I was nearly forty. Still, he was only suggesting a night out on the town, and I thought I deserved a bit of fun.

The evening started off rather badly. There were a few people ahead of us at the restaurant who also had reservations, and Robert was shockingly rude to the maître d' when he didn't seat us immediately. He was just as abusive to the waiter for hesitating a moment before bringing our menus. But once I told him that if he didn't change his tone I would have to leave, he began to calm down. In no time at all he was the same charming, self-possessed young man I first met.

As Robert relaxed into the evening and started telling me about himself, I could see he was a truly exceptional man. He was brilliant — his mind worked fast, he was well read and knowledgeable. He was also fiercely ambitious and seemed always to have gravitated toward the powerful and influential. From the names that Robert dropped, he seemed to have close personal friendships with all sorts of accomplished, successful people — politicians, businessmen, show-business celebrities. He had a wonderful position at *Jet* magazine, but that was only the beginning. He wanted to expand and grow, to move upward into the larger world of journalism, to follow in the footsteps of his hero Ben Bradlee, managing editor of the *Washington Post*. I was excited by Robert's extraordinary mind. I was fascinated by his ambition and barely concealed arrogance. When I visited his office and watched him put the magazine together, I was awed by his talent and drive. As young as he was, he was already a bit larger than life.

We spent a lovely week together, but then my engagement ended and it was time to leave. Robert, though, seemed determined not to let the momentum fade. He called to say that, coincidentally, he also had some time off — perhaps we could take our vacations together. As a matter of fact, one of his friends owned a beautiful condo in St. Thomas just two minutes from the beach, and we wouldn't have to deal with the hotels and the crowds. I mulled it over for a moment, then asked myself, well, why not? He was very good company. I had planned to be alone, but now that I had all this newfound freedom, why shouldn't I go off on a little fling with a gentleman with whom I didn't intend to spend the rest of my life? I told him that sounded fine, and he plunged ahead with the arrangements.

The moment we entered his friend's condo, Robert reached for the telephone and called his publisher in Chicago. I was not really paying attention, but he seemed to be saying that he had to leave the office in such a hurry in order to nail down a story. "I'm in St. Thomas," I heard him explain. "And guess who's with me?" The way he uttered my name sent a tiny shiver up my spine. It was as though he were throwing his boss a juicy tidbit that would more than justify his sudden departure. If my ears hadn't deceived me, someone was being manipulated here, if not his boss then myself. But I assumed Robert would clarify the situation for me during our time together, so I didn't question him.

When Robert opened his suitcase, I was surprised to see how little clothing he had brought with him. There were only a few dirty shirts, jeans, and socks, all rolled into a bundle as if they were being dropped off at the laundry. "Oh, there was a last-minute crisis at the magazine," he smiled, "and I didn't have a chance to pack. I didn't even have time to go to the bank." I was a bit embarrassed for him and said I would lend him some money so he could go shopping. I chose not to dwell on the subject.

When an older woman starts dating a younger man, most people believe it's primarily because of the sexual attraction. But, on the contrary, Robert and I did not have an incredible sex life. The important thing was that we enjoyed each other's company. We did everything together, and it felt perfectly comfortable. A few days before we left, Robert turned to me and said, "You know, you feel just like my wife. Would you ever think about getting married?" The question took me completely by surprise. We barely knew each other. I laughed and told him it was much too soon for that sort of conversation. "Well, maybe we can talk about it again some other time," he answered, backing off a little. "Come on, let's go swimming."

(I think that I'd better explain that despite the fact that throughout my life, especially on my vacations, I always seemed to be going swimming, I can't swim. But I can do a perfect imitation of a little old lady on the Florida shore, standing at the edge of the water, umbrella in hand, splashing herself with ocean water and loving every minute.)

At the end of the week Robert returned to Chicago and I returned home to California. But now he called every day, and we began seeing each other almost every weekend. I would fly into Chicago. He would visit me in Los Angeles or New York. It was all great fun, exactly what I needed, and when he started talking marriage again, I found myself listening. Maybe it wasn't such a preposterous idea after all.

I think I was in love with him. I also think I wanted to be married. Freddie was less than two years behind me, and that marriage had been such a disaster I must have felt some misgivings about trying again so soon. But my apprehensions were mainly about being single — I still hadn't lost the fear of going through the rest of my life alone.

I think, too, that Robert represented a segment of the black community I was raised to admire, and that also clouded my judgment. He was well educated. He was bright and ambitious. He was just the sort of young man I would have met and dated and eventually married had I done what I was supposed to when I graduated from high school and gone off to Howard University the way my parents planned. My mother and father were both very impressed by his credentials, and so was I. I believed in his future. I wanted to be part of it.

The difference in age didn't seem that consequential. As it turned out, Robert was only twenty-four, not twenty-seven or twenty-eight as he first led me to believe. But this was 1975, and there was an emormous amount of talk in the air about older women and younger men. It was becoming almost a trend, and I was perfectly comfortable being one of the more visible women involved in this kind of relationship. Besides, Robert had friends of all ages. He introduced me to as many people my age or older as he did his contemporaries, so it wasn't as if I would be walking into the world of someone fifteen years my junior. Eventually the age difference probably would catch up with us, but I thought I'd be able to handle it.

Mom was delighted that I was thinking about getting married again. Most of my friends were less enthusiastic. "Well, he seems like a nice guy, a very bright guy," they answered when I asked how they felt about it, lightly dancing around the question so they wouldn't have to say anything negative.

On one of our weekends together in New York, Robert asked his father to fly down from Boston to meet me. The man was not at all what I expected. How could this unpleasant, self-involved man who drank too much that evening and flirted with me shamelessly before his son's eyes be the same marvelous human being Robert described in such loving detail? Robert was much too upset by his father's behavior to deal with any of my nagging questions about him, and I thought it best not to press him.

We had discussed the possibility of marrying sometime during the summer if we were both still sure that's what we really wanted. But then Robert began to say he didn't want to wait.

"I miss you too much," he would say when he called from Chicago. "I have to be with you. This is only April — summer is still an eternity away. Why couldn't we do it sooner? Why not in May?"

We had known each other less than three months, but I was so flattered by his impatience that I agreed. Impetuous and immature? Absolutely!

Robert took charge of all the arrangements, and I went along with whatever he decided. The wedding was held in the chapel at Columbia University. A friend, Thad Garrett, a special assistant to Nelson Rockefeller, performed the ceremony. John Johnson, president of Johnson Publications, agreed to be his best man. Robert wanted a very small wedding, so virtually none of my family and friends were invited. I didn't object. From the time I was a child it had been made fairly clear to me that men are supposed to make the decisions. Even though I had been in therapy and had learned that I could make my own decisions, it was somehow easier to revert to the old Diahann and let Robert take charge. Perhaps because those old feelings of guilt about my success would not go away, I still found myself relinquishing power over my personal life almost as though I needed to give it away. Robert made all the decisions, discussing very little with me. As a matter of fact, not until some months later when I saw our picture on the cover of *Jet* did I realize that, without discussing the matter with me, Robert had granted Johnson Publications exclusive coverage of the wedding.

❧

After the wedding Robert began spending more time at my home in Beverly Hills than at his office in Chicago. Ostensibly he was in California to pursue a cover story about Quincy Jones, who was recuperating from very serious surgery. Quincy, though, was still too ill to give interviews, much less pose for photographs, and as the days went by the magazine started pressuring Robert to return to Chicago. He was adamant about staying, and there were any number of heated long-distance telephone arguments. When Robert wanted to do something, he could find all sorts of brilliant reasons to prove he was right, and he didn't want to go back to Chicago.

Finally, Robert announced that he was leaving the magazine to take a job in Oakland with a management consultant company that examined government contract proposals. I was very surprised, because he constantly spoke of journalism as his future and of his commitment to becoming a successful journalist. His ultimate goal was to work at the *New York Times,* but for the time being he had planned to remain at Johnson Publications, rising up through the hierarchy to become editor in chief of *Ebony* or *Jet.* We had even thought about looking for a house in Chicago. Now suddenly all that changed, and he was putting journalism aside to try something new. I didn't really understand, but he described his new job in such glowing terms, I never allowed myself to consider that he might have been fired for his high-handedness.

I moved to Oakland and retired from show business. Surprised? So was I, underneath it all. But there it was once more, that little voice inside, repeating again and again, "If this marriage is going to work, Diahann, you have to be there. You have to be totally supportive. You have to give up your life, your work, to be with your husband." There were still a few jobs here and there, but most of my concentration went into my new career as Mrs. Robert DeLeon. To be fair, Robert didn't actually insist on my giving up my career, but I mistakenly surmised that was what he really wanted. He was always terribly uncomfortable when I went off to play an engagement and we had to be separated for the week. So I primarily concentrated on sheets, pillowcases, and placemats.

The decision to retire was complicated and not very smart. I wanted to work, but it seemed to me that my career was floundering after the Academy Award nomination. I kept remembering a conversation I had with my friend Sue Mengers, when I ran into her on a plane a few days after being nominated. Sue Mengers was one of the most powerful agents in Hollywood, handling stars such as Barbra Streisand and Robert Redford. I was still so happy about my nomination that I forgot what every black actor who wants to make movies has to remember.

"When I return to California I'd like to call you," I found myself saying. "I'd like to discuss some business with you, perhaps representation."

Sue was very quiet, then, looking me straight in the eye, she gave me her answer. "I don't have the time to work that hard," she said. "Let me explain, Diahann. When I get up in the morning the only thing I have to do is return all the phone calls from the major studios and decide which of the offers are best for my artists. If I represented you, I would have to call the studios myself, and then call them again to try to develop a project that might or might not become a reality — and that takes a lot of effort and a lot of time. And, even then, chances are we would not be able to make it happen."

I was stunned, but I knew she was telling me the truth. I appreciated her honesty, and I've remained forever grateful.

Believe it or not, I started to enjoy being "only" a wife. There was a fascinating challenge to not working, to becoming "the wife of," and I attacked the role the same way I do any new job, throwing myself into it with every bit of energy and dedication I could muster. I decorated the apartment. I went to the market and cooked dinner. I entertained Robert's business associates and made sure not to wear anything too haute couture when I attended the cocktail parties. "Well, what do you have coming up?" they would ask. "What's your next project?" It felt a bit strange, but also rather reassuring, to be able to tell them, "I have no next project. I'm living in Oakland now with my husband."

Oakland was not Los Angeles or New York, and I had to make some adjustments. But I didn't feel as though I had walked into something I couldn't handle. During the day I went to the beauty parlor or shopped a little, or spoke to Suzanne on the telephone — her school was now only forty-five minutes away, and she was always popping in and out over the weekend. Robert was marvelous with her, and she adored him. We were building a life for ourselves, and for a while, at least, both of us were happy.

Trouble was not far off. Not unexpectedly, it began with money. Robert was reluctant to discuss our finances, but I assumed we would essentially live on whatever he earned and that he was prepared to work hard and struggle for a while until he made it on his own. To see us through this difficult period I thought it would be fine to supplement his salary with some of my own savings, matching the dollars he deposited in our bank account, but basically he was still the breadwinner and provider. That was my fantasy about how marriage was supposed to work. Robert, though, talked one philosophy, but lived another.

He was a young man with a rather modest income; however, he had very expensive tastes. He loved foreign sports cars, custom-made clothes, the finest restaurants, and when he preceded me to Oakland to find us a place to live, he looked at the most lavish homes in the most desirable neighborhoods. I, being frugal, thought it would be much more sensible to take an apartment until he saw what his job was like and was sure he would stay for a while, but one house he showed me was so beautiful I also fell in love with it. We agreed to share the cost from the sale of our respective homes, but then when it was time to put down the deposit suddenly there were all sorts of unforeseen complications. For some reason that was too murky to comprehend, Robert's share of the money would have to be delayed for a while. It seemed to have something to do with the fact he had never actually married his last companion, but Robert tap-danced so fast I couldn't get a clear picture. The one thing that did seem clear was that I was expected to complete the purchase. That disturbed me. So did the way the owner seemed to know I was selling a large house in Beverly Hills that once belonged to Barbara Hutton's son and wouldn't have any difficulty meeting his price. I told Robert that we ought to wait. He tried to hide his disappointment, but was quite upset.

When I returned to Los Angeles to begin closing up my home, Robert rented a small one-bedroom apartment in Oakland. But then in a matter of weeks he became quite friendly with the landlord and had arranged to move upstairs to the huge penthouse. The rent was very high, much more than he could afford, yet he insisted he had made the right decision. "You have to live in a certain style," he argued, making his case almost as though he were handing me a Christmas present. "You have to be comfortable. Now there will be plenty of room for Suzanne when she comes to visit. Besides, this place is a steal."

As the months went by it became increasingly apparent that we had two very different ideas about how the marriage would operate. He still refused to talk about it, but clearly he had absolutely no intention of living within our budget. The MG was traded in for a Jaguar, and in due course the Jaguar became the down payment on a Ferrari. The credit cards were flying. The bills at the end of the month were staggering. I hated myself for doing it, but I knew I was right: when I received the first payment for the sale of my house in California, I opened a separate account in a different bank and quietly made the deposit. At some point Robert couldn't contain himself any longer and asked what happened to the money. When I told him what I had decided to do, he was astonished. It never occurred to him, never, that I would make such a decision — that I wouldn't just deliver the money into his hands with my blessings.

⁊

From the very beginning, Robert tended to drink a little too much toward the end of the evening, but now he began drinking in earnest. I didn't realize how out of hand it had become until the night he invited Vida Blue, the Oakland pitcher, to dinner. This was a very important meeting for Robert — he was thinking about leaving his job to go into the public relations business and had arranged this meeting to discuss possible representation. When Vida arrived, Robert had not yet come home. I called his secretary and she said he was on his way, but an hour went by and then another hour and there was still no sign of him. Just as Vida was about to leave, the telephone rang — it was the Oakland police. They were holding a man for drunk driving. He had driven off the side of the road and down an embankment, and when questioned, claimed to be the husband of Diahann Carroll. Was this really so? And would I mind proving I was *the* Diahann Carroll by answering a few questions about *Julia?*

"All right, Miss Carroll," they finally told me, "we know you don't want this in the papers, so we'll bring him home and release him in your custody."

Vida Blue was shocked. "Does this happen often?" he asked. "I can't believe it. He's such a bright, intelligent young man."

I told him it had never happened before and I was sure there must be an explanation, but when the police escorted Robert to the door he was still inebriated. He tried to make light of it, to cover his embarrassment with fast talk and jokes, yet there was no disguising his condition. Nor for all his efforts to pull himself together was he able to conceal the hostility bubbling just below the surface of his banter. "Well, aren't I fortunate?" he sneered. "If I weren't married to Diahann Carroll, I'd probably be in jail right now. Isn't she wonderful? She can just sit here in this apartment and she's so powerful the police will bring me home, and it won't even be on my record, all because she's Diahann Carroll."

Vida Blue said goodbye. Robert went to bed, but I stayed up, thinking. It occurred to me that, among other things, Robert was self-destructive. It was as though he had sabotaged himself deliberately, as if some secret demon lurking in his soul had made him say, "I really have a meeting with a man as important to my career as Vida Blue? Well, I'm going to get clobbered and prove to everyone I don't deserve it." Obviously, his insecurities had surfaced.

The persona was securely in place the next morning and the catastrophe of the previous night was all but forgotten. But now that Robert's demon had broken free, he began drinking more and more heavily. Sometimes his frustrations took a personal turn. "I can't get away from you!" he lashed out at me one evening when he had consumed just enough alcohol to speak the truth. "I can't get away from your name! Everywhere I go it's the same damn thing. My boss took me out for a drink, and all the women in the bar were only interested in one thing — that I was your husband. I could have had any of them if I wanted. But I don't need you for that! I can get women on my own!"

The drinking and hostility became even worse after his mother suddenly died of a heart attack. Robert loved her deeply and was inconsolable. He had thought there was time to do all the things he planned — to buy her a beautiful home and take her on trips and make her proud of him — but now it was too late.

Robert never really collected himself after that. There didn't seem to be any way to get through to him. I tried talking, and when that didn't work I mirrored his own behavior back at him in the hope he might see what he was doing to himself.

I don't know why I decided to stay. Was I that much in love with him? Was I really that unable to confront what I had gotten myself into? That afraid to be alone? To this day I don't know for certain. Let's just say I realized there were far more problems in the marriage than I had anticipated, but I hoped that with enough time, effort, and luck somehow we might manage to work them out.

Nine months after we arrived in Oakland we packed our bags and left. There were no explanations. Robert simply came home one evening and proclaimed, "I've quit my job. We're moving back to L.A. We're leaving immediately." (I discovered much later that he had to leave — he was heavily in debt.) I called the movers, and we sneaked out of town like thieves in the night.

❧

Once we arrived in Los Angeles, Robert announced he planned to set up an office and start his own public relations business. When he asked what I thought of the idea, I told him it sounded fine. I assumed I was answering his question, but that wasn't what he was waiting to hear. A few weeks later he couldn't restrain himself any longer and just blurted it out. "You know what kind of money I have," he fumed. "You know I don't have enough to put an office together. Why are you making me come to you and ask for your help?" I told him that if he needed money to start his business I would back him until he got on his feet. We rented a five-room suite on Sunset Boulevard and proceeded to furnish it immediately.

Robert was foolishly optimistic; he was positive he only had to pick up the telephone and many of the important people he met during his tenure at Johnson Publications would immediately become his clients. It was a rather naïve expectation. He was almost in shock when the clients he sought explained that they had press agents and couldn't really leave them for a young man who had just arrived in town and had no contacts.

"I'm really sorry, Robert," said Sammy Davis, who was very fond of him and wanted to soften the blow. "You should have discussed this with me earlier. And for what it's worth, I think you ought to do everything you can to form this business on your own. Don't become Mr. Carroll. That's the worst thing you could do to yourself."

Robert was too panicked to listen to Sammy's advice. Now that contacts like Sammy Davis and Quincy Jones weren't falling into line, he needed someone else to open the door for him, and that someone was to be me. He knew that David Horowitz was not only my longtime press agent but also one of my dearest friends. He also knew how negatively I felt about mixing business and marriage. But Robert was desperate. He dare not fail!

When Robert saw my resistance, he wrote me a very long letter that flattered and cajoled and unashamedly played upon all my guilts and fears. "I am uniquely qualified to represent you," he wrote. "I believe that you possess rare talents that, unfortunately, have largely gone unnoticed by the public. Your career is now at an interesting point. I would like to work with you as a team. . . . When it's all said and done, there are only the two of us and if we don't do for each other, no one else will."

I don't know what angered me more: the high-handed way he was trying to pressure me or his assumption that I wasn't able to see how transparent his desperation had made him. (Oh, God, how ugly desperation can make people behave!)

"Well, what did you think of the letter?" he asked a few days later. "What are you going to do?"

"I feel exactly the same as I felt when we discussed this before," I told him. "I'm not going to do anything. For the sake of your dignity, Robert, the people in this town have to know you're your own man. How can you even think about sending out a client list of one, and that person is your wife? Please believe me, you couldn't make a bigger mistake. I won't have anything to do with it."

He slammed the front door behind him and sped off in his Ferrari. When he returned home late that night, he was very drunk.

As far as he was concerned, our marriage was a trade-off, a simple matter of give and take. He would give me a young, attractive husband. I would give him my name and my contacts. But part of him also wanted me to put away my low-cut dresses and trade in my identity as Diahann Carroll for the more acceptable role of Mrs. Robert DeLeon, helpmate and wife, the woman who ran his home. The conflict tore at him, but his ambition drove him, and he was moving so fast there was no way for him to stop. And once he began to see I didn't run my life or my business in that manner, he didn't know what to do about us . . . and neither did I.

Now that his control was slipping, Robert had to find other, more devious ways to try to manipulate me. We had agreed that our home was our home and we would confine our business to the office, yet one evening Robert appeared unexpectedly at the door with two new clients and one of their girl friends. I was wearing a bathrobe and no makeup, but as soon as they stepped inside they took out their cameras and asked me to pose for them. It was extremely painful for him — for both of us. As soon as they left, he grabbed a bottle from the bar and poured himself a stiff drink. My silence upset him, but there was nothing to discuss. It was obvious. It was ugly. And soon it became uglier.

We were in very deep trouble, yet I continued to hang on. As the months went by, the situation became intolerable. Robert drank more heavily — not infrequently he was too drunk to find his way home at night. His self-hatred and self-destructiveness seemed to control him now, and as a living reminder of everything in himself that he loathed I soon became the constant object of his rage. Nothing I did was right — not the clothes that I wore or the meals that I served or the way I took care of his daughter when she came to visit. He complained about me to his friends, belittled me in front of them, and finally he started bringing other women to our home. I endured it as long as I could, but then one night after a dinner party at Sammy Davis's home, I just exploded.

Robert was insistent that we go to Sammy's party. He worshiped Sammy and wanted Sammy to think well of him, but it was almost as though he deliberately set out to discredit himself. We were discussing South Africa over the dinner table when Robert broke into the conversation and began attacking me for my ignorance and stupidity. Later on we moved into the living room to watch a movie, and some other guests arrived, including a man I hadn't seen for years, who was once my agent. When he gave me a hug, Robert rushed over and raged at him, "What do you think you're doing? Take your hands off my wife!" The man was stunned. So were Sammy and everyone else.

"Come on!" Robert snapped at me. "We're going home. I want to get out of here, and you're coming with me."

I was embarrassed and humiliated, but this time he had gone too far. "You can leave if you like," I seethed, "but I'm staying to see the movie. Here are the keys. I'm sure someone will drive me home later."

Robert seemed surprised that I was no longer quite content to suffer in silence, yet he continued to make such a dreadful scene there was really no choice but to do as he asked. It was a long time coming, but I was so furious by now that the moment we arrived home I began breaking everything in sight — glasses, lamps, vases, the door to the shower — then pushed all the furniture — every piece — into the pool. I had deep cuts on my arms and hands and was bleeding all over the house, but I was too frenzied to care. I just kept breaking and breaking and breaking until there was nothing left to destroy.

Robert was amazed. He had never seen me this way before and didn't know what to make of it. Eventually he calmed me down and became very quiet and attentive. It had finally sunk in that he had pushed me over the edge. Where we went from here was a question still to be answered, but there was no doubt in either of our minds that something would have to change.

Maybe Robert wanted to change. Maybe he tried. But he was so desperate to get to the top of the mountain he couldn't control himself. Whatever the cost, he had to make the deal. And nothing was too sacred to stand in his way.

Any lingering doubts about that were dispelled once and for all by what happened a few months later. Robert was trying to raise money to buy a radio station, and we had come to New York so he could talk with some people interested in backing him. He had also managed to involve a very wealthy banker from San Francisco, whom we had met when we were living in Oakland. The man was flying in to join Robert for an important meeting in Philadelphia, and Robert had invited him to stay with us overnight at our New York apartment. "I don't know if that's really such a good idea," I told him. "That gentleman makes me extremely uneasy. He's always just a little too flirtatious. Couldn't we put him up at a hotel?" Robert assured me I was only imagining things, and the man arrived at our apartment with his luggage.

The afternoon of the meeting, their plans suddenly changed, and it was decided that Robert would go to the meeting in Philadelphia without our houseguest. Not wanting to be left alone with the man, I asked Robert to explain that I had a dinner engagement and wouldn't be able to entertain him.

"You don't have to worry," Robert assured me. "He's not going to be here — he's spending the evening with a friend."

Half an hour later, the telephone rang.

"What are you doing for dinner?" the man asked me. "You're busy? That's too bad. Would you care to meet me? . . . Maybe you can get out of it. I'm only in New York this one night, and I'd hate to spend it alone."

I knew what I suspected, but wasn't completely certain I was right. Luckily, my cousin Pat was still at her office.

"I'm probably blowing this thing way out of proportion," I apologized, "but I could really use your help tonight." She said she would meet me for dinner and keep me company until Robert returned. When the man called back, I said I wasn't able to change my plans, but if he didn't mind being bored by a couple of garrulous women, he was welcome to join us.

"Well, Pat, what do you think?" I asked her when he left the table to make a telephone call. "Am I being slightly ridiculous about this?"

"Let me put it this way," she answered. "I believe I'm a fairly attractive young lady, but he doesn't even know I'm here."

"Then I'm not imagining all this?"

"Certainly not. He's not even trying to hide it."

"Then I think you'd better come home with me."

Robert was scheduled to return around eleven, but by two o'clock in the morning he still hadn't appeared. Pat pulled me aside and whispered, "I really do have to leave. But I think you'll be all right. He's not going to be too overbearing, and Robert ought to be here any minute."

After she left, I told the man I was very tired and had to go to bed. He smiled over at me and said, "Maybe there's something I can do for you."

The insinuation was brutally clear, but it seemed best not to confront it directly.

"Like what? This is my home. You are my houseguest. Can I get *you* a nightcap before I retire?"

The smile on his face had coarsened into a leer. "But isn't there *something* I can do for you? *Some* way I can repay your hospitality?"

"I really don't know what you're talking about, and I think we'd better say good night."

"You're really going to bed then?"

"Yes, I am."

I locked the bedroom door behind me and spent the rest of the night staring at the clock. Finally, about seven in the morning,

Robert stumbled home. He was very drunk. I asked him all the questions — Where had he been? Why hadn't he called? How could he have left me alone with this person? — but he had no answers. He disappeared into the guest room to confer with his friend. When he returned a few minutes later, he looked like a naughty child who had just been punished.

There was really no way to overlook or extenuate or pretend not to understand what had happened. It was so blatant, so ugly, so totally insane. I suppose I should have hated him for it, but more than anything I felt sorry for him. He was so desperate and confused, such a helpless victim of his own blind ambition that it was almost as if he didn't have a choice.

It seemed to me that if there were any chance at all of saving this marriage we would have to get out of each other's way for a while. Maybe if I put enough time and distance between us, Robert might begin to come to his senses. I needed the break as much as he. Retiring from the business had turned out to be a very bad mistake. Without the work to keep me focused I had lost much of my own clarity, and I had to try to find it again.

When we returned to Los Angeles, I told Robert that I'd be moving to New York for six months.

"I want to develop some projects and see what I can do about salvaging my career. You have the house here in California, the office, the car. You should be perfectly comfortable while you go on with your business. Once we're out of each other's way, maybe we'll both be able to think a little more clearly about what we're doing together. I'm not asking for a divorce. We don't need lawyers or papers. This is strictly between the two of us."

Robert had never heard this sort of dialogue from me and wasn't at all prepared for it. He was absolutely devastated. As he brooded over my decision, he became certain I was leaving him for good and the marriage was over. I tried to make him understand that the move to New York was a positive step, but he couldn't seem to hear me.

"What will people think?" he kept asking, as if that were the decisive factor. "What will they say if you're in New York and I'm here in California?"

"Of course people will suspect we're in trouble," I reasoned with him. "But the important thing right now is to see if we can work our way out of it."

Robert became increasingly despondent as the weeks went by and I began implementing my plans to move. Now that he saw everything slipping through his fingers, he seemed overcome by a sense of futility and failure. The fact that I appeared to grow stronger as his own strength and self-confidence waned made it even more difficult for him.

"You're always going to be all right, aren't you?" he asked me at the dinner table a week or so before I was due to leave. He was very drunk. He had been drinking constantly for days. But for a brief moment, as he stared over at me with a strange, ironic smile on his face, he seemed to be cold sober.

"I don't understand you, Robert. What do you mean?"

"I mean you're always going to land on your feet."

"I would think you'd be proud of that."

"Well, it's just that I didn't know that about you."

I couldn't really believe he had said it. "Don't you want me to land on my feet?"

"That's not what I'm saying. I'm saying that no matter what happens to you, no matter how bad things become, you will never fail."

I had started rehearsing again with Phil Moore, and it was time to leave for our appointment. Robert had his own plans for the evening. "I'm not trying to keep tabs on you," I told him. "I don't want to know where you're going. But I think it would be a good idea if you took me to Phil's, then picked me up when you're through. Maybe the drinking won't get so out of hand tonight if you know you have an obligation." Robert pretended not to hear me, so I went off in my car.

I returned home quite late, but Robert wasn't there. I woke up around dawn, and he still hadn't come home. "Oh, God, he's probably drying out in jail somewhere," I thought, then reached for the telephone to tell our attorney and friend Leo Branton. When Leo finished checking the jails, the hospitals, and the morgue, he called to tell me, "At least we know Robert isn't in trouble. We just have to find him. Don't worry. I'll let you know the minute I hear anything."

I waited by the telephone as the hours dragged by, and then it finally rang. It was Dr. Wexler, our therapist.

"Oh, I'm really glad it's you," I told him. "Robert has stayed out all night again. I think we ought to come by for a talk."

"Diahann?"

"Yes."

"Are you alone? Is anyone with you?"

"Well, the houseman is here. And I think Louise is up in her office. But why do you ask?"

"All right, I want you to call them into your room. Then I'd like you to sit down. Wait for me. I'll be right over."

"What is it? What's wrong? Is it about Robert? Did he have an accident? What happened?"

He waited for a moment before he decided to tell me.

"We've lost him."

It was as if he were speaking in a foreign language. The words didn't make sense.

"What do you mean, we've lost him?"

"We've lost him."

"Do you mean that he's dead?"

"Yes."

It seemed that Robert had been speeding along Mulholland Drive, the narrow, winding road that snakes its way high across the mountainous hills separating Los Angeles from the Valley. He had lost control of his car and plunged over the side, plummeting down hundreds of feet onto the jagged rocks below. They had just found his body in the wreckage.

The telephone cord twisted around me like a coil of barbed wire. Screaming and thrashing like a crazy woman, I struggled to tear myself loose. Louise and the houseman tried to subdue me, but I ripped at their hair, pulled down the drapes, and smashed everything in sight.

How could Robert be dead? How could his young life suddenly be over? Yes, he had used me. Yes, he had treated me badly. Yes, we didn't know how to live with each other — maybe the marriage was doomed to fail from the start. But this was no way for it to end. Not like this, not with his broken body trapped in the ruins of his Ferrari. It couldn't be true. It wasn't possible.

Dr. Wexler appeared and pumped me full of sedatives. No one would take me to Robert until the morticians had finished their work and brought him to the funeral parlor. I was certain they had made a mistake, that for one reason or another someone else was behind the wheel that night and Robert was still alive. The undertaker sat me down in his office and asked me question after question until I demanded to see the body. He led me into a roomful of stretchers and pulled back the sheet. There was no mistake.

Maybe for the first time in his brief, tortured life, Robert was finally at peace.

❧

I closed the front door behind me, put on my widow's black, and began learning how to be alone. The vodka and bottles of wine helped some, especially after dark, but they weren't the answer. Neither was sitting there in a daze and staring blankly at the walls. But I couldn't seem to get a handle on anything. Nothing made any sense. Friends tried to pry me away from my seclusion by inviting me out for a drink or a walk, but I couldn't bear being with anyone, not even the people I loved. For the last two years, so much of my existence had centered around my marriage, and whatever our problems, now that Robert was gone it was difficult to regain my footing in the outside world. It was better to seal myself off in the silent isolation of my home.

"You really have to stop this," my mother finally told me. "It's been going on much too long. There's nothing you can do for Robert anymore. It's over. I want you to stop wearing those black clothes. You're still a young woman. You have a whole lifetime ahead of you. This isn't doing anyone any good."

Robert's things were everywhere. Every corner held its own painful memory of this unhappy, tormented soul who, for good reasons or bad, had been my husband. There was his date book on the desk, still opened to all the appointments he would never keep. It was still so hard to believe he was gone. But as the months went by I gradually started giving everything away.

Slowly, tentatively, I began to come back to life. When David Frost called to say he was in town for a few days and wanted to know how I was getting along, I asked him to dinner. Our romance was ancient history by now, but he had always remained a dear friend, and once I heard his voice, I knew I was ready to see him. I was surprised by my excitement as I went about planning the evening. It had been so long since I entertained that I had quite forgotten how much enjoyment it gave me. I worked out a menu that avoided the onions and mustard and garlic that David abhorred, telephoned the Wine Merchant and discussed their recommendations, laid out a beautiful table with my finest china and crystal.

Seeing David that night was exactly what I needed. Up to then

I hadn't been able to talk about Robert with anyone. It was too painful, too ugly, still too confusing. But, as always, David was so warm and caring and full of concern that I told him the entire story. He listened quietly, then asked what I was doing to put my life in order. Was I keeping myself busy? Was I spending enough time with my family and friends? Did I need any help? Had I started seeing anyone?

The last question brought a smile to my face. David understood me so well. That was how I usually dealt with my problems when the pressure became too hard to handle. "No, David, I'm not," I answered, "and I'm not sure that I will. Now that I'm finally alone it's no longer so frightening. And I'm quite pleased about that, I really am." As I walked him to the door, he put his arm around me and said, "If you don't mind some advice, I think you ought to go back to work as quickly as possible." Of course, he was right!

❧

Carol Burnett and Dick Van Dyke were completing a limited run of Bernard Slade's comedy *Same Time Next Year* at the Huntington Hartford Theatre. When the producer told me they wanted to do another four weeks with Cleavon Little and myself, I wasn't at all sure I was up for it but decided to take the chance.

It turned out to be the best thing I could have done. I was required to go to the theater every day to rehearse. I had to learn my lines. I had to work in the evenings with my drama coach. There was hardly a moment to think about anything else. The sense of futility and helplessness would still overtake me at times and threaten to drag me down. One night, on the way to the theater, I heard myself say, "Why don't you forget about rehearsing today and just keep driving? It doesn't matter if you learn the lines. It doesn't matter if you do the part. None of that really means anything." But the sane, logical side of me knew that I couldn't give in. If I was ever going to find myself again, it would have to be through my work. That was the only thing that would save me.

All my energy and concentration went into the show. It became my only reality. I couldn't wait to get to the theater. I was always the first to arrive and the last one to leave. It felt so good to be busy I didn't want the days to end. But then four weeks after we opened the run was over and I was back in the house staring at the walls again.

I had to stay active and keep working. But that was easier said than done. I had heard the warnings my entire adult life: "A performer must never retire. For anyone in show business, it's absolute death." Yet I didn't understand just how true they were until I tried to come back.

In the past, agents I didn't feel were right for me would ask my manager when he called about representation, "So where has she been? Why haven't we seen her? . . . Has she taken any pictures lately? . . . Well, why don't you tell her to drop by. We'd like to meet her."

"But, Roy, what do they mean, they'd like to *meet* me? They know me. They've known me for twenty years."

"Well, the truth of the matter is they want to see how you look."

It was a bitter pill to swallow, but there it was. I had entered my forties, and my age was working against me. So was everything else. The feeling in the business was that I wasn't entirely serious about running a career. Yes, I sang and I acted, but like so many other performers, my main contribution seemed to be all those well-publicized romances splashed across the newspapers and magazines. I also had a reputation for allowing personal relationships to interfere with my work. (I hate to admit it, but the reputation was justified. When I briefly came out of retirement to do four summer shows for CBS, I consented to make Robert my executive producer. He was totally inexperienced, and his inexplicable behavior alienated almost everyone on the set. The shows were a complete embarrassment — I couldn't bear to look at them.)

I had been away only about three years, but when you're gone, you're gone. Even the success of *Claudine* had become totally meaningless. Not that one good film means very much in the life of an actor, but I hadn't made the right moves to take advantage of it. The moment had passed, and no one was really interested in me any longer. For all my years in the business, no one even seemed to remember who I was. It was as if I no longer existed.

The realization was frightening, but it also felt like a challenge. "All right," I told myself, "you've made some very bad mistakes, but if you can't redeem them, then maybe you don't deserve a career. Maybe everything they say about you is true. Well, Diahann, you were fortunate enough to be blessed with a gift — now let's take that and try to make it work for you again, because if that goes there's nothing else. And for God's sake, for the next five years of your life please do not become involved in anything that remotely resembles a romance. Clearly, that's one area where you are unequivocally a failure. You've had your go at it — you've had experiences and relationships and marriages. Now let's get down to some solid work. A career is a business. Let's start running it that way. Stop kidding yourself that it will always be there no matter what."

I began exercising every day to get my body into shape. I started taking singing lessons again. I looked for new material and put in a lot of time and effort revamping my act. I accepted almost any job I was offered. Naturally, certain jobs I once worked were no longer available. The jobs that did come my way were often for one-fourth of my old salary.

It was almost as though I were starting out all over again, but I accepted the jobs anyway. I didn't really have a choice. The bills flew in from everywhere after the death of my husband. He had borrowed a great deal of money without my knowledge, and I was determined to try to repay his creditors.

A few old friends were willing to take a chance on me. Bob Hope selected me as his opening act in Palm Springs and exhorted the audience to welcome me back. Gary Smith and Dwight Hemian, who produced television specials, called me. But I was still dealing with a series of not very first class one-nighters and the odd week here and there at not very first class hotels. I remember the devastation on Louise's face when we walked into some of those dressing rooms.

The absolute bottom was the evening I played an automobile show at a huge warehouse of an exhibition hall. When I walked out onto the stage, the only thing I could see were two shiny cars revolving slowly in front of me. The audience was several stories above me peering down at the top of my head.

"How can I perform like this?" I asked myself. "How am I supposed to make contact?"

I tried. I really did. But then as fate would dictate, an old dog wandered in from the street, sidled onto the stage, and plopped itself down. I stopped in the middle of the song and sat down at the piano to regain my composure. My conductor Ernie Freeman looked over and whispered, "Keep going. Just keep going."

I knew he was right. I owed it to the audience. I owed it to myself. If I didn't finish the performance I wouldn't be paid, and I needed the money badly. I made the effort, but it was all so hopeless that a few minutes later I threw up my hands and ran off. Sitting there in the awful little makeshift dressing room, I burst into tears.

"How did this happen?" I sobbed. "How did I get into this situation? If I can't work any other way, I'll do something else." But I knew I was prepared to do only *this!*

For the next three days I locked myself in a hotel room to figure out my next move. The answer was obvious. Ernie had told me on stage. Don't stop. Just keep going.

Slowly — very slowly — the jobs became better and the money improved. And little by little, as my situation grew less desperate, I became more comfortable on stage and began finding myself as a performer.

I had always sung fairly well and used good arrangements and worn beautiful gowns. But that wasn't enough for me any longer. Now that I started studying my tapes at the end of the night, I realized I was much too set in my ways. Once my performance began, nothing could pull me out of it. Song followed song and patter followed patter as if I were on automatic pilot without any real awareness that there was a whole roomful of people out there watching me. I was too aloof, too disconnected, too far away from the truths of my own personality. I remembered the words that had been used to describe me over the years: "distant," "remote," "reserved," "unapproachable," "standoffish." That may have been appropriate when I was standing in a pin spot at the Persian Room — it was what the audience wanted and expected then. But the world had changed, and so had I. I remembered, too, the words my first manager told me: "The audience is an unconscious genius. They really do know what you're putting out. They may not be able to verbalize it, but, believe me, they know what they're getting and they know what they're not getting."

I began to loosen up, to take chances, to trust my sense of the moment and reveal more of myself so as to close the gap with the audience. I came onstage now fully aware that I was trying to recoup my career, and while I couldn't allow myself to dwell on it, it was never far from my thoughts. The industry's rejection had frightened me badly, and I needed the audience more than ever.

And the more I needed them, the more I gave. And the more I gave, the better and more real I became.

Everything was fine as long as I was working. The work was fulfilling, particularly because, once again, I was surrounded by my team. But then when the job ended and I returned from the road, there I was, back to being a young widow alone in an empty house. Like so many others in my profession, I didn't have a life outside my work and was so afraid I wouldn't find one that I couldn't bring myself to try.

It took a while, much longer than it should have, but I eventually faced up to the fact that nothing was going to change unless I made it happen myself. Little by little, I began to reach out to the people I loved instead of waiting for them to find me while I sat there languishing in my self-imposed misery. I was an unattached single woman now — that was my reality. The business of coming home to a husband was over. But I didn't have to be alone. I had my family. I had my friends. It was time to stop brooding about what might-have-been and should-have-been and move on.

I'm still not sure why, but I returned to the world a very different human being from the woman I had been. God knows it was long overdue, but I finally seemed to have done some growing up. For the first time in twenty years I was no longer possessed by the overwhelming desperation to be married or engaged or off on some new romance. A chapter had closed with Robert's death, and I was able to look back at all that and see just how destructive it had been. I had made one horrendous blunder after another, yet had never allowed myself the time to stop and reflect and try to benefit from my mistakes. When it came to my personal life, I had accepted the failures and pain as if they were a natural part of the territory and marched onward. When a relationship ended, I had barely given myself time to catch my breath before I moved on to the next.

But that period of my life was over. I was finally able to walk into a restaurant alone without feeling that everyone was staring at me because I wasn't with a man. I was finally able to stop breaking out in a cold sweat because I didn't have a wedding ring on my finger to prove I really mattered and wasn't just a "flash-in-the-pan" out there singing a little song.

I was happy about the freedom. I was happy about the peace of mind. And maybe that was enough. If there were still some leftover hopes about love and relationships lurking inside me, somewhere, at least they no longer ruled my life. Perhaps I had learned enough from my mistakes with men to finally get it right, if and when the chance came round again. If it happened, that would be wonderful. But if it didn't, I knew now that I could have a full life without it.

And then the rest of my life began.

Chapter Nine

I t was the fall of 1982, and I was in New York for a brief vacation between nightclub engagements. I wanted to see some of the current plays, and a friend recommended *Agnes of God,* John Pielmeier's drama about a young nun who gave birth under mysterious circumstances and may or may not have killed the baby to hide her shame. The play starred two of my longtime favorites, Elizabeth Ashley as the psychiatrist appointed by the court to determine if Agnes should be brought to trial, and Geraldine Page as the mother superior who tries to block her investigation. The part of Agnes was played by Amanda Plummer, an exciting new talent who was receiving a lot of attention.

The play was fascinating, and all three performances were marvelous. But as I sat there on the edge of my seat watching the drama unfold, I found myself more and more caught up in the character of Dr. Livingston, the psychiatrist. I knew this woman so well and felt such a deep emotional kinship that it was almost as if the part had been written for me. I understood the confusions and failures in her personal life, especially in her relationships with men, and I understood how the one thing that saved her was her work. I was so in tune with the character that I began scrutinizing Elizabeth's approach to the role, agreeing with some of her choices, disagreeing with others, deciding how I would have liked to play this or that moment had I been onstage.

I knew I could do this part and do it well, but I was also positive that both because of the color of my skin and the fact that I had never done a drama, I would never be given the opportunity. The realization was so frustrating that during the intermission I left and took a walk. When the play ended I was still too upset to go backstage to pay my respects.

A few days later I was in Hyannisport singing at the Melody Theater when I received a phone call from my dear friend Josephine Premice. Josephine had spoken to the producer Ken Weissman, and he mentioned that he wanted to talk to me. I remembered that Ken Weissman had produced *Agnes of God,* and I thought this would be a very good opportunity to apologize for my rudeness in not going backstage. When I reached him on the telephone he immediately asked if I might have any interest in taking over the role of the psychiatrist for one week while Elizabeth Ashley went on vacation. I was too stunned to speak.

"But why me?" I finally managed to ask.

"Well, why not?" he answered. "We were looking for someone who can project the strength the role requires, for someone with some drawing power who might appeal to an audience we may not have reached. I saw one of your films on television the other night and suggested your name, and we all agree that if you're interested we'd like you to do it."

I couldn't believe what I was hearing, yet somehow was able to say yes without any difficulty.

The decision to go into the part for only one week may have seemed a bit foolhardy for several reasons. Dr. Livingston is an extremely demanding role — she is on the stage for literally two hours and twenty minutes, never leaving it once. It had been almost twenty years since I last appeared on Broadway. I had never done a straight dramatic play before — practically all my recent experience was performing in nightclubs with all the necessary glamorous accoutrements of that part of the business. On this stage, it would be only me.

I had only about two weeks of rehearsal time to whip the part into shape, and I wasn't entirely sure I could make it work. But, whatever the risk, I had to accept the challenge. The opportunity was too precious to waste.

Over the years, Harry Belafonte has argued with me about many of my choices, but this time he was totally supportive. So were so many other people in the business, like Bill Cosby and Richard Kiley, who cared about me. "There you go again," they kept telling me. "Always taking chances. Maybe you're a little crazy to come back to Broadway like this, especially in a three-character drama, but we're pulling for you. Even if you fail, we love you for trying."

So I did it. And that first day of rehearsal, as I stood in the empty theater, in the darkness under the naked work light, and began reading the first scene, I remembered my audition for *House of Flowers* so many years before and the words of Chuck Wood, my teacher and mentor: "The greats have been here. The greats are coming. Don't embarrass them by doing anything less than your best. If you make any contribution at all, it will only be through giving the work everything you have in you."

I tried to do that, but it was truly more demanding than I expected. As well as I understood Dr. Livingston — maybe *because* I understood her so well — the nuances of her character turned out to be extremely difficult to pin down. The questions about her were endless and sometimes there were no answers. Then there was the obvious fact that Geraldine Page and Amanda Plummer had worked together for many months and had already found their dramatic moments. Now, I had to discover my own, and my interpretation of the role was, of course, different from what they had come to expect.

When we finished rehearsing for the day, I would return to my apartment and work until three or four in the morning with Alice Spivak, the dear friend who had coached me for *Claudine*. There were moments when I was petrified by what I had undertaken, and Alice was always there to help make me believe that I could do it, and do it well. Alice pushed and pulled my mind in all the right directions, and although I certainly hadn't mastered the part by the time we opened, at least I was on the right track.

Nevertheless, when I finally stepped into the spotlight, a small voice in the back of my head whispered, "How could you paint yourself into this corner? Are you out of your mind?" Yet I went on. Another night I was so scared that I wanted to kill myself. Yet there were also other nights when the three of us walked onstage and our eyes met, and I knew for certain that the magic was about to happen. And that was truly glorious.

The public reaction to my performance was so gratifying, and I was so happy performing this difficult and challenging role that when the week ended, I didn't want to give it up! I wanted to keep on playing it. I wanted that more than anything in my life! Ken asked Elizabeth, and she agreed to take another week's vacation if she got paid. Without hesitating for one minute, I paid her salary for that week — it cost me several thousand dollars, but I would have paid more just to be able to do the play again.

When the two weeks ended, I put *Agnes* behind me. But then during the spring I received another phone call from Ken Weissman. He said the company was planning to take *Agnes* on the road, and would I care to come back to the play for the rest of the New York run?

I was dying to do it. But there were many reasons not to. My nightclub work was going extremely well — the economics of the Broadway theater are such that I would earn less in one week than I earned in one night and be required to work a hundred times harder. I also had to consider the consequences for my personal manager, Roy Gerber. Roy had devoted such effort and care to reestablishing my nightclub career, and going back into *Agnes* would require a considerable financial sacrifice on his part as well as my own. It could also jeopardize all the work he had done so lovingly and well to get me back into the nightclub circuit, and there was a good chance that the momentum might no longer be there when I returned to the clubs after the play closed.

But I had to do it. I can't explain it, I just had to.

Roy brushed aside my concerns with a wave of his hand. "Don't even think about that," he told me. "You just do whatever you feel you need to do as an artist."

I returned to the theater and picked up the role where I left off. I still had a great deal of work ahead of me before I could call the part mine, but little by little it fell into place. After the first three weeks I was just about on the verge of a real performance. It was far from complete — I was finding it, then losing it, then finding pieces of it again. When I stepped onstage it was like jumping off the edge of a cliff with my arms waving — I never knew from one night to the next whether I'd fly or crash down to the bottom. But I was beginning to feel unafraid enough to experiment a little during the actual performance rather than just during the rehearsals and my preparation with Alice.

Geraldine must have sensed my growing confidence, because now she began playing her scenes with me a bit differently each night — challenging me, pushing me, forcing me to grow by adjusting to the unexpected. I wanted to kill her, but I also loved her for having enough faith in me to believe I could handle it. It was a priceless learning experience, and I'll always be grateful.

❦

Agnes of God turned out to be a lifesaver. Because of *Agnes,* I moved back to my home in New York, where I find the life-style more to my liking. It made me begin to feel positive again about myself as an actress. And then, after six months, the run came to an end. The prospect of the closing matinee was so painful that I accepted a job singing the same night so I could dash out of the theater immediately after the performance and not have to face the long, bittersweet goodbyes with my backstage family.

I decided to remain in New York for a while. My daughter was there, and we rented a summer house in Connecticut. It was wonderful to be able to spend a substantial amount of time with Suzanne, but I found the adjustment to not working quite difficult. *Agnes* had given structure and purpose to my life, and now that they were gone I fell into the same depression most performers experience while they wait for their next project. And since work had always been the center of my life, I found myself at loose ends once again. To escape the anxiety, I retreated into my bedroom and began watching a lot of television. That's something I never have a chance to do when I'm busy working at night, but now that I was just biding my time I formed a new camaraderie with my television set.

As I watched *Knot's Landing, Dynasty, Dallas, Falcon Crest,* and the other nighttime soaps, I began to notice something. Jane Wyman, Joan Collins, and many of the other actresses were playing a new sort of woman I had never seen before on series television. They were the pivotal characters at the center of the action, not on the periphery, patiently sitting at home waiting for their husbands. They were strong and gutsy and very often ruthless. They ran their own companies and had their own wealth and were just as power-hungry as the men. A new, important era was starting to happen, and I longed to be a part of it. I wanted to be the first black bitch on television.

"Well, why not?" I found myself asking. The shows had touched on just about every other controversial, highly dramatic subject. It was only a matter of time until they overcame their timidity and introduced a black character who was just as unscrupulous and nasty as her white counterparts. Why shouldn't it be me?

I was especially interested in *Dynasty*. I adored the look of the show — *Dynasty* was luxurious and rich, and the camerawork and lighting were brilliant: every shot was beautiful. The actors looked as if they belonged together, as if they were having a wonderful time with their roles. I could picture myself in that setting, dealing with those characters. And, needless to say, the wardrobe was spectacular!

It was quite late the night the idea hit me, but I reached for the telephone and called Roy.

"What do you think?" I asked him. He loved the idea. "Do you suppose Aaron Spelling might go for it?"

"Let's give it a try," he answered. "I'll talk to him tomorrow."

"Anything happen?" I asked him a few days later. Roy told me that Aaron seemed receptive but we would have to wait. I have never earned a master's degree in "Waiting," but I had no choice — so, I tried to put it out of my mind. I remembered all too well that in Hollywood a possibility can be alive on Tuesday, dead by Wednesday afternoon, then spring to life once again Friday morning.

I began to emerge from my cocoon and decided to give a small dinner party (small dinner parties are very therapeutic for me). I was in the kitchen in the midst of making my first osso bucco when the telephone rang. It was Barbra Streisand. Barbra and I had known each other peripherally for many years and always enjoyed talking whenever our paths happened to cross. We originally met when I was starring in *No Strings* on Broadway and she was still a young girl trying to find a foothold in the business. I was being interviewed on a late-night television show hosted by Mike Wallace. "Everyone keeps saying this kid is really good," Mike told me during the commercial break, referring to the new girl singer on the show. And then Barbra walked out onstage, with a run in her stocking, sat down on a stool, and with an air of supreme self-confidence began to sing.

As soon as that incredible voice came out of her mouth, I looked at Mike and said, " 'Really good' is an understatement. She's definitely got it." God had been kind to me. He had given me a good instrument, and I could sing. But He had not blessed me with a voice like that.

"I want you to do something for me," Barbra now said. "The Golden Globe Awards are coming up soon, and I'd like you to sing 'The Way He Makes Me Feel,' my song from *Yentl*."

I was more than flattered — I was honored, because I knew how carefully Barbra considers every decision she makes. And I knew that *Yentl* was especially dear to her. Not only had she starred in the film, she was also the coproducer and director, and had spent several years, and a hell of a lot of money and energy, to make the film against almost everyone's advice.

"I'm thrilled," I told her. "I really am. And I want to thank you for asking me. But — and I say this with great respect — I will have to think about it. You know that I never touch any of your material. Once you sing a song, it has been sung. May I call you back later tonight? I need to have a glass of wine and think calmly."

"Okay," Barbra laughed. "We'll talk later. But I hope you say yes. I want someone who is an actress as well as a singer, and you and I are about the only actress-singers around!"

I had my glass of wine and put the finishing touches on the osso bucco. After talking it over with Roy and my guests, I managed to overcome my anxieties and called Barbra to tell her that I would be more than happy to come to Los Angeles and sing her song at the Golden Globe Awards.

It was one of those nights when everything goes right. Bruce Hutchinson and Arthur John did a magnificent job on my makeup and hair. Arnold Scaasi insisted on sending a spectacular gown (even though I explained that I had just come out of a play and couldn't really afford it), and the cameraman made me look terrific. Thank God that Barbra won an award seconds before I came onstage — because she wasn't sitting at the table watching, I was able to sing her song without feeling vocally intimidated.

I was still so up by the end of the evening that I said to Roy, "Come on, let's take the whole gang out somewhere for supper. I've heard about a new place called Touch. Why don't we go there?"

Someone called to make the reservations, then told me, "They're booked for the night unless you're part of the Aaron Spelling party."

"Well, tell them, yes, I most certainly am," I answered, without thinking twice.

Roy almost fell through the floor. "*Yes?* What do you mean, *yes?*"

"Don't stop me now!" I whooped. "I'm on a roll!"

I had known Aaron Spelling casually for twenty years and was certain that my little lie wouldn't cause him any embarrassment. And, in fact, when we walked into Touch he was waiting for me with a smile on his face.

"Diahann, it's so good of you to come," he laughed, throwing his arms around me. "You and your friends are my guests for the evening."

"Oh, Aaron, please, I couldn't do that. There are too many of us! I really only wanted you to help us get a table."

"I won't have it any other way. This is your table right here." Was there ever a more gracious man?

As my luck would have it, Aaron was throwing a supper party for the entire *Dynasty* team. Everyone was there — John Forsythe, Linda Evans, Joan Collins, and the rest of the cast, Esther and Richard Shapiro, who created the show, Elaine Rich, the executive producer, and Nolan Miller, the elegant man who designs those marvelous clothes.

Elaine Rich recognized a friend at my table and came over to say hello. We talked for a while, and I finally asked her, "Are you aware of the fact that I'm trying to invade your show?"

"Of course I am," she answered. "We all are. It's very much a part of our meetings."

I realized then and there that the discussions must have gone much further than I had thought.

Aaron had wine and dinner sent to our table and then invited me to meet everyone. I didn't know what to expect, but they were all warm and friendly and put me immediately at ease.

"I'd like you to know," Esther Shapiro told me, "that we've all heard about the idea, and we like it."

I felt so relaxed I found myself saying, "Esther, forgive my presumptuousness, but if you don't do it with me, please, please do it with someone. *Dynasty* is an international success, and we tend to forget in America that most of the people in the world are not white. I'd like her to be black because that happens to be me, but should you decide not to go that way, then I beg you to think about an oriental or some other Third World person." Esther nodded. This had also been discussed.

The next day when Roy and I talked, I asked him to speak with the *Dynasty* people and reiterate that it was important to me that the black woman they create be strong and powerful.

I flew back to New York, then returned to California a few weeks later to take care of some personal business. Late one afternoon Roy called me at home.

"What are you doing right now?" he asked.

"I'm in the office answering letters and paying bills. Why?"

"Well, come downstairs. I want to talk to you for a minute. Do you have any Dom Perignon in the refrigerator?"

"Yes, I do. But you don't drink."

"Let's be extravagant. I'll be right there."

I wouldn't allow myself to think about it. Roy had recently mentioned that Aaron was seriously considering me for the show. I had heard through the grapevine that Lew Erlicht, the head of ABC Entertainment, had liked me in *Agnes* and indicated he would be interested in having me on the network if someone could find the right vehicle. But having experienced many disappointments over the years, I no longer allowed myself to become too hopeful.

Roy arrived. I opened the Dom Perignon and poured him a glass of Perrier. He raised his glass and said, "Congratulations. You are a member of the *Dynasty* family."

To keep my body from floating to the ceiling, to keep from jumping up and down and laughing or screaming, I turned my head over my shoulder toward Roy, and, with all the coolness I could muster, said "Really, as of when?"

"As of immediately."

"I don't believe you!"

Roy put in a call to Aaron Spelling, then handed me the phone.

"Roy is here trying to tell me I'm a regular on *Dynasty*," I explained. "Is that really true?"

"Oh, yes," Aaron answered matter-of-factly, as if it were the most natural thing in the world.

And then I finally screamed!

❦

Aaron Spelling and his associates turned out to be a remarkable group of people. They obviously understand television ratings, but they were willing to take a top-ranking series and risk trying something new that might or might not be accepted. (Roy had made the same suggestion to all the top nighttime soaps and had been turned down by all of them with the explanation that only peripheral roles were being considered for Third World actors — definitely *not primary roles!*) Aaron and company took a chance with me, and I was damned if I wasn't going to give them my best.

My feeling of being "a part of it all" began immediately. Elaine and Esther called to discuss the name of my character and her personality. We did not settle immediately on "Dominique." The first name they tried was "Johnny." I tried that one — I walked around the house and asked everyone to call me Johnny. It didn't work — I never once turned around to answer to that name. It just didn't fit. Finally one afternoon Elaine called and said, "How do you like Dominique?"

I loved it and told her so. "Wonderful," replied Elaine. "Now you come up with a last name."

I tried and tried, but before I could think of a name Elaine called back. "We've got it," she said, happily.

"Great. Are you going to tell me?"

"Deveraux."

"Fabulous! Where did you find it?"

"In the phone book."

Now that we had the name, our next conference was about the personality that went with it. We made a list of many powerful women we knew, and took a little from each. From Bricktop, the black international celebrity of so many years ago, we took the European nightclub background, the singing, the aura of show business. She knew everyone and could pick up the phone and call dozens of important, titled people all over the world and Dominique had to have that kind of power. We pulled a little from Regine, the nightclub owner in Paris. We took a little from Suzanne DePass, who assists Berry Gordy, the Motown genius. Suzanne's position is one of monumental power. And the bitchiness — well, that sort of came naturally. It was such a pleasure to be given an outlet to act out such wonderful, caustic, sarcastic, deliciously bitchy lines, that I ate it up.

And a few weeks later I went to work. I had assumed that I would start with the new season, but the producers decided that I would be part of last season's cliffhanger. I was a little nervous when I got the script with my first scene on the show. After all the discussion, I hoped it turned out that they would allow me to be as ambitious and unscrupulous — and ultimately as complex and interesting — as I had envisioned. And my hopes were answered.

The first time my character appeared, I was decked out in a lavish, $150,000 lynx coat and a half-million dollars' worth of jewels (there was a gun-toting policeman following me around the set every minute!). I arrived at the hotel La Mirage with a full set of monogrammed Cartier luggage. The camera first focused on the bellman, then the luggage, then my feet, the bottom of the coat, and then slowly panned up my body until it stopped on my face. Even on the set, you could hear the gasps, you could feel the audience at home asking, "Who the hell is that?"

I slowly walked up to the desk, and, in my best, most imperious and elegant voice, full of authority, haughtiness, and class, said, "Good evening, I am Dominique Deveraux."

One other scene that season was with Joan Collins, and we had a ball doing it. Decked out in a fabulous gray suit trimmed with silver fox, I waltzed in to meet with Joan's character, Alexis Carrington. (Joan and I have known each other for over twenty years. The first day I came on the set, she reminded me that it was only a couple of years before that she and I had sat in my living room, celebrating Suzanne's birthday and wondering what was going to happen to our careers — and now here we were, working together.) I sat down, and with much ceremony, tasted her champagne and proceeded to pronounce, "Your champagne is burned, and I only eat Petrossian" (meaning a kind of caviar). Joan looked stunned, and America said, "Who is this crazy broad? Perhaps she really is a black bitch!"

Obviously I was rich, demanding, strong, and, yes, probably bitchy, and someone to be reckoned with. But what was I doing here in Denver? America (and I) would have to wait until that next season to find out.

It was a delicious way to be introduced, and we were all overjoyed when the ratings shot through the roof. As the next season progressed, they took my character even further, overriding the unspoken taboo against interracial relationships and making me a blood member of the Carrington family. When I read the script where Dominique confronts her dying father and demands he acknowledge her, I was astonished that a network television series could be this honest, this forthright. Maybe in the larger scheme of things none of this is important, but I think it represents some kind of progress.

It's been fifteen years since *Julia,* and *Dynasty* is an entirely different experience. I have never known such openness and camaraderie, such a free and easy exchange of ideas between the creators and the actors. The cast is really a repertory company — everyone is supportive and helpful with critical comments that encourage mutual respect. For someone like me who is used to working all night and sleeping in the daytime, believe it or not, I can't wait to get up at four in the morning and rush to the set.

❦

Dynasty is a dream come true for me. I am part of a worldwide successful television series without all the pain and criticism of *Julia.* I still perform, often flying from the set on a Friday to Chicago or New York or Las Vegas to do my show. And I have come to terms with who I am, and who I am not.

There has to be something good about growing older, and I suppose it's that you become more mellow, less exacting of yourself and others. I no longer take everything head on or drive myself into a frenzy when something doesn't work out the way I want. Every unpleasant incident does not mean the end of the world. Every negative comment does not put a knot in my stomach and make me question whether I deserve a place on the planet. I am much more relaxed now and see those distractions for what they are.

When I look back over all the changes in my life since I appeared in *Agnes of God,* it seems like a miracle. I've never felt such fulfillment; sometimes it frightens me. That little voice in the back of my head keeps saying, "Be careful. Don't let yourself get carried away. Don't become too comfortable." Some people are reluctant to give up their pain because they've lived with it for such a long time, and I'm afraid I fall into that category. But for all my apprehensions, I'm beginning to let go. I'm really beginning to feel secure about myself as a performer and a woman. I'm beginning to have some faith in the future. And I have to tell you, it feels absolutely wonderful.

That's not to say that there are no regrets — not guilt, but regret. It hurts me that after my parents divorced, my dad decided to divorce me, too. I suppose that for some strange reason he felt that when he divorced my mother, he had to divorce Lydia, my sister, and me, as well. (For over a year during the divorce, my father decided that Lydia and I could reach him only through a post-office box — no telephone number and no address.) I was devastated. I felt abandoned once again. We had been so close when I was a child. He was there for me, and now, I still miss that dad. It surprised me that after he had left me once, when I was two years old, he could now leave again, seemingly without much thought. I suppose that by this time in my life, as I turn fifty, I should be used to living without that closeness, without having a father around to share my life. Today, we speak on the phone only two or three times a year. It still feels strange, after almost fourteen years without him, but I'm trying to adjust.

I regret not being closer to my sister, Lydia. The difference in our ages (I married Monte when she was almost seven, and was gone during most of her childhood) may be one reason. Another may be the fact that, as an early success, I took up much of my parents' attention. But Lydia was always adored and loved and fussed over, both by my parents and myself. I loved having my own little "baby" around to play with and cuddle. And, in truth, I was thrilled when I discovered that my mother was pregnant. Even then, at that young age, I knew that this would take some of the pressure off me, that having another child around would have to make my parents let go of me just a bit.

But, as I got older and moved away from home, as I became more and more successful, we grew apart. I understand well that it must have been hard — and probably still is — to be "Diahann Carroll's sister." It is almost impossible to try to retain a relationship with someone who is always traveling, always in the limelight. It must be difficult to make a successful life for yourself, always aware of the shadow of someone who has achieved "fame." How complex fame can be, creating havoc in the lives of the people we love. Thus, although I cannot and would not honestly apologize for my success, I do regret that we are not closer.

And Suzanne, my love, my child. I cherish all the moments I have shared with her, and I regret that there were not many more. I guess it is every working mother's lament not to have enough time for her children. And, if your mother is also famous, the pressure has to be compounded. We both know that my work has been my life, and that has meant that there was never enough time for a lot of other things. Even though I took Suzanne with me almost everywhere I traveled, there were occasions, more than I want to remember, when I had little time to spend with her. I regret that lost time — I regret the hugs that I had to give over the telephone, the kisses that I had to send in the air.

But I must have done something right. I married Monte, which gave Suzanne a wonderful, lifelong father and friend. And some of the experiences that Suzanne and I had must be responsible for the wonderful person she has turned out to be. She is world traveled and world educated — at the moment she is a journalism student (no small feat, this show-off mother hastens to add!), and is living in New York. I am proud of her and wish for her to have a daughter as wonderful as my own.

My last regret is that I did not meet Vic Damone years ago — actually, I *did*. About six years ago I went to Puerto Rico, and who should be singing there but Damone himself (I always call him Damone, because Vic is not my favorite name!). Louise and I went to see his show but because I was exhausted, we left right after to return to our suite. I was starving, but we found that it was too late to order from room service. Not five minutes later there was a knock on the door and a parade of waiters began to enter with trays full of the most fabulous food! It seems that Damone, a longtime performer who knew that I would be hungry this late at night, had commandeered the hotel kitchen staff and ordered this lavish meal.

That's Damone. He is thoughtful, kind, loving, and as attentive a man as I have ever encountered. He is familiar to me, as if I have been waiting for him my whole life. We met again after I had started *Dynasty*, when I was singing in San Francisco, and have since established a relationship which is the most precious I have ever known. Together, and between us, we have five children, careers, houses that await our arrivals, and a bond that I am going to work my damnedest to keep for the rest of my life.

The rest of my life. A phrase like that always brings to mind that life has its inevitable ups and downs, its special moments, good and bad, that will always be there. I've certainly had those downs, but I've had the ups, too, and I don't take them for granted, not for a second.

I like myself today. And I love my life. Who wouldn't? Today I feel as if someone up there is saying, "It's her time. She's been through a lot of tests — some of them she flunked, some of them she passed. And, now, it's her turn."

It's taken me a while, but I really and truly have peace in my life — and that's really saying something, isn't it, Carol Diann Johnson?

Index

ACKNOWLEDGMENTS

This book would not have been possible
without the following people who have shared my life:

*My dad, John Johnson, Louise Adamo,
Harold Arlen, Harry Belafonte, Judith
Bernstein, John Berry, Donald Brooks,
Joyce Brown, Sammy Davis, Jr., Ophelia De
Vore, Judy Feiffer, David Frost, Roy
Gerber, Annie Gilbar, Joe and Corinne
Guercio, Bob Hope, David Horowitz, Bruce
Hutchinson, Phyllis Adams Jenkins, Arthur
Johns, John H. Johnson, Hal Kanter, Mrs.
Landecker, Joe Layton, Peter Matz, Harold
Melvin, Phil Moore, Josephine Premice,
Margot Rebeil, Elaine Rich, Ray Roberts,
Richard Rodgers, Diana Sands, Arnold
Scaasi, Chuck Scott, Esther and Richard
Shapiro, Nat Sobel, Aaron Spelling,
Alice Spivak, Geraldine Stutz,
Hannah Weinstein, Charles R. Wood,
and Damone.*